WHAT IS A FAMILY JUSTICE SYSTEM FOR?

In a time of austerity, medical emergency, and limited public funding, this book explores the role of the family justice system and asks whether it has a function beyond decision-making in dispute resolution. Might a family justice system even help to prevent or minimise conflict as well as resolving dispute when it arises? The book is divided into 4 parts, with contributions from 22 legal scholars working across Europe, Australia, Argentina and Canada. Part 1 analyses what constitutes a family justice system in different jurisdictions, and how a welfare element is included in the legal framework; Part 2 looks at those engaged with a family justice system as professionals and users; Part 3 examines new ways of working within a family justice system and questions the move towards privatisation; and Part 4 explores recent major changes of direction for the family justice systems of Australia, Argentina, Turkey, Spain, and Germany.

Oñati International Series in Law and Society

A SERIES PUBLISHED FOR THE OÑATI INSTITUTE FOR THE SOCIOLOGY OF LAW

Recent titles in this series

Collective Bargaining and Collective Action: Labour Agency and Governance in the 21st Century?
Edited by Julia López López

Fundamental Rights and Legal Consequences of Criminal Conviction
Edited Sonja Meijer, Harry Annison and Ailbhe O'Loughlin

Digital Family Justice: From Alternative Dispute Resolution to Online Dispute Resolution?
Edited by Mavis Maclean and Bregje Dijksterhuis

The Legacies of Institutionalisation: Disability, Law and Policy in the 'Deinstitutionalised' Community
Edited by Claire Spivakovsky, Linda Steele and Penelope Weller

Gender and Careers in the Legal Academy
Edited by Ulrike Schultz, Gisela Shaw, Margaret Thornton and Rosemary Auchmuty

Contesting Austerity: A Socio-Legal Inquiry
Edited by Anuscheh Farahat and Xabier Arzoz

The Right to the Continuous Improvement of Living Conditions: Responding to Complex Global Challenges
Edited by Jessie Hohmann and Beth Goldblatt

Supporting Legal Capacity in Socio-Legal Context
Edited by Mary Donnelly, Rosie Harding and Ezgi Tascioglu

What Is a Family Justice System For?
Edited by Mavis Maclean, Rachel Treloar and Bregje Dijksterhuis

For the complete list of titles in this series
see www.bloomsbury.com/uk/series/oñati-international-series-in-law-and-society/

What Is a Family Justice System For?

Edited by
Mavis Maclean
Rachel Treloar
and
Bregje Dijksterhuis

Oñati International Series in Law and Society

A SERIES PUBLISHED FOR THE OÑATI INSTITUTE FOR THE SOCIOLOGY OF LAW

• HART •
OXFORD • LONDON • NEW YORK • NEW DELHI • SYDNEY

HART PUBLISHING

Bloomsbury Publishing Plc

Kemp House, Chawley Park, Cumnor Hill, Oxford, OX2 9PH, UK

1385 Broadway, New York, NY 10018, USA

29 Earlsfort Terrace, Dublin 2, Ireland

HART PUBLISHING, the Hart/Stag logo, BLOOMSBURY and the Diana logo are trademarks of Bloomsbury Publishing Plc

First published in Great Britain 2022

A catalogue record for this book is available from the British Library.

Library of Congress Cataloging-in-Publication data

Names: What is a family justice system for? (Conference) (2020 : Online) | Maclean, Mavis, editor. | Treloar, Rachel, editor. | Dijksterhuis, B. M. (Bregje Monique), 1975- editor. | Oñati International Institute for the Sociology of Law, sponsoring body.

Title: What is a family justice system for? / edited by Mavis Maclean, Rachel Treloar and Bregje Dijksterhuis.

Description: Oxford ; New York : Hart, 2022. | Series: Oñati international series in law and society | Includes bibliographical references and index.

Identifiers: LCCN 2022015573 (print) | LCCN 2022015574 (ebook) | ISBN 9781509950973 (hardback) | ISBN 9781509951017 (paperback) | ISBN 9781509950997 (pdf) | ISBN 9781509950980 (Epub)

Subjects: LCSH: Domestic relations courts—Social aspects—Congresses. | LCGFT: Conference papers and proceedings.

Classification: LCC K672 .W43 2020 (print) | LCC K672 (ebook) | DDC 346.01/5—dc23/eng/20220531

LC record available at https://lccn.loc.gov/2022015573

LC ebook record available at https://lccn.loc.gov/2022015574

ISBN: HB: 978-1-50995-097-3
ePDF: 978-1-50995-099-7
ePub: 978-1-50995-098-0

Typeset by Compuscript Ltd, Shannon

To find out more about our authors and books visit www.hartpublishing.co.uk. Here you will find extracts, author information, details of forthcoming events and the option to sign up for our newsletters.

Acknowledgements

WE WISH TO thank the Onati Institute for enabling us to hold our first online workshop, and for dealing with the challenges arising with skill and enthusiastic commitment. Despite the different way of working due to the Covid-19 crisis we were able, as always, to enjoy and learn from the stimulating and constructive exchange of ideas and information during this difficult time, which we now present.

We also thank Professor Barbara Willenbacher of the Institute of Sociology, Leibniz, Germany, who contributed to the Workshop for her comments referenced in chapter fourteen.

Finally we thank Professor Encarna Roca Trias, Deputy President of the Constitutional Court, Madrid, who attended the Workshop for her comments on the role of the family court in Spain, which are included in the concluding chapter fourteen.

Mavis Maclean, Rachel Treloar and Bregje Dijksterhuis
November 2021

Contents

PART C
INNOVATIVE PRACTICE

PART D
MAJOR POLICY CHANGE

List of Contributors

Gaelle Aeby, CETEL, University of Geneva

Masha Antokolskaia is Professor of Law at the Vrije Universiteit of Amsterdam, Netherlands

Benoit Bastard is Directeur of Researche Emerite at CNRS, Ecole Normale Superieure de Paris-Saclay, France

Marit Buddenbaum is a doctoral researcher Vrije Universiteit Amsterdam, Netherlands

Michelle Cottier is Professor of Private Law, Centre of Legislative and Evaluation Studies, CETEL, University of Geneva, Switzerland

Lieke Coenraad is Professor of Dispute Resolution, Vrije Universiteit, Amsterdam

Bregje Dijksterhuis is a Lecturer at the University of Amsterdam, Netherlands

Belinda Fehlberg is Professor of Law, University of Melbourne, Australia

Alexander Flos is a Lecturer in Law at the Vrije University of Amsterdam, Netherlands

Malgorzata Fuszara is Professor in the Institute for Applied Social Science, University of Warsaw, Poland

Annette Kronberg is Professor of Law, University of Southern Denmark and Utrecht University

Richard Ingleby is Adjunct Professor of Law, University of Western Australia

Verda Irtis is Associate Professor of Sociology, Galatasary University, Istanbul, Turkey

Christina Jeppesen de Boer is Lecturer in Law, Utrecht Centre for European Research into Family Law, Netherlands

Jane Krishnadas is a Senior Lecturer in Law, University of Keele, England

Jacek Kurczewski is Professor of Sociology and Anthropology of Custom and Law, University of Warsaw

Mavis Maclean is Senior Research Fellow, University of Oxford, England

Thomas Meysen is Director of SOCLES International Centre for Socio Legal Studies, Heidelberg, Germany

Elena Lauroba is Professor of Law, University of Barcelona, Spain

Teresa Picontó Novales is Professor of Law, University of Zaragoza, Spain

Bindhu Sahdeva, is a Researcher, CETEL University of Geneva, Switzerland

Rachel Treloar is a Lecturer in Law, Keele University, England

Introduction

MAVIS MACLEAN

THE MEMBERS OF the Family Group of the Research Committee on the Sociology of Law have been thinking hard about the place of family law in society for many years now, starting from concerns about the relationship between law, family and the state, then looking at specific issues, including parenting after separation and divorce. More recently we have looked at the broader problems of delivering access to family justice in times of austerity, complicated by the need for a justice system to be able to help individuals and families with a diverse range of values and expectations. Our last volume, *Digital Family Justice*, looked at the rather varied contribution being made by the use of technology to developing cost-effective digital justice.[1] This volume has arisen in the context of continuing widespread concern about increasing demand for access to family courts, and the public and private costs which follow, and tries to raise and address the questions which might help us to find a way through this barrier to achieving access to justice. If we wish to move on from focusing on policy questions which only look at how to cut costs, we will need to step back and think first about what it is that we want from a family justice system? And only then consider how such a service could be provided in a cost-effective way.

This introduction sets out the work of the 2020 IISL Workshop convened by a group of family lawyers, mainly members of the RCSL Legal Professions Working Group, who set out to take the first step of asking: What is a family justice system for? What is it asked or expected to achieve? And how might this work be evaluated across a number of jurisdictions in Europe, and also in Australia and Canada? In *Digital Family Justice* published in the IISL Hart Series in 2019, we began by tracing concerns about the attempts to promote Alternative Dispute Resolution (ADR), which had developed in order to enable those with family disputes to reach a settlement without using traditional court-based decision-making, but instead working with a skilled and impartial mediator. Sadly these attempts, although supported by a number of governments in the hope of reducing conflict and increasing acceptance of personal responsibility, as well as reducing demand for costly court process, have failed to gain widespread support. This may be because mediation requires the parties

[1] Maclean and Dijksterhuis (2019); see also Maclean and Kurczewski (1994); Maclean (2005).

to do the work of rethinking and compromising, without a 'champion' to give a party confidence by supporting their individual position. There has also been concern about ADR as a move towards 'private ordering' whereby parties can reach a decision which they and society as a whole may accept, but which may not necessarily be supported by a legal framework, for example concerning gender equality in financial arrangements after divorce. Then followed attempts to modernise family justice by moving from ADR to developing Online Dispute Resolution (ODR) – making greater use of technology to provide legal information and advice as well as administrative support, in order to reduce pressure on court time. Here too the degree of success was limited, as information without advice and support in taking the next step to resolve a matter was not enough in most cases. After the onset of the Covid-19 pandemic in early 2020 remote court hearings became increasingly important for family matters, as many courts closed except for hearings online.

But these earlier discussions on the alternatives to court, both ADR and ODR, have helped us to understand that dispute resolution is only part of what is needed by those who approach a family justice system. If we start by looking at the people who are seeking the help of the courts, we can see that they are experiencing a major life change, such as divorce, with particular difficulties if they are parents, and they are likely to be confronted by challenging decisions about how to manage their financial arrangements as well as the care of their children. If problems arise these may be resolved privately, perhaps with the help of family and friends, or they may develop into disputes which reach high levels of conflict requiring external intervention. In what follows we wish to explore at what stage, and in what way, a family justice system becomes involved in these private matters, as well as in the public duty to protect children.

A number of questions have arisen: Does a family justice system have functions other than decision-making in dispute resolution, whether traditional, alternative or digital in form? Might a family justice system help to prevent or minimise conflict as well as resolve dispute when it arises? How might a family justice system develop such functions in a period of austerity, medical emergency and limited public funding? Could these kinds of interventions by a family justice system be offered through direct provision, with referral to other services, or by acting as a hub for information enabling increased self-help? What is the level of responsibility to be accepted by a family justice system to provide help and support directly or indirectly? Above all, we ask whether a justice system can embrace a welfare function? If so, where does the boundary lie between justice and welfare and where can the necessary resources and experts be found? Does public responsibility extend beyond protecting the vulnerable, often meaning women, children and those who lack legal capacity, to include public involvement in private quarrels? Or might a family justice system withdraw from the private sphere, perhaps using legislative reform to promote private autonomy by clearly imposing defined financial obligations after divorce, or by requiring structured individual responsibility for decision making through mediation rather than adjudication? Should we add to our consideration of what we may call the Welfare Justice Axis a second complex relationship evidenced by the emerging debates about the relationship between autonomy and economy? Might a more proactive family justice system, accessible early in the development of a problem into a dispute, be costly at the point of use but cost-effective over time by saving public money at a later stage when more substantial intervention by other services such as health or education could otherwise be required? In addition, we see an ongoing tension between the dominant trend towards privatisation, whether sought for its own sake or because it is thought to save resources, and the need to maintain control in cases of domestic violence and child abuse. From country to country different configurations are emerging.

From our earlier work on access to family justice[2] we have already learned a great deal about different ways of responding to family matters where the law offers a framework for resolution. We saw how ADR, even though not used as widely as policy makers had hoped in many jurisdictions, can help to broaden the focus of justice to think more about problems as well as disputes, how the child-centred approach in Scandinavia enables parenting issues to be dealt with by expert welfare services rather than courts, and how financial advice services have been developing online to help families make the best use of their available resources. At the Workshop, held at a time of crisis during a pandemic, we could see an urgent need to ask more clearly the underlying question: what is the role of a family justice system? But even the well-evidenced and clearly argued research papers presented at the Workshop cannot, of course, provide a single answer. It is indeed rarely the sole purpose of research to provide answers, but as can be seen from our previous work, what we can do is to generate the next set of difficult but essential questions. Here we ask what a family justice system can offer, and how to set about the work needed, bearing in mind that family justice is very different from other parts of the justice system. Family justice looks to the future, not the past. In criminal justice the important question is what an individual did or did not do on a particular day. In family justice the focus in children cases is on the best interests of the child, ie what a number of individuals are likely to do in the future. This is a far wider and less clearly defined remit, which requires reaching out and asking for a range of information and nuanced advice in coming to a decision, rather than being limited to a precise view of a specific act. At the same time, in matters of family finance there may be wider societal issues about whether the justice system should be promoting a particular form of financial relationship between spouses, during or after a marriage, whether to rely on existing norms, or whether to strive to move forward towards greater gender and age related equalities.

[2] See Maclean, Eekelaar and Bastard (2015); Maclean and Eekelaar (2016).

I. STRUCTURE OF THE VOLUME

In Part 1 the contributors look at the boundaries of a family justice system in different jurisdictions, and the place of public and private values in a legal framework. Part 2 looks at those who take part in a family justice system, whose who work there and those who use a family justice system. Part 3 looks at different ways of working within a family justice system and raises the question of whether the move towards privatisation derives from the intrinsic value of individual autonomy, and acceptance of responsibility in family matters, or whether it is more often a response to the increasing burden on the state of providing a welfare-minded proactive family justice system. Finally, in Part 4 we hear of some of the major changes of direction for the family justice systems in Australia, Argentina and Germany. Our concluding chapter incorporates the wise words of Justice Encarna Roca Trias, Deputy President of the Constitutional Court of Spain, and a distinguished family law scholar, who emphasises the permanence of the fundamental role of the judiciary, and the immense importance of the need to guarantee the human rights of those who are experiencing a family law conflict.

A. Part 1 Boundaries – Defining the Function and Purpose of a Family Justice System: Justice and Welfare?

We begin with Rachel Treloar's account (chapter one) of the impact of recent attempts in Canada to develop new ways of working with post separation parenting disputes, by providing additional services outside the court. Treloar draws on her own work in British Columbia with highly conflicted separated parents, and describes the new potentially helpful ways of making court more accessible and friendly with new information and early resolution services. But sadly this approach has left those who still need the help of the court with few places to turn to. The range of services include parenting education, mediation and collaborative law, as well as arbitration, parenting coordination, expert assessment and children's lawyer. But the parents must use their own resources to access these services, and if they fail to resolve their problems the court has become the place of last resort, with the remaining state funding being used for ADR and online information, neither of which are enough to help parents with complex or high-conflict problems. Treloar suggests that it would be more prudent to ensure that all families receive sufficient help to navigate difficult family cases, especially given the high financial health and social costs of litigation. The dominant approach is to 'nudge' parents towards out-of-court resolution, and under the forthcoming federal Divorce Act, parents will have a *duty* to attempt to do this. But reforms which emphasise individual problem solving and remove family disputes from formal justice change the very meaning of justice, Autonomy and Economy may prove a dangerous alliance.

In chapter two we hear of a very different way to try to maintain a minimal role for the family courts in the Danish system by relying on a larger administrative component provided by the state. Annette Kronborg and Christina Jeppesen de Boer describe how a Family Court has recently been added to the system based on the Family Law House with a new mandatory triage process which identifies 'green' cases needing information, 'yellow' cases which also need help including counselling or mediation, and the urgent 'red' cases which need immediate referral to court. The triage follows on from self-referral, and is completed online. The aim is a holistic, unified and focused system with a child-centred approach. To the outsider it appears an attractive model, providing welfare with justice and autonomy with economy. But sadly in practice there are still some practical problems with communication and cooperation between the existing agencies that have been brought together in this attempt to provide a holistic service, and there is continuing tension between the aims of promoting the welfare of the child and respecting the rights of the adults.

The second two chapters in Part 2 look at the gap between the principles underlying public law and the private values expressed in seeking the management of family disputes.

In chapter three Bregje Dijksterhuis and Alexander Flos from the Netherlands ask how far family justice systems should reflect social norms and behaviour in making financial arrangements after divorce. They draw on their research into conflicted financial arrangements to describe the role of the notary in providing information and advice to couples on making fair and informed prenuptial agreements to avoid conflict on divorce. But the legal framework is changing in a way that accepts and reflects current social norms relating to the economic position of men and women during marriage and afterwards, but does not support gender equality, leaving a third of divorced mothers reliant on state benefit. For example, in 2020 the legal duration of spousal support was reduced, and since 2018 the law has moved from supporting universal community of property to limited community of property. So even here a system which as part of the regulated attempt to avoid conflict may have reduced resort to the courts, has nevertheless failed to guarantee a just outcome in the opinion of those who support gender equality.

In the following chapter (chapter four) Michelle Cottier, Bindu Sahdeva and Gaelle Aeby look at a parallel dilemma in Switzerland where there is a constitutional mandate to implement gender equality and private post-divorce arrangements are common. But social norms are not in alignment with the constitutional position. The divergence here is even more pronounced than in the Netherlands, as the aim of the Swiss justice system is not to follow social norms but to proactively implement gender equality. In accordance with the ideal of basing divorce on mutual agreement, 90 per cent of all divorces in Switzerland are based on a settlement made by the spouses themselves, and the role of the justice system is reduced to providing a framework for the spouses' settlements and judicial sanction of their agreements.

B. Part 2 Participants – Who Uses and Who Works in the Family Justice System?

Here we turn to patterns of court use, and begin to ask whether what we see reflects the impact of Autonomy and or Economy? In chapter five Benoit Bastard looks at the changing role of the judiciary and the family courts in France, drawing on his research into the continuing impact of the recent reforms in France which placed divorce by mutual consent in the hands of lawyers, without recourse to court hearings and judicial decision-making in most cases. The judges have not indicated that they have suffered in any way from this change, as they had been overloaded with work; however the cases they no longer deal with are the more consensual cases which had taken little of their time. The pace of reform continues, while the main part of the work of the courts concerns parenting disputes. In 2021 there was no change in these cases, and there will be no change to the rules which support the best interests of the child, but the procedure will be simplified by reducing the time before a consensual divorce can be granted to six months, and the first stage in the process which attempts conciliation will no longer take place. The judges remain concerned about the increasing debate on domestic violence, but for the legislator divorce is increasingly seen as the personal business of the spouses, and the courts are to disengage themselves further. Nevertheless, pressure on the French justice system continues to be at crisis level and reforms continue to flow, while the family judges continue to manage family situations which seem to them more than ever to be seriously dysfunctional and conflicted. The mediators, who were social workers by origin, are less visible. In this context the process of 'privatisation' has continued without the debates and difficulties which might have been expected. In addition, the restrictions associated with the Covid-19 crisis have accentuated and confirmed the long-term tendency to reduce the oral nature of debates.

In chapter six Malgorzata Fuszara and Jacek Kurczewski describe a very different set of issues in Poland about which family issues are brought before the courts, where the divorce rate is low as befits a strongly Catholic society. Here survey research by the authors looks at the nature of public readiness to turn to the courts to settle family disputes. The long standing tradition of reluctance to do so springs from the high value given to protecting the privacy of family life, and reluctance to turn to the state courts during the communist period for help except in extreme circumstances such as risk to personal safety. The financial cost to the individual of going to court is not a major factor in keeping people away, as court fees are not high and there is no requirement to use a lawyer. Multivariate logistic analysis of their survey data indicates that of gender, age, employment, education, and standard of living and urbanisation, it is education which emerges as the dominant factor associated with privacy, with higher levels of education being associated with a greater willingness to approach the court. But, overall, private forms of dispute resolution are preferred.

In chapter seven Teresa Picontó and Elena Lauroba start from the opposite perspective, and look at how frequently cases proceed from ADR towards the court system in Spain, taking into account the impact of the Covid-19 crisis. Mediation, even though encouraged by the government in Spain, is not widely used, and is not permitted in cases where there is domestic abuse or where the safety of children is at risk. The authors describe how any case of abuse will not go to the family court, but to a specialist gender violence court. But the new role of parenting coordinator is attracting a great deal of attention, with a lively debate about whether this is role is basically a social work task (welfare) or whether there is a more juridical function (justice). Meanwhile the impact of the Covid-19 crisis has had a profound effect on the work of the family justice system, causing delay in resolution while family conflict increases.

C. Part 3 Innovative Practice

After entering the court, what new procedures are developing with the involvement of different professionals and lay advisers in legally assisted decision making? How is efficient use of resources supporting the aim of Autonomy?

In chapter eight, which opens this Part, Masha Antokolskaia and her colleagues look at the new ways of supporting parents in developing their own arrangement within the shelter of the court, described as a 'non-adversarial divorce procedure' in the Netherlands. An obligation to submit a parenting plan had been placed on separating parents in the Netherlands, but a subsequent evaluation found that little help had been made available with addressing this task. This chapter describes new pilot schemes in two Dutch family courts, experimenting with non-adversarial procedures somewhat resembling Australian family dispute resolution, whereby parents receive support in preparing workable arrangements for the children. To avoid escalation of conflict, the parents first have a non-adversarial hearing where they are represented by an impartial family representative – a lawyer-mediator or mediator – who represents the whole family, including the children. If they can reach agreement at that stage the family representative will apply for a consent order, If not, the matter proceeds to the new style of interventionist family judge, the *regierechter*, who can make an immediate decision or allow the parties to start an adversarial procedure with two lawyers.

But are there other ways of enabling access to justice while controlling costs? In chapter nine Jane Krishnadas asks who needs what, where and when? She then describes the project which she started in Keele University in England in which she developed the concept of the Community Legal Companion. CLOCK (the Community Legal Outreach Collaboration Keele) was designed by applying a transformative methodology to identify resources and navigate legal needs through the family justice system. CLOCK is a community law based project whereby law students with training from local solicitors and court staff in a growing number of universities are able to support parties in a number of ways: trying to access the limited legal aid that is still potentially available where there is evidence of domestic abuse; helping at court counter services which are now short of staff; and also trying to direct parties to sources of help in the community. Jane Krishnadas developed this work from her experience with women's groups in India, and the UK, challenging the colonial public and private sector divide, and developing a collaborative, intersectional, relational and transformative mechanism for access to family justice, The approach has been of great value in responding to the increased exposure of children to harm during the Covid-19 pandemic crisis, and particularly at the intersection of private and public law.

D. Part 4 Major Policy Change

The final Part prepares us for thinking about future developments by looking closely at examples of recent major policy changes and their user impact, including the aims and aspirations, and also the outcomes, both positive and negative. The Part begins with an account in chapter ten of a new approach to family justice, 'Developing Holistic and Inclusive Family Justice in Argentina'. Julietta Marotta uses this phrase from Patrick MacDonald (see MacDonald, 2010) to describe the deeply considered Argentinian plan to move to full access to holistic and inclusive family justice, incorporating an appropriate legal framework with more accessible courts and trained judges, plus multidisciplinary assistance and empowerment of the parties involved in the conflict. In the case of domestic violence, the legal framework itself was transformed by Law 26485 in 2015 on the Right of Women to live Free of Violence, and a framework for implementation was provided through a network of legal aid offices created over the last 10 years, particularly the two centers created to assist victims of domestic violence. The legal aid provision enables a women to have interdisciplinary support from a lawyer, a psychologist and a social worker. Of course there are problems in practice of coordination, motivation and resources. But the policy and planning is exciting, and marks a major step forward along the welfare and justice axis.

In chapter eleven Verda Irtis raises questions about the family justice system in Turkey arising from the tensions between the traditional influence of the religious advisers to the family courts appointed since 2012, and the new developments of mediation, and the use of technology which have become increasingly important since the Covid-19 pandemic. The justice system is in danger of becoming increasingly fragmented and losing its cohesion. And in chapter twelve Belinda Fehlberg and Richard Ingleby note the gap between the vision set out for Australian family justice at the time of the establishment of the Family Court of Australia in 1975, with specialist judges and court staff including welfare officers and counsellors as well as legal advisers, and the situation by the time of the recommendations of the Australian Law Commission Inquiry in 2019 for addressing the division of responsibility between federal and state authorities began to be put into effect, together with a new requirement to use ADR before making an application to the court. In this context they raise the question of how a legal system can best deal with malfunctions by its judicial officers. Richard Ingleby argues that 'there needs to be more extended and precise discussion of what the aim of a court should be as a prerequisite for particular changes' (Ingleby, 2020: 181). The contributors to this volume strongly agree!

But a positive note is provided by a description of a radical and highly successful reconsideration of what a family court is for, from Germany. Thomas Meysen (chapter thirteen) describes the approach to family justice set out in the German legislation of 2009. The Act for Proceedings in Family Matters served to emphasise the importance of basic personal conflicts, but also to strengthen support and prevent conflict (Bundestags Drucksache 16/6308, p 64). The courts are required to serve a secondary non-justiciable role, not addressing the solution or decision, but rather the reasons which hinder parents from coming up with the solutions themselves. There must be a first hearing within a month, in order to prevent further escalation of a conflict, and there is an acknowledged need to restore the ability for self-determination, but with process not decision as the primary orientation. Agreement is the goal, and counselling (or mediation if desired) is the pathway. On first appearance in court the message to parents is to try counselling first, before coming back to court! The best interests of the child would normally include contact with both parents. Counselling is provided by the Youth Welfare Offices, free, with direct access to parents. And a study to appraise the system (see Ekert and Heiderhoff, 2018) found a high percentage (60–70 per cent) of the professionals think the proceedings are practicable, and that more agreements are reached, though they are less confident about prevention of conflict or success in high-conflict cases. The association of welfare with justice is strong and clear, while autonomy is supported but free from the economic pressures on the public or private purse as Germany draws on the pre-existing network of Youth Welfare Officers, and the right to use these without charge is statutory. The approach is attractive in its direct commitment to social support to enable parents to understand their conflict, and hopefully move towards resolving it. It offers high normativity, clear orientation for parents and professionals, with early intervention by welfare services providing what has been called 'fenced in voluntariness' (see Loschky, 2011), ie guided autonomy without direct cost to individual parties. It would of course be useful to have the views of parties, and more information about the working of the welfare services.

We also note the views of Barbara Willenbacher on the need to balance prevention, management, settlement and adjudication on the one hand, with enforcement, sanctioning and defending on the other. At the Workshop Professor Willenbacher gave a more detailed account of how the majority of all actions at the Family Court are regulated bureaucratically, following and enforcing rules for divorce, pension splitting, levels of child support and so on, while the mediating / counselling roles of the Family Court are mainly concerned with parenting arrangements. A sanctioning role emerges when a child is taken into care, and single mothers and migrant families are over-represented in this group, a matter often neglected in public discussion by partisans of mediation and consent. Furthermore she feels that the Family Court has a repressive controlling function with respect to domestic violence, mainly through the use of restraining orders. In the German family justice system parental autonomy is limited in the joint legal custody presumption, and child support rates are set by regulation, but compliance by low income fathers is low, and in contact cases the negative impact of domestic violence is not well acknowledged. Recent government-funded research has reported the statements of fathers about their relationship with the mothers, but not the statements of the mothers. The German system, like all family justice systems, is far from perfect. But the availability of the counselling services makes a major difference to our axes of concern by enabling justice to sit alongside welfare and for a degree of autonomy to flourish for its own sake without economic incentive.

The volume ends (chapter fourteen) with brief observations from the editors, who are most grateful to Justice Encarna Roca Trias, Deputy President of the Constitutional Court of Spain for her contribution to the Workshop. She emphasised the enduring and permanent role of the judges in family conflict, and also the long standing and ongoing need to guarantee the human rights of people in involved in family conflict.

II. QUESTIONS FOR THE FUTURE

An international collection of sociolegal research reports could simply describe the different ways of carrying out the necessary functions of the justice systems in the countries studied. We have been encouraged by the research presented at our Workshop to go further, and to try to develop some old and identify some new questions about what a family justice system is for.

Is the purpose of a justice system concern to promote societal values? To protect the vulnerable? To enhance the life chances of children and young people? To control unacceptable behaviours? Maintain the rule of law? Provide access to justice? Or all of these and more … while making sure the quality of judicial decision making in family matters is good enough.

Our key original question was about how justice in family matters sits alongside welfare considerations, and if so which element along this axis dominates in the case of conflict between the two? For example, how does a legislative provision such as the Children Act 1989 (England and Wales) ensure adherence to the principle of welfare paramountcy in any decision in a matter concerning a child when the judge has no expertise in child development? Welfare advice must play a part. But who will give it? Who will pay for it? What authority will it have?

A second important question has emerged, about how far the current emphasis on autonomy in decision making supports the value of respect for the rights of the individual, and how far it is used to justify reducing the cost of a justice system by keeping people out of court. How do autonomy and economy fit together? And how do our two axes of welfare/justice and autonomy/economy intersect a time when family problems appear to be more turbulent and difficult to manage, and resources are increasingly limited? The kinds of issues arising between conflicted separated parents seem to be revealing extreme behaviours, including domestic abuse and violence, which are less manageable through out-of-court ADR, and there appears to be an overlap between the rights of adults in private disputes and the public responsibility for child protection. Where will our thinking go next? The growing interest in universal holistic provision and concern for the experience of those who need a family justice system, together with better understanding of the assumptions of those who provide it, may help us to move in a positive direction. The Covid experience has stimulated radical thinking and stimulated changes in practice. Perhaps the need to think about what might be 'good enough justice' during this time of crisis when courts have been closing may encourage us to consider radical and effective solutions. But only when we have identified our goals for a family justice system can we begin to evaluate its effectiveness.

REFERENCES

Ekert, S and Heiderhoff, B (2018) *Die evaluaering der FGR Reform Abschlussbericht zum Forscungvorhaben* (Berlin, Ministry of Justice).

Ingleby, R (2020) 'Case Management: Never mind the quality feel the width', *Aus Law Journal* 94, 179.

Loschky, A (2011) 'Die Beratung mit angeordneter Teilnahme' in K Menne and M Weber (eds), *Professionelle Kooperation zum whole des Kindes. Hinwirken auf elterliches Einvernehmen im familiengerichtlichen Verfahren (FamFG)* (Weinheim, Basel, Beltz Juventa), s 137–150.

Maclean, M (ed) (2005) *Family Law and Family Values* (Oxford, Hart Publishing).

Maclean, M and Dijksterhuis, B (eds) (2019) *Digital Family Justice* (Oxford, Hart Bloomsbury).

Maclean, M and Eekelaar, J (eds) (2016) *Managing Family Justice in Diverse Societies* (Oxford, Hart Bloomsbury).

Maclean, M, Eekelaar, J and Bastard, B (eds) (2015) *Delivering Family Justice in the 21st Century* (Oxford, Hart Bloomsbury).

Maclean, M and Kurczewski, K (eds) (1994) *Families Politics and the Law* (Oxford, Oxford University Press).

Macdonald, RA (2010) 'Access to civil justice' in *The Oxford Handbook of Empirical Legal Research* (Oxford University Press) 492–521.

Part A

Boundaries

1

Recent Family Law Reforms and High-Conflict Post-Separation Parenting Disputes in Canada

RACHEL TRELOAR

THIS CHAPTER BEGINS by examining ongoing efforts to make British Columbia's family justice system more user-focused and accessible, and the recent statutory changes to Canada's Divorce Act (1985).[1] Next, it turns to high-conflict post-separation parenting disputes and considers the aims and purpose of Canada's family justice systems, the tools available to the courts and the current approach to high-conflict disputes. Then, drawing from the author's research conducted with parents in British Columbia (BC) who had at one time experienced high-conflict disputes regarding arrangements for their children, it provides an overview of what parents said was, or would have been, helpful at the time. The chapter concludes by suggesting that while recent transformations are generally positive and likely to be helpful to the majority of divorcing parents, the system remains under resourced. Although the main purpose and intent of these reforms appears to be to further the best interests of children, a focus on information provision and early resolution out of court has left parents who do require court assistance and extra-legal support with few places to turn, while they continue to experience court delays and ongoing difficulties.

The chapter argues that in a democracy, according to the rule of law, a justice system must have a welfare function. While Canada's family justice system provides some protection for those deemed 'most vulnerable', by promoting party 'autonomy' and cost saving through out-of-court dispute resolution, the system may delay the resolution of more complex and high-conflict disputes, thereby adding costs and creating new vulnerabilities. Further, by shifting state resources to information and online dispute resolution, the minority who do require the assistance of the court are left with individualised 'justice' and 'welfare' as their only options (ie a market-based approach), but only if they can afford it. Access to justice is widely regarded as a human rights issue. And,

[1] Divorce Act (RSC 1985, c 3 (2nd Supp)).

as Justice Encarna Roca has noted (see chapter fourteen, p 260), we must not forget our obligation to ensure the human rights of those who are experiencing a family law conflict.

I. BACKGROUND AND CONTEXT

In Canada, family law is an area of shared jurisdiction between the federal and provincial/territorial governments. There are two court systems, each with specific responsibilities and jurisdiction with respect to family matters. The federal Superior Court has jurisdiction over divorce by way of the Divorce Act (1985), as well as related matters such as child and spousal support, 'parenting time' and 'parental decision-making responsibilities'[2] when they are part of a divorce application. The division of family property is regulated by provincial and territorial statutes, regardless of whether divorce is involved. Provincial or territorial legislation applies to unmarried couples as well as married couples who are separated, and the courts also deal with child-related matters. Therefore, family legal disputes may be addressed through federal or provincial/territorial statutes. Each province or territory is responsible for the administration of justice, including the court system, and sets out its own family law legislation. Provincial Court rules are less complicated and less formal, cases are usually heard more quickly, and court costs are lower. Nevertheless, despite differences in legislation, court structures and rules, as well as programming and service delivery, provincial/territorial justice systems share similar objectives with their federal counterparts.

Broadly, Canada's family justice system includes federal, provincial and territorial government ministries/departments and their staff, those working in the formal legal system (eg judges and lawyers), as well as paralegals, legal advocates,[3] Alternative Dispute Resolution (ADR) practitioners and front-line workers in community agencies. The unique geographic and cultural terrain of Canada presents challenges with respect to provision. That, along with political and legal variations at the provincial level, means that there are differences in the availability of programs and services across Canada. This contribution will use the BC (Canada's westernmost province) family law system as a provincial example. While family legislation varies across provinces and territories, a common aim is to ensure the best interests of children, with ADR as the preferred option for resolving disputes.

Canadian democracy is governed by the rule of law, a key principle of which is that every person is to be afforded the same protections of the law and its

[2] Revisions to the Divorce Act include new language for parents' responsibilities. Previously, the Divorce Act used the terms 'custody' and 'access'.

[3] Family law legal advocates are typically community agency staff with knowledge and experience of court processes who can help people understand their options and rights. While advocates cannot provide legal advice, they may assist with negotiations and provide court support.

process. Legal aid plans prioritise services to areas that are constitutionally guaranteed,[4] with the remaining funding going to civil legal aid. Starting with significant cuts in 2002, family law legal aid has been decimated in BC (as in other provinces), to the extent that the current legal aid system falls far short of its international obligations.[5] Factor 7 (Civil Justice) of the World Justice Project Rule of Law Index[6] measures the extent to which 'ordinary people' can resolve their grievances effectively and peacefully in the civil justice system, including whether civil justice systems are accessible and affordable. Timeliness of court proceedings, effectiveness of enforcement of orders, and the accessibility, effectiveness and impartiality of ADR mechanisms are also included in the measures. Canada ranks twelfth out of 24 among countries in the EU, EFTA and North America, and nineteenth out of 37 high income countries.[7] Thus Canada lags behind other 'developed' nations in ensuring that all citizens can effectively access the civil justice system. As in the UK, cutbacks to legal aid and reduced court funding have resulted in court backups and an increase in self-represented litigants (SRLs). In Canada, 58 per cent of family law litigants are now self-represented (Statistics Canada, 2021a).

II. REFORMS: CANADA AND BC

A. The BC Family Law Act

The BC Family Law Act (2011)[8] (FLA) is the primary family law legislation in BC and it applies to everyone in a family-like relationship.[9] Following extensive review and consultation,[10] the FLA received Royal Assent in 2011 and came into full force in March 2013. The statutory reforms were designed to reflect social change, place the safety and best interests of the child first, and keep families safe.[11] Amongst the changes, the FLA clearly sets out parental responsibilities and both defines and addresses family violence. The FLA explicitly promotes out of court dispute resolution as cheaper and faster, and as reducing the emotional consequences for all involved (Bond, 2013). However, the reforms

[4] For example, when a person is charged with an offence for which incarceration is likely on conviction, or when a person is facing extradition.

[5] See the World Justice Project: worldjusticeproject.org/rule-of-law-index/country/2020/Canada/Civil%20Justice.

[6] ibid.

[7] ibid.

[8] Family Law Act (SBC 2011, c 25).

[9] The federal Divorce Act only applies to those who are married.

[10] For a more detailed overview of the development of the FLA, see Treloar (2015) and Treloar and Boyd (2014).

[11] British Columbia, Legislative Assembly, *Official Report of the Debates of the Legislative Assembly*, 27 (14 November 2011) at 8709 (Hon S Bond) and 17 November 2011) at 8845 (Hon S Bond), online: Debates of the Legislative Assembly (Hansard) www.leg.bc.ca/documents-data/debate-transcripts/39th-parliament/4th-session.

were not accompanied by new funding for the services and programmes required by families as they face the emotional and legal process of divorce. Concomitant with a shift toward a neoliberal approach to governance, family justice in BC has moved away from state intervention and service provision toward a market-based approach (Treloar, 2015; Treloar and Boyd, 2014). The reforms involved an explicit shift of responsibility without a shift of resources. Solving family legal disputes is understood to be matter of personal and family responsibility, with consensual dispute resolution the preferred option. Those who are unable to resolve disputes early, cooperatively and without recourse to the courts, are left with few places to turn.

In family cases, BC provides limited legal aid only in cases of family violence (and even then only to get a protection order); situations where children are unlawfully removed from the jurisdiction; or where there is an unreasonable denial of access. However, it is well known that abuse can continue well beyond separation, and thus the need for legal advice and representation is likely to remain after a protection order is in place. A test case of the constitutionality of this denial of legal aid where violence is a factor is set to be heard by the BC Supreme Court in March 2022.[12]

In 2017, The BC New Democratic Party (BC NDP) came into power, introducing a number of promising developments in line with their social-democratic values. While the 2017 budget did increase legal aid funding by approximately $5 million dollars, the increase fell far short in replacing the $40 million cut by the previous government. Although the BC government announced increased investment in the justice sector, including for increasing digital access to justice services for remote parts of the province and for family dispute resolution services (mainly for indigenous child welfare), legal aid funding still falls well short of what is needed to ensure that qualifying individuals have access to legal advice and representation.

Resources have been moved to online information and dispute resolution which are most useful for those with more straightforward issues and some ability to cooperate with respect to their children. There are very limited programmes or services providing targeted support unless there has been violence, and even then support is piecemeal. Parents' access to the family justice system is limited unless they can resolve their disputes independently or pay for legal assistance themselves. Of course, a party's personal resources have a significant impact on both process and outcome. Personal resources influence the available dispute resolution processes and the nature of the final agreement reached. There is a risk that where one party has fewer resources than the other, that party may be pressured into settling on the other's terms. When resolution is prioritised over justice, particularly when there are inequities in material and personal resources

[12] Single Mothers' Alliance v BC. See www.westcoastleaf.org/our-work/legal-aid-test-case and the BC Supreme Court ruling allowing the case to go ahead, www.bccourts.ca/jdb-txt/sc/19/14/2019 BCSC1427.htm.

between parents, those with fewer resources may find themselves on the losing end with respect to outcomes.

Nevertheless, since 2017 the BC government, the Legal Services Society (the legal aid provider), and other academic and professional groups, have been trying to broaden the scope of legal services within existing funding, and new initiatives are being piloted. Government has been working to find justice system 'efficiencies', simplify court rules and further promote ADR. While there is evidence of systemic change, it is unlikely that previous legal aid cuts will be fully restored. Instead, government is focused on early resolution and improving dispute resolution services. Indeed, the BC Ministry of Attorney General's service plan for 2018–2021 emphasised that the Ministry 'serves families with children experiencing separation or divorce by providing information and mediation services to help resolve family law disputes outside of court' (British Columbia Attorney General, 2018: 18). Notably, no mention was made of legal advice or assistance if it is necessary for the parties to go to court. The most recent service plan (British Columbia Attorney General, 2021) focuses on fairness and 'the most vulnerable', saying that 'fairness in the justice and public safety sector is bolstered by improving the public's access to justice, including affordable, effective and lasting resolution to civil and family disputes, as well as criminal legal proceedings. A fair justice system protects the public, including the disadvantaged and victims of crime' (British Columbia Attorney General, 2021: 6). However, while increased access to justice is listed as a key ministry objective, performance measures are linked to out-of-court dispute resolution, assessment and other forms of early intervention. Clearly, access to justice still means access to information and dispute resolution.

In January 2019, an External Review of Legal Aid Service Delivery ('Roads to Revival')[13] was conducted for the government by Jamie Maclaren, QC. Maclaren, who has a long history of involvement with pro bono groups, was given the mandate to review the effectiveness and efficiencies of legal aid service delivery models from the perspective of those who use legal aid services. The overall aim was to advance the rule of law and access to justice in the province. He assessed legal aid services and systems by applying Access to Justice BC's Triple Aim Framework,[14] which has three core objectives: better user outcomes, better user experiences and lower system costs. Overall, the goal of the framework is to encourage a 'user centric' perspective. The Triple Aim Framework has been endorsed by Provincial Court Judges and a number of key justice system organisations. Maclaren's main recommendations involved developing community legal clinics staffed by lawyers and advocates and a more balanced service-delivery mix, rather than the current fee-driven model.

[13] See news.gov.bc.ca/files/Roads_to_Revival-Maclaren_Legal_Aid_Review-25FEB19.pdf.
[14] See accesstojusticebc.ca/the-a2j-triple-aim.

Also in 2019, the BC government launched a pilot project in the capital: the Victoria Early Resolution and Case Management Model (Court Rule 5.01). The project was designed to encourage consensual dispute resolution and to assist parties in obtaining 'just and timely decisions'[15] in Provincial Court. While the original wording was 'just and timely decisions', the website currently says 'earlier and more durable resolutions. This reduces conflict and builds skills that can help prevent future conflict.' The change of wording focuses less on 'justice' and 'timeliness' (ie the legal system), and more on conflict resolution between the individuals involved. The process introduces early resolution requirements for family law matters proceeding through Provincial Court in the Victoria registry. Specifically, these matters are child support, spousal support, parenting arrangements (including parenting time and parenting responsibilities) and guardianship of a child. In addition to the early resolution requirements, the new process introduces a family management conference which will replace the initial appearance and is intended to provide increased case management (specifically, by exploring dispute resolution and ensuring parties are prepared if they need to proceed to trial). The stated purpose of these new processes is to 'build knowledge, support problem solving and help parties prepare for next steps'.[16] It is expected that once the model has been evaluated and fine-tuned it will be rolled out across BC, although it is likely that the impact of the Covid-19 pandemic will delay this expansion.

In 2020, the FLA was amended to add arbitration of family law disputes, and the pilot project was expanded to a second courthouse in Surrey. All of these changes are part of a larger project by the Ministry of Attorney General and the Provincial Court to reform the Provincial Family Court rules, to encourage out-of-court dispute resolution, and to ensure that litigation is viewed only as a last resort. Key policy changes are being trialled in the Victoria Provincial Court registry, as a first step. Under the new rules, there is a process for seeking protection orders or for extraordinary and time-sensitive parenting matters. A judge will hear only those matters first, with the outstanding matters dealt with through the early resolution and case management process.

As with the current process, the province's four Justice Access Centres will provide legal information, needs assessment, referrals and consensual dispute resolution services free of charge. The Ministry's webpage[17] says: 'People with lower incomes may be eligible for free limited legal advice or representation through Legal Aid BC. […] Parties may choose to hire a lawyer, a private family mediator or take part in a collaborative law agreement with private family lawyers.' In accordance with a shift to the individualisation of Family Justice Services in BC,[18] the 'choices' to hire a lawyer, mediator or arbitrator, or to

[15] See www2.gov.bc.ca/gov/content/life-events/divorce/family-justice/your-options/early-resolution (page date: 7 July 2021).

[16] ibid.

[17] ibid.

[18] See Treloar (2015), (2018); Treloar and Boyd (2014) Treloar and Funk (2008).

participate in collaborative family law are at the expense of the parties.[19] This means that those without the funds to use market-based services get only limited assistance and may need to represent themselves in court, likely affecting the outcome.

In previous work with this group, completed for a 2018 Oñati workshop (Treloar, 2019), I examined 'MyLawBC', an interactive digital platform modelled on the Dutch Rechtweiser. This was developed in 2016 to offer parents online information, with the aim of encouraging them to resolve family disputes themselves. In line with this focus on self-help and early resolution, MyLawBC has been further expanded, offering parents the opportunity to develop their own parenting plan online. They can also access up to five free hours with a qualified mediator. If the issues are not resolved using mediation, the parties may then file an application and proceed to court. A family justice counsellor[20] will help the parties make sure they are ready for court. This process is intended to be helpful both to the parties and to the courts as it means key issues will have been identified and materials organised.

The addition of online dispute resolution (ODR) may be helpful to parties who have fairly simple disputes and can communicate effectively, perhaps with a little structure and support, but it does not reduce my concern about parents with complex or high-conflict disputes being left with few places to turn. Indeed, a 2019 evaluation report prepared by RA Malatest and Associates[21] supports that concern, finding that '[t]he resources currently offered are helpful to those whose legal issues align with the resources, but there is considerable demand for pathways and tools that address more complex and a greater variety of legal issues' (at p iii). A large number of MyLawBC users who were surveyed indicated that the available pathways did not list or address their legal issues. Thus resourcing out-of-court support and information means shifting resources away from those who *do* need to go to court, leaving them with little or no support, even in highly complex and difficult circumstances.

B. The Divorce Act

I now turn to Canada's Divorce Act.[22] Bill C-78[23] amended the federal Divorce Act by updating language with respect to children's arrangements, establishing

[19] These expenses are either shared equally (eg mediation) or are the individual responsibility of each partner (eg lawyer, CFL professionals).

[20] In BC, Family Court Counsellors are conflict resolution professionals employed by the province. Most have an undergraduate degree and additional training in conflict resolution.

[21] See lss.bc.ca/sites/default/files/2019-06/MyLawBCevaluationReport2019_0.pdf.

[22] Divorce Act (RSC 1985, c 3 (2nd Supp)). Available at laws-lois.justice.gc.ca/eng/acts/d-3.4.

[23] Bill C-78: An Act to amend the Divorce Act, the Family Orders and Agreements Enforcement Assistance Act and the Garnishment, Attachment and Pension Diversion Act and to make consequential amendments to another Act. See canlii.ca/t/53rg6; openparliament.ca/bills/42-1/C-78.

new rules for family relocation, providing a new means to get or change child/spousal support orders, and laying out an explicit definition of family violence. The Divorce Act now specifically states that a court 'shall give primary consideration to the child's physical, emotional and psychological safety, security and well-being'[24] and the statute was reformed with four broad objectives in mind: promoting the best interests of the child; addressing family violence; reducing child poverty; and making Canada's family justice system more accessible and efficient. The changes, which updated federal family law for the first time since 1986, received Royal Assent on 21 June 2019 and were to come into effect in 2020. Due to the Covid-19 pandemic, government delayed the changes to 1 March 2021.

Amongst the changes is new child-focused terminology (such as 'parenting orders', 'parenting time' and 'parental decision-making responsibilities'), which is now used in place of terms such as 'custody' and 'access' in order to emphasise relationships with, and the best interests of, children, rather than the rights and entitlements of parents. Parenting orders set out each parent's decision-making responsibilities (eg decisions regarding health care, education, culture, language, religion or significant extra-curricular activities) and specifies the details of children's time with each parent ('parenting time'). The Divorce Act does not contain any presumptions about how parenting time should be divided. Parenting orders may specify the mechanism by which parents will attempt to resolve any disagreements regarding parenting. Parents also have new 'duties' under the Divorce Act. These duties will be discussed in the next section.

A clear emphasis on children's best interests and addressing family violence is now apparent in both statutes. Like BC's FLA (2011), the court can *only* consider the best interests of the children, and the court must assess a list of specific factors (Divorce Act, s 16(3)). If family violence is present, the court must also consider a second list of factors (s 16(4)). Again, the Divorce Act is very similar to the FLA with respect to family violence. The provincial statute also focuses on parental responsibilities and on out-of-court dispute resolution, while the federal statute emphasises the accessibility and efficiency of the family justice system as well as child poverty reduction. It aims to reduce child poverty through various measures, including new enforcement measures to ensure that child support is paid, streamlining of administrative processes including the recalculation of child support payments, and an emphasis on parental duties.

Concerns about the cost of welfare provision have led legislators in many western countries to direct judicial outcomes by ensuring that both parents fulfil their financial obligations to provide for their children, therefore protecting children from poverty. Considerable research indicates that mothers are more likely than fathers to experience financial disadvantage following separation (Scott, 2020a). As mothers are the recipients of child support in most cases, non/under-payment is a complex and gendered problem. While most payors (usually

[24] Divorce Act, s 16(2).

fathers) do fulfil their child-related responsibilities post-separation, some go to considerable extremes to avoid or try to reduce their financial responsibilities.[25] Furthermore, there is a link between post-separation financial abuse and coercive and controlling behaviour – a key feature of intimate partner violence (Scott, 2020b).

Reducing child poverty is a grand ambition, but I am not convinced that parents' behaviour can be changed by creating new norms or by legislating parental duties. Indeed, in this context, there may be a significant tension between government goals and those of the parties involved. More specifically, despite the appearance of new norms with respect to parental 'duties', where mothers bear the primary responsibility of providing for children when fathers will not,[26] and have less financial resources with which to access the justice system or to obtain needed support resources, this legislation will not provide children with a route out of poverty. Furthermore, the interpretation of legal norms may not recognise gender asymmetry in how parents carry out their duties.

In 2014 the OECD found that Canada had the second highest poverty rate compared to similar countries. International studies indicate that people living on low income over the long term are likely to remain disadvantaged with respect to health outcomes and life expectancy (Statistics Canada, 2021b), making a national poverty reduction plan essential. With 'Opportunity for All', the Federal government did set out such a strategy in 2018, and the Poverty Reduction Act was passed in 2019. However, despite ambitious poverty reduction targets and slight decreases in relative poverty since, lone mothers remain one of the groups most affected.[27]

According to Hakovirta (2011), in Canada, when child support is received it closes the poverty gap by 23.9 per cent, indicating that child support may be a key source of income for recipient parents. However, using measures of relative poverty reduction, child support can only lift one in four children over the poverty line. Consequently, without a broader range of policies to lift lone parent families out of poverty, the Divorce Act is unlikely to achieve its stated objective of reducing child poverty. Indeed, family law legal aid is more often used by women, so a lack of it is most likely to hurt women and their children (Track, 2014; Treloar, 2015). Also, without adequate access to legal assistance and advice, even middle-income parents who must seek the assistance of the court in order to resolve their family law disputes may find themselves in

[25] For example, *Colucci v Colucci* (2021 SCC 24) involved a father who underpaid child support over a 16-year period, failed to disclose his income and rarely made voluntary payments, resulting in a debt of more than CDN $170,000. Once the children were grown the father successfully applied to the Ontario Superior Court to reduce the child support arrears retroactively. The decision was overturned by the Court of Appeal for Ontario and the Supreme Court of Canada unanimously upheld the decision.

[26] Although some fathers live in poverty themselves and cannot even afford a small monthly child support payment, and thus requiring them to do so would do little to alleviate child poverty.

[27] Statistical data beyond 2018 is not yet available, however recent data suggests that is still the case. See www150.statcan.gc.ca/n1/pub/36-28-0001/2021005/article/00002-eng.htm.

significant financial difficulties (Trebilcock, Duggan and Sossin, 2012) or facing poverty, especially if they are among those who require the assistance of the courts to resolve complex and ongoing family law problems.

III. HIGH-CONFLICT DISPUTES

Johnston and Roseby (1997) define a high-conflict divorce as involving long, bitter and protracted disputes with high levels of litigation and re-litigation. There is often distrust and difficulty communicating and cooperating with respect to children. There may also be verbal and/or physical abuse. They note that while approximately one quarter to one third of parents report significant conflict post-separation, for about 10 per cent of divorcing parents hostility and conflict may last throughout their children's growing up years. One or both parties may drive this conflict.

In Canada, each province or territory has a slightly different approach to high-conflict and complex family law disputes. For example, British Columbia requires parents (and lawyers, if they have them) to attend a Judicial Case Conference (JCC) with a Supreme Court judge or master in the event of a contested divorce. An applicant may also apply for a JCC in order to get help resolving the dispute and potentially settling it. Both parents must attend a three-hour Parenting After Separation (PAS) program before their provincial court appearance is scheduled, although there are exemptions (eg in cases of domestic violence).

A range of programmes and services to help address high-conflict disputes outside court have been introduced across different parts of Canada, including: parenting education programmes; mediation; collaborative family law; arbitration; parenting coordination; expert assessments; and children's lawyers. Generally, parents must use their own resources to resolve family legal problems and the court is regarded as a place of last resort for only the most complex or conflicted cases. While the state has essentially withdrawn from support and intervention in family law disputes, what funding is available has been shifted to ADR and to the development of online informational resources. These resources tend to be used by parents who can communicate adequately regarding their children, and are in fairly straightforward and low-conflict situations. However, parents with complex or high-conflict disputes often require additional resources specific to their concerns (Treloar, 2019).

In Canada, the predominant approach to high-conflict post-separation parenting disputes, as reflected in recent family law and policy reforms, is to 'nudge' parents toward out of court resolution, while also extolling the many advantages of doing so. Indeed, under recent changes to the federal Divorce Act, parents have a new *duty*[28] to attempt to resolve their disputes out of court if it is

[28] www.justice.gc.ca/eng/fl-df/pdf/fsdpo-fiopa-eng.pdf.

safe to do so. The choice of the word 'duty' in this instance is significant, in that its meaning is similar to 'responsibility' but with moral undertones. While the term responsibility has often been used with respect to the family, the term duty carries an additional connotation of a duty to the state, leaving no doubt that the obligation is a legal one.

Under section 7 of the Divorce Act, additional parental duties include:

- exercising parenting time, decision-making responsibility or contact with a child under a contact order, in a manner that is consistent with the best interests of the child;
- protecting children from conflict arising from the proceeding;
- trying to resolve parental disagreements through mediation, collaborative approaches or arbitration rather than by going to court;
- providing each other with complete, accurate and up-to-date information as required under the Divorce Act; and
- complying with court orders while they are in effect.[29]

Therefore, I suggest that the role of Canada's family justice system is to activate parents to fulfil their responsibilities to their children *and* to the state, ideally making joint decisions about what is in their children's best interests, and doing so without recourse to the courts. This raises the question of whether federal and provincial reforms, in emphasising individualised problem solving and removing family disputes from the formal system, change the very meaning of justice (Diduck, 2016). I believe they do because, as Alison Diduck points out in the context of reforms in England and Wales, reforms that rely on an individualised and degendered notion of autonomy, and marginalise legal principles, are 'becoming the very essence of family justice' (Diduck, 2016: 133). With family disputes now conceived as interpersonal rather than legal disputes, the responsibility for resolving disputes and the consequences of not doing so fall entirely to the parties. Diduck further argues that 'in promoting justice-as-autonomy in an otherwise law-free environment, usually in money, property and child-related matters' (2016: 143) principles of gender and generational justice may be ignored, primarily disadvantaging women and children.

In this reconstruction of autonomy, parents who are unable to resolve their disputes, for whatever reason, will be seen as failing to fulfil their moral duties and therefore as undeserving of precious family justice system resources. Yet, as Lister and Campling contend, 'autonomy, and the agency that derives from it, is only made possible by the human relationships that nourish it and the social infrastructure that supports it' (2003: 114). Therefore, when relationships involving children 'fail', in order for both parties to be similarly positioned with respect to autonomy in the decision-making process and able to make joint

[29] ibid. See also Divorce Act, s 7: laws.justice.gc.ca/eng/acts/d-3.4/FullText.html.

decisions about what is in their child's best interests, a certain amount of social infrastructure is required, including early and timely access to quality professional legal advice and support services. Without this, a parent lacks meaningful 'choices' and their autonomy is limited.

Parents in high-conflict and complex disputes often do attempt ADR and engage in self-help (Treloar, 2019). However, they are not always able to resolve their disputes without going to court. Those who do may find that the outcome is not enforceable or sustainable (Treloar, 2019). Thus given the many financial, emotional, social and health care costs of protracted conflict and family law litigation,[30] ensuring that families with complex or high-conflict situations receive sufficient assistance to successfully navigate difficult family changes is essential. Although this broader approach might impact on the justice system budget, it could save costs elsewhere (eg the health care, income support, housing, education and employment budgets) while also reducing the likelihood of family poverty. Furthermore, if a fair and informed settlement is the outcome sought, some families will be excluded by virtue of their financial situation in combination with specific factors of their case. For example, where one parent lacks legal capacity, the other parent is likely to bear greater responsibility overall, in addition to their own costs. Similarly, in cases where a child has complex medical needs and parents cannot agree on parenting arrangements, one or both may bear significant additional costs as they attempt to resolve their disputes. Few publicly paid health professionals are willing to become involved in complex legal cases, meaning that private experts must be hired at significant personal expense. Given that parents and the courts have a legal *duty* to put children's interests first, resources must be available to ensure they are able to do so. I now turn to findings from my empirical research with parents, summarising their perspectives of what helped, or was needed, at the time of their high-conflict dispute concerning children.

IV. PARENTS' PERSPECTIVES: WHAT HELPED, WHAT WAS NEEDED

The qualitative study on which this section draws was conducted with parents residing in BC, who at one time experienced a high-conflict separation or divorce involving children and who looking back regard the experience as having been transformative (ie it changed them in a positive sense). I conducted in-depth semi-structured face-to-face interviews with 25 participants (18 mothers and 7 fathers) using a general interview guide, to answer the following research questions: How do mothers and fathers make sense of their high-conflict process, and how can it be transformed into a positive experience? Specifically, what facilitates this process, what challenges are encountered and how are they overcome?

[30] See eg Currie (2009); Genn (2019); Moore and Farrow (2019); Wickrama et al (2006).

Study participants were recruited to the study via professional contacts (lawyers, mediators, collaborative practitioners, helping and health care professionals), community agencies, advertisements in newspapers and by referral from other participants. At the time of interviews (2012–2014), participants were aged between 42 and 72 years and were 4 to 23 years post-separation. At separation, the age of the youngest child of the participants ranged from unborn to 14 years of age and 18 participants had a child under 5 years of age. Due to the sensitivity of the topic and to protect the anonymity of the parties, when writing about the experiences of study participants I gave each a pseudonym and changed minor details. As participants all separated under the former provincial family legislation (Family Relations Act),[31] the study also considered whether recent provincial reforms would have helped them.

Three key themes emerged from the study. First, that financial and child-related issues were interrelated (Treloar, 2022); second, that constructions of expert knowledge have implications for justice and voice; and third, that positive personal change occurs over time when a parent is supported with resources that address their specific needs and challenges (Treloar, 2018). Generally, parents who participated in the study did not feel heard or that outcomes were just. Nevertheless, despite the difficulties then encountered (and in some cases still encountered), parents detailed both what was helpful and what they felt they needed at the time. The next two sections summarise what parents found helpful and the changes they would have recommended based on their experiences in the family legal system. Since participants' responses to questions about what was helpful have been published elsewhere (Treloar, 2018), I provide only a brief summary as context for the second section.

A. What was Helpful

Participants described therapy, counselling and community support groups as most helpful, along with the support of friends and family. Some drew on spiritual practices or undertook new challenges that helped them to build resilience. Most said that they had well-developed internal resources, such as self-trust, self-sufficiency, resourcefulness and optimism – all qualities typically associated with resilience. However, it is important to be critical with respect to incorporating personal responsibility for change and the development of 'resilience', into policy and practice. While resilience and personal change are invaluable, without greater attention to litigants' broader needs, in the contemporary social and political environment both the responsibility for change and the costs will fall entirely

[31] Family Relations Act (RSBC 1996, c 128). Online BC Laws. Retrieved from www.bclaws.gov.bc.ca/civix/document/id/consol21/consol21/00_96128_01. Because of the timing of their separation, some parents also dealt with disputes under the FLA. However, the other reforms discussed in this chapter came into effect after the study was completed.

on individuals and families. It is also important to note that while many parents did find counselling helpful, legal expenses left other parents without any spare funds for counselling or support programs other than those offered by not-for-profit agencies. While these services are often excellent, many organisations lack sufficient funding and do not have the resources to help with complex situations.

Participants' experiences of lawyers varied, and a small number barely used lawyers at all. Although from the legal perspective their problems *are* legal ones, for the parents I interviewed their difficulties encompassed extraordinary challenges, often in combination, such as parent and/or child health and/or mental health problems, financial problems, domestic violence, abduction and addiction. These complexities help to explain not only why some parents require legal assistance and advice specific to their circumstances, rather than generic information, but also why extra-legal support is required as parents attempt to move forward despite ongoing challenges.

B. What was Needed at the Time

Turning to participant responses to the question: 'What would have made the process easier for you and what did you need at the time?', participants identified three general but interrelated areas as requiring change. These were changes to the legal system or processes, social support needs and personal development processes, which for some participants were linked to need for cultural change. Participants were clear that they needed a guide through the process as well as support programs, and that they needed a voice with which they could be heard within the legal system. Some identified stereotypes and cultural beliefs, especially gendered ones, as linked to personal change and issues around being heard. Since the focus of this chapter is the family justice system, I will now turn to summarise what would be helpful changes to family justice system processes, as articulated by study participants.

i. A Timely and Responsive System

Participants overwhelmingly said that a less adversarial and institutional system was needed. The current system should be replaced by a more timely and responsive system using triage, which provides early resolution and support, fast-tracking into the courts when appropriate, and more timely decisions. Paradoxically, the focus on out-of-court dispute resolution often delayed resolution. For example, Greg said that mediation and collaborative law were not helpful. Instead, a more timely and specialised court with a single judge assigned to his case would have done much to prevent the development of conflict in the first place. Although BC does not have such a system, active management by a single specialist judge would likely go some distance in ensuring timely and sustainable outcomes.

Mothers who had experienced domestic abuse felt that some professionals allowed, or even enabled, their former partner to continue the abuse through the legal system, and that more awareness and education was needed.

> For a high-conflict divorce like I had, if they can spot that right away it would be really good if they don't start suggesting mediation because all it does is allow the abuser another venue for browbeating the other person down. It just creates … it keeps getting farther and farther apart and it puts them in a position where they start to feel more and more powerful. (Emily)

Helen spoke about the emotional and financial consequences of her drawn-out legal process and envisioned a process that was less damaging to parents and children,

> I would take all of it out of this adversarial system, without question. And I would think about how you could minimise the damage. It is traumatic enough for anybody to go through the division of your life. The children are the ultimate commitment; they are not taken into account. It's a ruin … living in the toxic process that ensues.

Once a successful professional, Helen exhausted all of her resources, which had '*irreparable* consequences … even though I was successful in what I set out to do, in the issues that were dealt with, the fallout is a pretty sad story with the prolonged and ongoing poverty'. Having been screened out of mandatory mediation due to family violence and other factors, Helen did need to go to court, but given the complex circumstances involved, legal aid was not a viable option. Rather, she needed a more timely, responsive and child-focused court that would allow her to move forward and rebuild life for herself and her children.

ii. More Accountability and Enforcement

Participants wanted better enforcement of orders or agreements, saying that parents must be held accountable for their child support obligations. A number of participants went to considerable expense, and expended precious time, to make agreements or obtain orders, which were then ignored with impunity. Ideally, participants wanted child support to be an administrative matter[32] that took them out of the middle, and would spare them the difficulties and expense of chasing recalcitrant former partners. Kathy described how it took her several years to get financial disclosure or child support, while her high-income earning husband went to court self-represented:

> that was my big beef with the system. Not held to account and in fact, almost the opposite because he was unrepresented in court except in the beginning when he had *the* top lawyer in the city, um, they bend over backwards to ensure that this lay person understands the system and is not being browbeaten by the opposing counsel.

[32] As in Australia, for example. See Kaspiew (forthcoming, 2022).

Meanwhile, Kathy needed to return to work after decades as a stay at home parent, with little formal training, in order to support their children and pay her own legal expenses.

Participants also felt that professionals within the legal system must be held to account, including psychologists who prepared section 15 (Child Custody and Access Reports) reports. Two participants filed complaints due to poor practice and ethical concerns. As Wanda put it,

> be fair, get all the facts, don't take just a snapshot because a snapshot is taken out of context. Um, just get to know people … to make such weighty decisions based on just a snapshot is … was just devastating for me. […] It cost me my life savings, it cost me my health.

Under the FLA (s 211) these reports are now called 'Views of the Child Reports'. Research conducted by RISE Women's Legal Centre (Hrymak and Hawkins, 2021) with input from social scientists, suggests numerous concerns remain regarding the fairness of processes used in these assessments and outcomes, particularly where allegations of family violence were involved. The authors rightly argue for provincial guidelines in line with international standards and social science research. Arguably, provincial guidelines should apply even when violence is not a factor.

iii. A Guide Through the Process/System and a Way to Have Their Voice Heard

The majority of participants said they needed an advocate to explain and demystify the legal system, as well as a guide or coach through the broader personal, legal, and family processes. Guidance on selecting an appropriate lawyer for the case would also be helpful. For example,

> It would have been good to have an advocate but I didn't know in those days that those even existed. So that was my other challenge. I was not informed enough about, you know, how I could support myself, really. And so I think I needed people with better education, better knowledge, better understanding of the situation and people that would talk to me. And I found that a lot of them didn't really … besides saying you need to do this and that and that … nobody really listened or even really asked me how things were going or what I was going through. (Marla)

Several participants found legal advocates invaluable, especially those who have been abused. The advocate both understood the issues involved and helped them to be heard in the legal process. As one mother put it, 'it was so nice just to have someone like … "you know what? I get it."'

Some parents were able to access counselling, coaching or support groups. Those who were able to obtain needed support were also able to learn new skills and consider their own role in the conflict. For example, Alan explained that having grown up as an only child his conflict resolution skills were limited, 'being able to fight and remain friends is something I never learned. So that may have complicated things.' Counselling and coaching helped Graham realise that he was overly reactive early on and to manage his response,

> I often felt like an army soldier out in a great big field with a red x on my back, you know, and a little pellet gun, trying to make my way through somewhere. You are being hunted. You are constantly being sabotaged at every corner ... One of the things that would have made it easier for me in the process is me ... from everything I've learnt in the last couple of years, it would be completely different. Yeah, there would still be a little bit of stress but not like there was. I would be able to handle the stuff a lot better, I wouldn't be fighting at all. I wouldn't be giving in but 95% of it was pointless fighting ... or arguing. Not even to win, there was nothing to win. It was just defence, I was always defending.

However, others went without support altogether and abandoned the dispute. With little support or money, Lisa said 'I couldn't have done anything different at that time.' However, some support would have been invaluable, 'you know, if I had had *anybody* who would take me aside and had looked and just said you're doing fine. Just relax a bit, it's going to be okay, you can manage.' Thus those who had support through the personal, legal, and family processes found it central to moving forward in the midst of their challenges. Clearly, greater provision of support for those in high-conflict or complex disputes would ease conflict and support parents through the decision making process, especially if those providing support have the specialised knowledge and skills to assist.

iv. Attention to Stereotypes and Unconscious Bias (Professional and Cultural)

Parents who were unable to agree on what is in the best interests of their children described feeling stigmatised, even when it was clear that the conflict was primarily driven by the other parent. Krista wished there wasn't 'such a heavy bias on proving that the system wasn't biased in favour of women. I think just being heard. Just having people listen when you're telling the truth.' Parents in high conflict tend to be judged as poor parents, both within and outside the legal system, regardless of the circumstances involved.

Lone parents, especially mothers, face similar judgements. Helen described the stigma of being a lone parent and seen as needy and dependent (a view she finds deeply offensive), while Sofia said that she thinks lone mothers are judged and stigmatised unjustly. She also believes that society has a 'positive father bias'. Combined with gendered expectations of women, who are expected to 'make nice' regardless of the circumstances she sees this as particularly unjust. In contrast, two fathers described navigating gendered stereotypes of fathers in high-conflict situations: one as a potential child sexual abuser (social worker) and the other in relation to child support (Family Maintenance Enforcement worker). While extremely stressful and upsetting at the time, in both cases, things were eventually resolved in their favour.

A number of participants thought there was a need for more professional education, especially in relation to unconscious bias and the dynamics of abuse. Participants also said that broader cultural change is needed (eg attention to gender and cultural stereotypes, and attitudes toward and assumptions about those who are divorced and lone parents). It was felt that stereotypes were pervasive; that unconscious bias can impact both the legal process and legal outcomes; and that some legal professionals were providing advice or making judgments based on personal experience or opinion. In addition, a small number of participants mentioned that the media and social movements contributed to these stereotypes.

Overall, participants consistently said they needed a more timely and responsive legal system; a guide through the process and a way to have their voice heard; and greater accountability and enforcement. More broadly, participants said that broader cultural change and greater attention to stereotypes and unconscious bias is needed, including among family justice system professionals. The study findings highlight the need to unpack personal narratives to illustrate the diversity and complexity of these cases and improve access to justice, including broader supports and the opportunity to be heard.

V. DISCUSSION AND CONCLUSION

Returning to Diduck's 2016 critique of dispute resolution as autonomous family justice, with family legal disputes now understood to be interpersonal problems that should be resolved out of court, Diduck warns that 'What were once claims for legal entitlements become non-justiciable, and become either moral claims … or emotional claims' (2016: 136) that should be resolved on an individual or relationship level (eg by counselling) so that the parties can move forward in their lives. However, this discourse keeps family disputes in the private realm where resolving them is less a matter of law and principles of justice, and more an issue of individual behaviour or problem-solving (Diduck, 2016), such that 'All of those avenues lead away from formal law […] supported by the ideology of autonomy' (2016: 136). While most parents in the research study did find counselling and family support to be invaluable, and felt that their complex family issues did not belong in court, removing disputes from the legal system on the basis that family disputes should be solved consensually and out of court is not the solution for most high-conflict family law disputes.

In Canada, as elsewhere, both austerity and broader changes in the aims and forms of family justice services have highlighted a number of systemic problems that have only grown more obvious during the Covid-19 pandemic. While there have been a number of promising developments, more must be done to help service users with complex problems to navigate their difficulties without completely depleting their emotional and material resources in the process.

The focus on early assessment and the signposting offered through justice access centres (where they exist in BC), the presence of some screening for suitability for ADR (including for power imbalances as well as domestic violence), the simplification of forms and processes and the more integrated approach to legal and non-legal issues, are all positive developments. However, funding for legal aid, community based organisations and family services, remains inadequate and cuts by the previous government have not been sufficiently restored.

Family justice system reforms in Canada and in BC aim to create a less adversarial and costly justice system, with early resolution and out-of-court dispute resolution being key objectives. Courts are trying to develop a justice system that is easier to navigate and more user friendly. While there *has* been a clear shift to a more holistic and user-centric approach, with only the most contentious and complex cases going to court, we need to do more to ensure that the families and individuals behind those cases are able to access the support and services they require to move forward in their lives. Personal, material and systemic resources play a significant role in determining the type of dispute resolution process and other services available to each party as well as the nature of agreements that are reached.

As Mavis Maclean commented during our online Oñati workshop in 2020, we need to rethink what exactly access to justice requires access to. In my view, if access to justice simply means access to information and consensual dispute resolution, then it is not enough. While ADR and ODR may be useful tools that assist in advancing access to justice, they are no substitute for provision of a guide through the process, quality personalised advice and broader support services. These are especially needed by parents with high-conflict or complex disputes, who under the rule of law must be afforded the same protections of the law and its process.

I conclude that while recent transformations are generally positive and helpful to the majority of divorcing parents, the system remains under resourced. Although the intent of these reforms appears to be to ensure the best interests of children and to reduce costs both to court users and to the system, a focus on information provision and out-of-court dispute resolution has left parents who do require court assistance and extra-legal support with few places to turn, while court delays and their difficulties continue. As I have previously argued,[33] access to justice, including the broader programmes and services families need to navigate their difficulties, is essential to ensure that outcomes are fair and just. Thus with respect to the question, 'what is a family justice system for?' in Canada, whilst idealised notions of family and of justice lie within the collective imagination, in practice the family justice system largely operates as a mechanism to nudge disputing parents toward cooperative solutions that are least costly to all. Whether that is justice depends on where you stand. For parents in high conflict or who have highly complex disputes, it means courts for a few, and either privatised solutions or nothing for the rest.

[33] See eg Treloar (2015).

REFERENCES

Bond, S (2013) 'B.C.'s new family law reflects modern society' (Op-ed), *Vancouver Sun*: vancouversun.com/Opinion/Op-Ed/bcs-new-family-law-reflects-modern-society.

British Columbia Ministry of Attorney General (2018) 'Service plan 2018/19 – 2020/21': www.bcbudget.gov.bc.ca/2018/sp/pdf/ministry/ag-pssg.pdf.

British Columbia Ministry of Attorney General (2021) 'Service plan for 2021/22 – 2023/24': www.bcbudget.gov.bc.ca/2021/sp/pdf/ministry/ag.pdf.

Currie, A (2009) *The Legal Problems of Everyday Life: The Nature, Extent and Consequences of Justiciable Problems Experienced by Canadians* (Ottawa, Department of Justice): www.justice.gc.ca/eng/rp-pr/csj-sjc/jsp-sjp/rr07_la1-rr07_aj1/index.html.

Diduck, A (2016) 'Autonomy and family justice', *Child and Family Law Quarterly* 28(2), 133.

Genn, H (2019) 'When Law is Good for Your Health: Mitigating the Social Determinants of Health through Access to Justice', *Current Legal Problems* 72(1), 159.

Hakovirta, M (2011) 'Child Maintenance And Child Poverty: A Comparative Analysis', *The Journal of Poverty and Social Justice: Research, Policy, Practice* 19(3), 249.

Hrymak, H and Hawkins, K (2021). 'Section 211 Toolkit' (Vancouver, BC, Rise Women's Legal Centre): womenslegalcentre.ca/wp-content/uploads/2021/04/Rise-Womens-Legal-Centre-Section-211-Toolkit-1.pdf.

Johnston, J and Roseby, V (1997) *In the Name of the Child: A Developmental Approach to Understanding and Helping Children of Conflicted and Violent Divorce* (New York, Free Press).

Kaspiew, R (forthcoming, 2022) 'Australia's Family Law System: A User Centred Perspective' in M Maclean and R Treloar (eds), *International Research Handbook on Family Justice Systems* (Cheltenham, UK, Edward Elgar).

Lister, R and Campling, J (2003) *Citizenship: Feminist Perspectives* (2nd edn) (New York, Palgrave Macmillan, 2003).

Moore, L and Farrow, T (2019) 'Investing in Justice: A Literature Review in Support of the Case for Improved Access' (Toronto, ON, Canadian Forum on Civil Justice).

Scott, A (2020a) 'Surviving Post-separation Financial Violence Despite the Family Court: Complex Money Matters as Entrapment', *New Zealand Family Law Journal* 10(2), 27.

Scott, A (2020b) 'Hidden Hurt: The Impact of Post-separation Financial Violence in Aotearoa New Zealand', *Australian Journal of Family Law* 33, 282.

Statistics Canada (2021a) 'Profile of family law cases in Canada, 2019/20', 28 June: www150.statcan.gc.ca/n1/pub/85-002-x/2021001/article/00011-eng.htm.

Statistics Canada (2021b) 'Study: Lone-parent families, older people and people living alone are more likely to remain in low income, 2018', *The Daily*, 11 June: www150.statcan.gc.ca/n1/daily-quotidien/210611/dq210611b-eng.htm.

Track, L (2014) 'Putting Justice Back on the Map: The Route to Equal and Accessible Family Justice' (Vancouver, BC, West Coast LEAF): www.westcoastleaf.org/wp-content/uploads/2014/10/2014-REPORT-Putting-Justice-Back-on-the-Map.pdf.

Trebilcock, M, Duggan, A and Sossin, L (2012), *Middle Income Access to Justice* (Toronto, University of Toronto Press).

Treloar, R (2015) 'The Neoliberal Context of Family Law Reform in British Columbia, Canada: Implications for Access to (Family) Justice' in M Maclean, J Eekelaar and B Bastard (eds), *Delivering Family Justice in the 21st Century* (Oxford, Hart Bloomsbury).

Treloar, R (2018) 'High-Conflict Divorce Involving Children: Parents' Meaning-Making and Agency', *Journal of Social Welfare and Family Law* 40(2), 340.

Treloar, R (2019) '"My Problem, My Solution"? Private Ordering and Self-help in British Columbia, Canada' in M Maclean and B Dijksterhuis (eds), *Digital Family Justice: From Alternative Dispute Resolution to Online Dispute Resolution?* Oñati International Series in Law and Society (Oxford, Hart Bloomsbury).

Treloar, R (forthcoming, 2022) 'The Complex Interrelationships of Financial and Child Related Issues in Post- separation Disputes: Gender Matters' in E Aloni and R Tremblay (eds), *House Rules: Changing Families, Evolving Norms, and the Role of the Law* (Vancouver, UBC Press).

Treloar, R and Boyd, SB (2014) 'Family Law Reform in (Neoliberal) Context: British Columbia's New Family Law Act', *International Journal of Law, Policy and the Family* 28(1), 77.

Treloar, R and Funk, L (2008) 'Mothers' Health, Responsibilization, and Choice in Family Care Work after Separation/Divorce', *Canadian Journal of Public Health (Suppl Nov–Dec)* 33.

Wickrama, K, Lorenz, F, Conger, R, Elder, G, Abraham, W and Fang, S (2006) 'Changes in Family Financial Circumstances and the Physical Health of Married and Recently Divorced Mothers', *Social Science & Medicine* 63(1), 123.

2

Co-operation: The Glue that Unites the Danish Family Justice System

ANNETTE KRONBORG AND CHRISTINA JEPPESEN DE BOER

I. TOWARDS A MORE UNIFIED FAMILY JUSTICE SYSTEM

THE DANISH FAMILY Justice System was reformed in 2019. One of the main features is the strengthening of institutional co-operation between the authorities involved: the administrative family law authority and the court. There has been a political wish to establish a more unified system. The state administrative family law authority was reorganised and renamed the 'Agency of Family Law' (*Familieretshuset*) and at the ordinary courts a 'Family Court' was established. This court is not a truly specialised family court as it is established at the ordinary courts and have no specialised family judges. Judges in the Danish court system have successfully advocated to remain generalists circulating between different divisions within the court.

From the *travaux preparatoire* we learn that it is the intention of the legislature to create 'one unified family justice system' in which 'dialogue' between the Agency of Family Law and the Family Court is central. The purpose is to ensure that families encounter a unified system which seeks to find 'holistic solutions for families independent of the forum that takes the decision'.[1]

So, the Family Court and the Agency of Family Law have been given similar names which signals them as parts of the same system of family justice even though they are institutionally separate. The new Agency is located regionally, like the previous administrative authority. It is a public administrative authority belonging to the minister for social affairs and senior citizens. The family courts are part of the national court system with the minister of justice as the responsible minister. The glue that unites these two different institutions into a *unified* system of family justice is characterised as co-operation in the *travaux préparatoires*;[2] together and separate at the same time.

[1] Proposed Act L90 2018/19 with notes, pp 9–11.
[2] Proposed Act L90 2018/19 with notes, p 103.

The substantive difference and quality of these two systems is that the Family Court delivers justice and the Agency of Family Law provides conflict management such as counselling and mediation. A third actor, the municipality, is responsible for social work, which includes the protection of children at risk and the possibility of an out-of-home placement. The municipalities are not directly a part of the new family justice system. This is because divorce is regulated in private law and can be viewed to be 'socially acceptable'. It is based upon the parent's application and the protection of the 'family life' of parent and child, whereas social work is more about social problems. Nevertheless, many children in the family justice system are at risk and therefore part of the reform was aimed at strengthening the co-operation between the Agency of Family Law and the municipalities. According to the *travaux preparatoire* a central aim of the reform was 'to enhance co-operation between the family justice system and the social system'. A common understanding of 'decisions and measures which can be taken' by both actors 'to improve the actions taken for the family and the welfare of the child' is necessary.[3] In short, the individual characteristics of the three involved institutions are: the protection of the child at risk (the municipality); conflict management (the Agency of Family Law); and justice (the Family Court).

In this chapter we reflect upon institutional co-operation in the family justice system pursuant to the 2019 reform. We primarily take a legislative analytical perspective, supplemented however with raised critique and evaluations of the new system. First, we clear the way by taking a brief look at the political background to the reform, summarising the main elements of the reform, and providing a historical insight into institutional differences. We then turn to the legal framework for co-operation between the Agency of Family Law and the Family Court focusing upon the following aspects: fact finding, supervised contact, enforcement, and the role of the Agency of Family Law's Child Unit. Next, we turn to the framework for co-operation between the family justice system and the municipalities specifically looking into the following aspects: the screening process; complex cases; mandatory reporting; and the right of the municipality to initiate a family justice case. Finally, we reflect upon the success of a united family justice system, drawing upon insights from evaluations.

A. The Political Agreement behind the 2019 Reform

The 2019 reform was based upon an extra-parliamentary political agreement between most political parties in the Danish parliament, *Folketinget*.[4] This has become a common way to provide early grounds for legislation in family law.

[3] Proposed Act L90 2018/2019 with notes, p 11.

[4] www.regeringen.dk/publikationer-og-aftaletekster/aftale-om-%C3%A9t-samlet-familieretligt-system.

The agreement creates certainty that a broad majority in the parliament will vote in favour of a legislative proposal based on the agreement. There are several implications of this legislative mode. First, there is no commission of experts, as was previously common. Secondly, legislation passes through parliament swiftly with minimal debate – after all, they all agree. Thirdly, and perhaps not necessarily related, is that there is an intention to evaluate the changes within a few years. It may be suggested that this means 'evaluation' has come to replace caution when new fundamental changes are put into place.[5]

Historically, the agreement reached may be viewed as part of a train of events which has developed and favoured the administrative procedural regime in family law to include mediation and counselling as well as legal decision-making. The time was ripe to target the procedure to the needs of families by developing new types of categories that are different from the traditional ones, which remain grounded in the institution of marriage. According to the agreement the new family justice system was needed for the sake of children, and a particular problem concerns the enforcement of contact decisions involving the child being physically fetched, with the assistance of police and social authorities. The intention was to target resources to the *different* needs of families and children and to increase the number of child experts competent to spot such individual needs.

Consequently, the political agreement provided for a system with different tracks of procedures to respond to the different characteristics and needs of families in an initial screening of the application. In the new Agency of Family Law (hereafter referred to as the Agency) more efficient conflict management was to be established prioritising the individual child and family and offering (more) counselling and mediation. Within the Agency, a Child Unit (*Børneenheden*) was to be established providing a 'sanctuary' for the child. The purpose was twofold: to give the child his or her own entry into the family justice system, securing the welfare of the child during the procedure, and to ensure child involvement while minimising the number of professionals the child had contact with during the procedure.

Co-operation with the municipality (child protection) was to be strengthened to create a holistic approach towards the individual child, providing for more in-depth examinations in complex cases – an approach warranting more co-ordination between the institutions. In the new system a clear and differentiated court involvement was also needed in complex cases.

An important facet of the political agreement was the introduction of a three-month period of reflection (waiting period) before a divorce be granted for parents with minor children. In this reflection period no decisions could be given in respect of the child, and a new legal format was introduced involving the shared residence of the child with both parents in the reflection period, even if this were not factually the case. This 'legal fiction' was meant to strengthen

[5] In relation to a previous reform: Jeppesen de Boer (2014).

the parents in their legal position towards the child, ie to counter the assumption that the parent who leaves the home and the children will suffer legal disadvantage. As it turned out, the format resulted in increased conflict and was abandoned soon after.[6]

B. The 2019 Reform: Green, Yellow and Red Track Cases

The reform based upon the political agreement was adopted without much ado in 2018 and was implemented by the Agency Act which entered into force in April 2019. This Act addresses procedural issues only.[7] The Act implements a new design for the mandatory digital application to be used in a screening system. As before the reform, the general rule is that any application (divorce, parental authority, contact, parentage, maintenance) must be made digitally. What is new is that on the basis of the information (mostly ticking boxes) obtained from the applicant about the family circumstances, such as the applicant's perception of the level of conflict, the respect he/she has of the other parent, the vulnerabilities of the child, and in some cases based upon information from the municipality, the Agency will decide whether the case is simple (green), less simple (yellow) or complex (red).[8] The green cases are cases where the parties agree but need a registration, such as concerning consensual divorce, parentage, sole/joint parental authority, residence or contact. The yellow cases are cases without consensus where, nonetheless, it is timely to seek a mediated solution with the use of counselling and mediation. In these cases, the parties are primarily met by a child expert, not a legal expert. The Agency may register an agreement, grant a decision or submit the case to the Family Court if it is considered factually or legally complicated. Nevertheless, the Family Court has exclusive competence in some types of cases, for example, when parents disagree on parental authority or the child's residence. The qualification of the regime is based on the extent to which the issues are considered intrusive for the family, complex or burdensome to the child. Some of these are directly defined in the legislation, such as parental authority and the child's residence. Others depend upon the issue at hand, for example, a contact case could be burdensome to the child (Family Court) unless it concerns only minor issues, for example, costs relating to transportation (Agency). The civil status of the spouses as divorced or separated is not generally considered intrusive, so the Agency has competence to decide to grant

[6] *Lov om ægteskabs indgåelse og opløsning*, amendment Acts No 962 and 969 of 26.06.2020.

[7] *Familieretshusloven*, Act No 1702 of 27.12.2018.

[8] The Ombudsman has criticised the digital system for not respecting the right to representation since the digital application is based on the use of your personal ID number (CPR). Therefore, the application form was made accessible in a PDF file. See the Ombudsman critique: www.ombudsmanden.dk/find/nyheder/alle/mangelfuld_selvbetjeningsloesning. Presently, a mandatory digital proxy must be used.

divorce or separation unless the case is factually or legally complicated, as laid out in the guidelines to the Agency.[9]

The red cases are complex cases, and the Agency is obliged to contact the municipality the child resides in and, if needed, initiate co-operation with the municipality. All 'red' cases are decided by the Family Court.

Analogous to the different procedural regimes in the Agency, two different procedural regimes exist in the Family Court, which were implemented through a revision of the Procedural Act.[10] These consist of one simple regime where the court decision is made based on the fact finding by the Agency, and another regime where the Family Court initiates further fact finding and holds an actual hearing.

Administrative decisions made by the Agency are appealable to the Family Court.[11] The reform introduced a general division between fact finding and decision making, involving a general responsibility for the Agency to gather all relevant information for both their own decisions as well as for any subsequent decision of the Family Court. The enforcement of decisions is handled by the Family Court only and is regulated in the Procedural Act.[12] However, the child perspective may be elaborated by a child expert from the Child Unit of the Agency and a representative from the municipality may be present when a child arrangement is enforced with the assistance of the police.

In the revised system the regional Agency office and the regional family courts are obliged to hold quarterly meetings with the aim of discussing their co-operation. According to a provision in the Agency Act, annual reports of these meeting must be published. At the time of writing, the first report covering the initial co-operation 2019–2020 has been published.[13] The report is interesting because it demonstrates where better co-operation is warranted. The report deals with: (1) supervised contact (how can the Agency execute a decision taken by the Family Court?); (2) unity in case presentation (how to secure similar structure in data upload in the database of the Family Court in a transfer case?); (3) the functioning of the Agency's Child Unit in court, including the hearing involving a child (eg the difficulty of co-ordination of meetings with short notice); (4) the need for court decisions to provide and communicate comprehensive solutions rather than a limited decision or unmotivated settlement (to avoid the parties having to start over again with a new case in the Agency); and

[9] *Vejledning om Familieretshuset*, Guidance No 9404 of 26.06.2020 section 5.4.1. Some issues such as the obligation to pay spousal support and the right to succeed in a rented flat belongs to the status case. The division of property at divorce is dealt with in a wholly different procedure if parties do not reach agreement.

[10] *Retsplejeloven*, Consolidated Act No 1445 of 29.09.2020, chapter 42.

[11] *Familieretshusloven*, Act No 1702 of 27.12.2018, chapters 12–13.

[12] Chapter 42 b.

[13] Agency Act, art 44; '*Rapport om det familieretlige system og samarbejdet mellem familieretterne og Familieretshuset 2020*', familieretshuset.dk/media/1605/aarsrapport_frh_og_familieretter_2019_2020.pdf.

(5) the need for transfer of knowledge from the Family Court to the Agency when competence has been transferred (eg spousal maintenance).

Also, an advisory committee to the Agency has been established with a broad variety of competences related to divorce including members from other authorities.[14] The character of the advisory committee with its mix of public authorities and non-governmental organisations, such as the fathers' rights movement, may in practice due to its open structure involve knowledge exchange rather than a forum for qualified advice.

C. Historic Division between Municipality, Agency and Court

It is essential to briefly sketch the historic division between, on the one hand, the municipality (social work) and the Agency (family law), and between the administrative Agency and the Family Court.

Social work and related decision making takes place in the municipality, which is the smallest administrative unit historically developed from the parishes of the Danish state church.[15] In the nineteenth and into the twentieth century child protection was directed at poor families as a response from the socialist movement and their attention to the conditions of the working class and their children. Since then, social work has become more ambitious, offering child protection as well as family services. However, the legal framework of the child's family life after the parents' break up has not been integrated within the welfare work unless the child was already placed out-of-home prior to the breakup. The establishment of the legal framework (parental authority, residence, contact and maintenance obligations) after a divorce starts in the Agency.

To explain the existing division of competence between the administrative Agency and the Family Court we must turn to other developments. Two reform periods are significant: the family law reforms in the 1920s, and the 2007 structural reform that abolished direct access to the court system, obligating an initial request to the Agency for divorce, parental authority, etc.

The Agency is placed at the national level of state administration developed during the period of autocracy from 1660–1849, which continued after democratisation typically linked to the year of enactment of the constitution in 1849. As a parallel to the court's ruling on divorce, an administrative concession practice developed whereby the King as head of state could grant concessionary divorce. This concession practice formed the normative basis of the legislative reforms in Danish family law in the 1920s. The reforms maintained a parallel court and administrative state system, roughly speaking providing the

[14] Agency Act, art 45. *Bekendtgørelse om forretningsordenen for det rådgivende udvalg i familieretshuset*, Secondary legislative act, No 288 of 20.03.2019.

[15] For a more detailed description of the development, see Jeppesen de Boer, et al (2013: 144–50).

administration with authority to grant a divorce in case of agreement and the court in case of a dispute. The spouses thus had two gateways: one for agreement and one for dispute. This was changed into a one-stringed system in 2007 as part of a comprehensive structural reform. The 2007 reform was based on the development of mediation and counselling as a remedy for fulfilling individual rights to family life. The administration should take the role of gatekeeper of access to the court system with the aim of promoting parental co-operation and settlements, reserving the court procedure for those unwilling or unable to fit the norm of co-operation.[16] With the administration (now the Agency of Family Law) as the main family law institution, consensual divorce was seen as the 'ideal divorce' and the three institutions have since then maintained their characteristics focusing on the protection of the child (municipality), conflict management (Agency) and justice (Family Court).

II. CO-OPERATION BETWEEN THE AGENCY AND THE FAMILY COURT

During the legislative process leading to the 2019 reform, the courts were sceptical towards close co-operation with the Agency.[17] They did not want any responsibility for the quality of work in the Agency. In the preparation of the reform, the courts argued for the protection of their independence from the Agency, articulated in the Constitution as a matter of the division of power.[18] Thus, the court procedural rules are maintained in revised form in the Civil Procedural Act, in an interplay with the general rules on civil procedure which the judges are familiar with, supporting the understanding of the judges as generalist judges. The courts were critical of legislation that would introduce quarterly meetings, even when these were defined to involve only general co-operation, since they already had informal meetings with other partners without a necessary legislative obligation. The courts had no objection to sending the case file to the Agency when the case is closed to assure coherence.[19]

In the following we will focus on the legal framework of the co-operation between the Agency and the Family Court, as legally framed by the following four aspects: (1) the sufficiency of the fact finding by the Agency for a decision which is to be made in the Family Court; (2) the arrangement of supervised contact in the Agency as decided by the Family Court; (3) the return of the case from the Family Court to the Agency; and (4) the task of the Child Unit in the Family Court.

[16] For a more detailed description of the development, see Jeppesen de Boer, et al (2013: 138–43).
[17] www.ft.dk/samling/20181/lovforslag/L90/bilag/1/1964675.pdf at pp 112 ff.
[18] *Grundloven*, art 3.
[19] Procedural Act, art 449 e.

A. Fact Finding

Legislative provisions on fact finding can be found in the Agency Act and in the Civil Procedural Act. According to the Agency Act, the Agency is responsible not only for offering counselling and mediation in yellow and red cases but *also* for the gathering of information as a basis for decision making.[20] It should be noted that in the Agency procedure, parties are not legally obliged to tell the truth. Consequently, false oral statements are not punishable only written statements are.[21] Therefore, parties in an administrative procedure may not be as truthful as they would be in court, where they are legally obliged to tell the truth.[22] The extent of the Family Court's fact finding depends on the track in which the case is handled as decided by the Family Court.[23] This will be the simple procedure with no fact finding,[24] or it may be a more extended procedure with a hearing and fact finding that is independent of the fact finding in the Agency. A party may consider the fact finding in the Agency to be insufficient and request the judge to evaluate the case in the extended procedure. This extended procedure takes more time and may render the fact finding in the Agency a waste of time. Lawyers have recommended that the Family Court should conduct their own fact finding in red cases[25] but the parliament's response has been to allocate more resources to the Agency in 2020.[26] It is worth noting that what is called 'fact finding' in the Agency may in fact be integrated into the conflict management approach and thus support the favoured political solution, which is the parents' co-operation.

B. The Agency is Responsible for Supervised Contact

The division of competence between the Agency and the Family Court in contact cases has been the subject of earlier revisions. The 2019 reform divides the competence. A yellow case on contact may be decided by the Agency or the Family Court depending on how complicated the case is.[27] Red cases are always decided by the Family Court. An earlier reform in 2007 abandoned the principle that all contact cases (save enforcement) were to be dealt with by the Agency.

[20] Agency Act, arts 26, 28, 32.

[21] According to the Criminal Act, *Straffeloven*, consolidated Act No 1650 of 17.11.2020, art 163, any person who in writing or on another readable medium makes a false statement or representation or confirms the correctness of facts not known to him for use in legal matters involving public authorities is liable to a fine or imprisonment for a term not exceeding four months.

[22] Procedural Act, art 450 a.

[23] Procedural Act, art 451.

[24] Procedural Act, art 452.

[25] As reported in the Danish newspaper *Politiken* on 14 January 2021, '*Rystede advokater: Familieretshusene er en fuldtonet katastrofe*'.

[26] familieretshuset.dk/nyheder/%C3%B8konomisk-saltvandsindsproejtning-til-familieretshuset.

[27] As mentioned above, an example of a less complicated contact issue is transportation costs.

The court could decide on contact but *only* in the context of a simultaneous procedure on another matter, such as parental authority or the child's residence. This system of parallel competency did not work out well and was abolished soon after in 2012. The reason given was that contact cases were not suited to the court procedure given their undelimited, detailed and variable nature.[28] What also mattered was that the court has no means to provide supervised contact.[29] It is notable that these earlier negative experiences were not addressed in the *travaux preparatoire* to the 2019 reform. It is currently the responsibility of the Agency to establish supervision of contact if this is made a condition in the contact decision. This applies to decisions from the Agency and the Family Court alike.

The processing and delay in contact cases and contact supervision orders have been much criticised since the 2019 reform. Also, possible breaches of human rights have been noted by human rights organisations.[30] Many complaints were sent to the Ombudsman concerning the Agency in 2020 and the Agency has taken up a lot of resources at the Ombudsman's Children's Division.[31] Many parents have complained about long processing times, which made the Ombudsman initiate an investigation – among others – of cases where a decision was made on supervised contact but there was a long processing time before the contact was arranged. The Agency explained to the Ombudsman that they were working on improving co-operation with the courts to make the courts better in communicating the specific aim of the supervision order because this influences the arrangement to be made. Thus, the Ombudsman may have motivated the Agency to improve its co-operation with the Family Courts. At least, it generated a response from the head of the Agency on the Agency's website: 'we are working on it'.

C. Enforcement: Possibility to Remit Case

The enforcement of an agreement or decision concerning a child arrangement is purely a matter for the Family Court and as such is regulated only in the Procedural Act.[32] Enforcement must benefit the child, and enforcement is not possible if it is beneficial to the child to remit the case from the Family Court to the Agency for a reassessment of the agreement or decision.[33] Thus, enforcement can be rejected by the Family Court in favour of remitting to the Agency and

[28] Proposed Act L157 2011/2012 with notes, pp 15–16.

[29] Evaluation of the Parental Responsibility Act (*Evaluering af forældreansvarsloven*), *Familiestyrelsen* 2011, p 19.

[30] menneskeret.dk/udgivelser/ret-samvaer-familieretssystemet-menneskeretlige-rammer.

[31] en.ombudsmanden.dk/publications/annual_reports/annual_report_2020.

[32] Procedural Act, chapter 42 b.

[33] Procedural Act, art 456 p.

reassessment of the substance. The legal mechanism of remission (*hjemvisning*) replaces a rejection of enforcement and guidance for the parties to contact the Agency in order to apply for a new decision. Therefore, remission may be viewed as only a minor change. According to the *travaux préparatoires* the requirements for enforcement are extended with the reform but it is not clear whether there is a 'real' new legal standard for enforcement. It was envisaged that the practice of physical fetching of the child with the assistance of the police and the social authorities should be limited or stopped.[34] It is not yet known how these changes have worked out, but they are part of the ongoing evaluation of the reform.

D. The Child Unit's Task in the Family Court

The Child Unit in the Agency has two main functions.[35] The first is to support and counsel the child. Secondly, the Child Unit is responsible for the investigation of the child's perspective. The Child Unit offers the child a contact person, in order to minimise the number of adults the child has contact with not only in the Agency but also in the Family Court. The contact person from the Child Unit hears the child in procedures in the Agency and possibly also later in the Family Court.[36] The idea of minimising is not new. Before the reform there was a focus on hearing the child in a manner that made it unnecessary to hear the child again, for example, by sending notes from the hearing. Another example of the need for coordination is illustrated by case law, where a court decided on the matter of 'substitution contact' (to compensate contact that had not taken place) without hearing the child. The appeal court returned the case, remarking that the court should have awaited a planned child hearing in a concurrent procedure on parental authority in the Agency.[37]

Although the legislature's intention was that the same person will hear the child, the court has discretion to decide to use another child expert.[38] The aim of minimising the number of adults may be challenged by practical considerations – is the child expert available at the court's convenience? – but the court may also have concerns about the child expert's impartiality. Thus, the value of co-operation between the Agency and the Family Court is challenged by the values imbedded in court to qualify judicial fact finding involving a need to assess the impartiality of the child expert.[39] The various functions of the child expert may touch upon the sense of impartiality, which may be counteracted by the judge appointing a new child expert.

[34] Proposed Act L91 2018/2019, notes to the Act, p 165.
[35] Agency Act, chapter 5.
[36] Agency Act, art 16, 1st indent.
[37] Case *TFA* 2021.244/2 V.
[38] Agency Act, art 16, 2nd indent and Procedural Act, art 450 b, 2nd indent.
[39] Proposed Act L91 2018/2019, notes to the Act, p 151.

III. CO-OPERATION BETWEEN THE AGENCY AND THE MUNICIPALITIES

Here we focus upon the legal framework of the co-operation between the Agency and the municipality as legally framed by (1) the screening process; (2) mandatory co-operation in red cases; (3) the Agency's mandatory reporting to the municipality when a child is in need; and (4) the municipalities' competence to initiate a case on parental authority to prevent an out-of-home placement of the child. From the perspective of the Agency, one may ask how the conflict management approach is balanced with the welfare (child protection) approach that the municipalities represent.

A. The Screening Process

An allocation of a digital application into one of the tracks mentioned earlier is based on the information the applicant has sent to the Agency digitally. For this purpose, the Agency Act specifies that the Agency may contact the municipality and ask if a child protection case is pending in the municipality, if this is deemed necessary.[40] If a case is pending, the Agency case may qualify as complex. The intention was to identify complex cases early in the procedure. The type of information the municipality is permitted to give is defined in the Act to have a general character as *if* an investigation is pending or support is granted, but not more specifically on what type of support. The information may be given over the phone or by mail, or in another way. The Agency is not obliged to inform the applicant about the contact and the screening decision (green, yellow or red) is not a binding decision, which means that it cannot be appealed. However, the Agency can change the decision on its own motion, if so desired.[41]

It should be noted that it is common knowledge that the municipalities are overloaded with work, and so the lack of involvement of a family with a municipality may not be because there is no need.

If the municipality *is* involved with the family, this gives weight to the assumption that the right screening decision is the red track. Thus, the regulation mirrors the tendency to handle cases as yellow instead of red. The rule of making contact with the municipality to qualify the screening of the case could be perceived as a counterweight to the primary rationality of the conflict management approach in the Agency. The 2019 annual report from the Agency mentions that the number of red cases has been higher than expected.[42]

[40] Agency Act, art 9.
[41] Agency Act, art 4, 2nd indent.
[42] The Family Law Agency, Annual report, *Annual Report*: https://familieretshuset.dk/media/1460/2019_familieretshuset_aarsrapport_2019.pdf.

B. Red Cases

In contrast to the chapter in the Agency Act on green and yellow cases, the title of the chapter on red cases is 'Interdisciplinary case management'. In this track the focus is on the protection of the child and the Child Unit's investigation of the child's perspective. A child expert examination is usually made.[43] The disciplines mentioned in the Act are child experts and lawyers *within* the Agency and they are *obliged* to contact the municipality to qualify the needs of the child and to find a holistic solution for the family.[44] They may exchange information and arrange meetings with the municipality with or without the presence of the parties.[45] In our view, it is notable that the interdisciplinarity spread out from the Agency to the municipality is not developed in the *travaux préparatoires*. Further, developing guidelines for the municipalities in favour of local developments has been expressly rejected.[46] Well-functioning co-operation between the authorities already exists, but it is of a very different intensity in different regions, and it is not backed up by data or research. What does a holistic solution mean? As mentioned in the *travaux préparatoires* the focus is on child welfare, but what is meant by child welfare? In our opinion there is no single definition. Rather, it depends upon the legal question at hand. An illustration can be found in the different assessments of the child's interests in the case law of the European Court of Human Rights. The Court integrates the principles contained in the UN Child Rights Convention in the assessment of whether there has been a legitimate violation of parents right to private or family life according to Art 8 of the European Convention on Human Rights. We will not go into this here, but we will refer to an analysis that shows different focuses depending on the issue at stake.[47] Therefore, there is reason for a sharper focus on the potential of interdisciplinary cooperation between the Agency and the municipalities.[48]

C. Mandatory Reporting to the Municipality by the Agency when a Child is in Need

In Denmark all citizens are subject to a mandatory notification requirement in a case of potential child abuse and neglect.[49] Professionals who hold public office or who provide public services to children have a strengthened mandatory notification obligation: they must notify in all cases where a minor needs special

[43] Agency Act, art 28.
[44] Agency Act, art 29.
[45] Agency Act, arts 30–31.
[46] Legislative proposal L 90 2018/2019, p 30.
[47] Kvisberg (2019). Kvisberg shows that in case law after 2013, the Court has applied the *X v Latvia* principles in child abduction cases, while the requirements of *Neulinger and Shuruk v Switzerland* are still applied in public childcare cases.
[48] A Danish book offers a focus on the meaning of interdisciplinary social work: Ejrnæs and Svendsen (2021).
[49] Social Services Act, Serviceloven Act No 1287 of 28.08.2020, art 154.

support.[50] This obligation applies to professionals in the Agency and their duty is addressed several times in administrative guidelines.[51] In 2019, the municipalities in total received approximately 140,000 notifications regarding more than 75,000 minors, equivalent to approximately 6 per cent of all minors in Denmark. All notifications must be registered in a national database and screened within 24 hours to assess whether there is reason for immediate action.[52] The notifications play a central role in the municipalities' work with early detection of minors at risk,[53] and is not as such part of the Family Justice System. Nevertheless, since co-operation between the municipalities and the Family Justice System is a central factor in the 2019 reform it would have been relevant to investigate the notification practice in the Agency and how children at risk gain from the notifications through the social work of the municipalities. The number of notifications from the Agency was 350 in 2019 and 520 in 2020.[54] However, no attention has been directed in the *travaux préparatoires* or elsewhere to the benefit of notifications from the Agency or how they may or may not be a part of a co-operation between the municipalities and the Agency. One area which could be explored is the different perceptions of the parents' break up in the municipalities and the Agency. In social work divorce is characterised as a demarcated problem which may be addressed using resources from the child's network and counselling groups,[55] differing from a situation where the municipality investigates the living circumstances of the child in order to qualify the needs of the child. The Agency is specialised in handling divorce, offering networking and counselling groups in the Child Unit,[56] and may therefore see itself as the competent authority to address an exceptional situation as a delimited problem for the child, therefore failing to notify. Nevertheless, the raison d'être of the co-operation has not been developed.

D. The Municipalities' Competence to Request the Agency to Initiate a Case

In very extraordinary circumstances the municipality may request the Agency to initiate a case concerning parental authority if it believes the alternative is an out-of-home-placement of the child.[57] In the *travaux préparatoires*[58] the example given is that an applicant has withdrawn an application to terminate

[50] Social Services Act, art 153.

[51] Guidelines on parental responsibility, residence and contact, Vejledning No 10064 of 20.12.2020.

[52] Social Services Act, art 155.

[53] sm.dk/Media/D/1/VPA_Underretninger_og_social_foranstaltninger_herkomst.pdf.

[54] The notifications from the Agency do not have their own statistical code in the national statistics database (Statistics Denmark) but we have received the information from the Agency from their own data (statistical code 199111).

[55] Guidelines on support for children, youngsters and their families, *Vejledning* No 9142 of 26.02.2019, sections 123, 124 and 128.

[56] Agency Act, art 15.

[57] Agency Act, art 24.

[58] Legislative proposal L 90, 07.11.2018, Comments on art 24.

the other parent's contact with the child because of threats from this other party. Thus, the municipality may act, indirectly replacing the weaker party. Legislatively, this construction raises some questions, especially in relation to the enforcement of the decision since it is still only the parents who initiate enforcement. It is possible that the decision is simply respected but this cannot be taken for granted, and it may further complicate police involvement in the enforcement case. In June 2021, the Agency stated that the total number of cases that had been initiated cases was one, and the case had been closed before a decision was made. Furthermore, 19 requests from the municipalities were pending. We may conclude that this limited number seems to mirror the understanding of the right to initiate as being extraordinary.

IV. A UNITED SYSTEM AND CO-OPERATING INSTITUTIONS?

So, at the end of the day, how are the intended changes 'unity' and 'co-operation' in the Family Justice System reflected in the legislation and subsequent evaluation? The reform was implemented on 1 April 2019 and, at the time of writing, is now a little more than two years old. The reform was met by an unprecedented avalanche of critique, not only attracting criticism from lawyers but also creating headlines in the ordinary press. Adjustments were soon made to the reform. The obligatory reflection (waiting) period was abolished, together with other 'follow-up' adjustments in 2020.[59] Financially, the costs of the reform turned out to be grossly underestimated, with more than 200 new jobs being created in the Agency. In May 2021, the head of the Agency declared that the effort to diminish excessively lengthy procedures was a 'long haul' and normality was not expected before 2022.[60]

Before we sum up on the Agency's co-operation with the Family Court and the municipalities, we conclude on the whole that political unity and co-operation were important aims in the reform, but the content of unity and co-operation remains difficult to grasp and the reform may be understood as one of many other recent reforms in Denmark that have not been well-prepared,[61] but are characterised by the use of buzz words such as 'unity' and 'co-operation' in the *travaux preparatoires*.

A. The Agency and the Family Court

Our description of the legal framework for co-operation between the Agency and the Family Court in respect of fact finding shows that the different focus

[59] Act No 962 of 26.06.2020 (abolishment of the period of reflection) and 969 (abolishment of shared residence and follow up).

[60] familieretshuset.dk/nyheder/ombudsmanden-har-set-paa-sagsbehandlingstider-i-familieretshuset.

[61] This is the focus in Nielsen (2021).

in the Agency (conflict managing) and the court (justice) makes the Agency vulnerable to criticism of the legal quality of their fact finding, and lawyers may consider that the truth finding does not really start before the case reaches the court. Therefore, the system is not perceived as united. Thus, it may be necessary and opportune to address fundamental institutional differences to pinpoint the actual content of the politically wanted unity and co-operation. The annual evaluation of the user perspective of the Agency procedure from 2020 has a question addressed to the user concerning coherence between the authorities involved (Agency, Family Court, municipality). Sixty per cent of the answers indicate that there was little or no connection between the different institutions' case management.[62] In an evaluation from 2021, qualitative data show that users do not experience co-operation between the Agency and the Family Court. They experience two separate systems with different functions.[63]

The challenge to co-operation in respect of arranging supervised contact seems to be of simpler character than for the fact finding. The process of co-operation put in place by the 2019 reform could have been better planned before implementation but seems to have come about due to complaints from users over too lengthy procedures, supported by criticism raised by the Danish Ombudsman and the Danish Institute of Human Rights. Enforcement is yet to be evaluated but it may be noted that the changes envisaged were minor anyway given the fact that remission was a known concept before the reform. It is yet to be seen whether, and how, the Agency's Child Unit will bring about co-operation with the Family Court, taking note of the fact that the focus on limiting the number of child hearings was also present before the reform and, further, taking stock of the fact that judges may not be content with the initial hearing but may choose to appoint a new child expert due to concerns about impartiality.

B. The Agency and the Municipalities

In respect of the co-operation between the Agency and the municipalities we have seen that the co-operation during the screening process may be of limited value due to the voluntary and general nature of the questions the Agency can ask the municipality. Additionally, the challenges in establishing 'interdisciplinary' co-operation in the red cases are great. In our view, the character of co-operation mirrors the challenges in respect of the Agency's fact finding because it reflects upon institutional differences between welfare (municipalities) and conflict management (Agency). The Agency's mandatory reporting to the municipalities is not new and to our knowledge there have been no efforts

[62] VIVE 2020: www.vive.dk/da/udgivelser/foraeldres-tilfredshed-med-de-familieretlige-myndigheder-15220 Figure 4.6.

[63] oxfordresearch.dk/wp-content/uploads/2021/05/Brugerrejseanalyse-test-af-serviceniveau-i-familieretshuset.pdf, p 48.

to develop co-operation on this basis. Finally, the municipalities' competence to request the Agency to initiate a case has, until now, remained an extraordinary exception. In the evaluation from 2021 qualitative data show that users in general do not experience any coherence between the case handling of the Agency and the municipality.[64]

REFERENCES

Jeppesen de Boer, C, et al (2013) 'The private–public law divide: Does this legal design create an abyss to children's welfare?', *Nordisk Socialrättslig Tidsskrift* 7–8, 133.

Jeppesen de Boer, C (2014) 'Gezamenlijk ouderschap na scheiding: over de interactie tussen de doelstellingen van de Deense wet op de ouderlijke verantwoordelijkheid, de bevindingen in de uitgevoerde wetsevaluatie en de daaropvolgende wetswijzigingen', F&R maart 2014, DOI: 10.5553/FenR/.000016.

Kvisberg, T (2019), 'Child Abduction Cases in the European Court of Human Rights. Changing Views on the Child's Best Interests', *Oslo Law Review* 6(2), 90.

Nielsen, W (2021) *Entreprenørstaten* (GADs Forlag).

Ejrnæs, M and Svendsen, L (2021) *Tværfaglighed i social arbejde* (Samfundslitteratur).

[64] oxfordresearch.dk/wp-content/uploads/2021/05/Brugerrejseanalyse-test-af-serviceniveau-i-familieretshuset.pdf, p 50.

3

Family Justice Systems, Social Behaviour and Financial Arrangements after Divorce in the Netherlands

BREGJE DIJKSTERHUIS AND ALEXANDER FLOS

I. INTRODUCTION

THE SUBJECT WE delve into concerns such a familiar situation that it is best illustrated by a standard Dutch case: A husband, John (47) and wife Mary (45) have a typical Dutch division of labour: John works five days a week and Mary three days a week. Mary works as a teacher at a primary school (before their marriage, she worked full-time) and John is a doctor, and he often works overtime and at night. They have two children: Paul (2006) and Ellen (2008) and live in a house that John bought in 2005. They married in 2007 and they did not conclude a prenuptial agreement. In July 2021, when the children are 14 and 13, the marriage breaks down.

Much has been written in the socio-legal academic literature about the subject of the financial position of spouses after divorce and its gender connotation. The first wave of publications was in the 1960s and 1970s when the number of divorces surged in Western Europe. Women increasingly took on paid employment during and after the First and Second World War, which meant that they became more self-sufficient. This lowered the barriers to divorce. Also, new, less strict legal requirements for divorce were introduced (Maclean, 1991: 4; Eekelaar, 1978). Finally, pressure groups for women's rights were an important force behind the legal possibility to leave an unhappy marriage (or to not marry at all). From the start, there was also a concern for the position of the financially weaker spouse, which was often the woman. In the 1980s and 1990s, new publications appeared as more became known about the legal and socio-economic consequences of divorce. 'Ironically the prosperity that enables family ties to weaken and individual aspirations to be pursued is followed by widespread poverty after divorce for women and children' (Maclean, 1991: 128). Bastard and Cardia-Vonèche carried out interviews which found different coping mechanisms of divorced French women with children (Maclean 1991: 119–20); see for a more detailed account: Bastard and Cardia Vonèche, 1988 and Bastard, Cardia-Vonèche and Maclean, 1988).

Nowadays, how a family justice system should cope with the financial consequences of divorce in the Netherlands remains a much-debated topic, as the divorce rate remains high. Currently, 37 per cent of marriages end in divorce, on average after 14.5 years. There is a trend towards the average duration of marriages becoming longer and divorcing partners are older (Schrama, Dijksterhuis and Spalter, 2020: 9). It is mainly men who pay spousal maintenance (from here on maintenance);[1] maintenance obligations are imposed on women to pay to men in only 1 per cent of the cases. Maintenance is awarded by the judge in about one in six divorces (16–19 per cent)[2] although this is based on relatively outdated empirical data (Schrama, Dijksterhuis and Spalter, 2020: 9–10; Kolkman et al, 2021: 147–52).

In this chapter, two different family law doctrines related to the breakdown of marriages and finances are studied: maintenance and matrimonial property law.[3] These laws are not mandatory; spouses can make their own arrangements with regard to matrimonial property if they do not want the default rules to apply to their financial situation (Scherpe, 2012: 1). In contrast to child support, maintenance is not obligatory and the amount can be settled by the spouses. On these two topics, two new Dutch laws have been introduced that have serious financial consequences for (former) spouses.[4] Since 2018, the statutory community of property has no longer been a universal community but a limited community of property, and since 2020, the maximum duration of maintenance has been reduced from 12 years to five years. There are some exceptions, which will be explained in section III.A. Although in some (common law) countries these two doctrines are intertwined, for example in England and the Netherlands, they are two separate legal issues. The case of John and Mary highlights the recent changes in Dutch matrimonial and divorce legislation. As they married in 2007, the new legislation is not applicable to them and according to the universal community, Mary is entitled, in principle, to half

[1] Of course, the topic of child support is also relevant in this context, but in this chapter the legislation on this financial arrangement after divorce is not addressed (for more information see: Dijksterhuis, 2008; Dijksterhuis 2017b).

[2] In the Netherlands, the judge makes the decision in all divorce cases. But when former partners come to an agreement beforehand on, for example, maintenance, the judge only checks whether it is in accordance with the law.

[3] Although in some countries these two doctrines are intertwined, in the Netherlands they are separated in family law legislation. When determining the amount of maintenance, sometimes the outcome of negotiations on matrimonial property is taken into account and vice versa. The question of who is the financially weaker spouse can differ when looked at according to those two doctrines of financial family law. It is possible that one spouse has more property/assets, while the other one has a higher income, which is, together with 'need', the most important condition for the obligation to pay maintenance in current Dutch legislation system, although income derived from property can play a role when determining the amount of maintenance.

[4] These lawyers are also qualified as mediators. See also Maclean and Eekelaar (2016: 130).

of all their assets. The duration of maintenance is a maximum of five years, compared with 12 years according to the old legislation. If they had married in 2020, Mary would have no claim on the assets of John that he acquired before marriage, for example their house. She would only have a right to maintenance for less than a year because of the short duration of the marriage.

This new legislation signals a trend away from solidarity between (former) spouses towards a more individualistic approach. These changes were partly due to what was presented as bringing the legislation in conformity with (changing) societal views (Schrama, Dijksterhuis and Spalter, 2020: 12, 13). However, it is questionable whether the ideas behind these new systems and the assumption that they mirror the actual social practices and thus align with what spouses in reality do during marriage. Spouses can make unwise choices from a financial risk management perspective (WRR, 2017; see also Dijksterhuis, 2019b: 208). This chapter addresses the assumptions underlying these systems and the realities in the Netherlands. It will focus in the first part on prenuptial agreements, in particular the type which excludes the financial protection a (limited) community of property offers. The second part will focus on maintenance. In this chapter, we also discuss the role of the legal professions: the notary with regard to prenuptial agreements and the (legal) experts, mostly lawyers, when spouses divorce.[5] The key question is: Should family justice systems reflect social behaviour in financial arrangements after divorce?

II. MARRIAGE

A. Legislation, Prenups and the Notary

Matrimonial property regimes try to balance the independence and interdependence of spouses. On the one hand it is important for spouses to be able to decide for themselves how they shape their property relationship with each other. On the other hand, given the nature of their relationship, it is self-evident that spouses should support and help each other. The most important types of solidarity are matrimonial property regimes in which spouses share (parts of) their assets during or after marriage. These especially protect a spouse who during marriage does not carry out any paid work or carries out lower paid work because of responsibilities such as housework or nursing children.

In the Netherlands in recent years the legislator has opted for less interdependence between spouses. Since 2018 universal community of property is no longer the legal default system in the Netherlands. Universal community of property means that spouses share in principle all their assets, including

[5] The role of the judge is also relevant, as the judge is involved with the division of assets upon divorce and determining or confirming the agreement of former spouses. Their role is not addressed in this chapter, however, as this would be too comprehensive.

premarital assets, but this was considered outdated, particularly due to the increase in divorce and because it is often considered nowadays to have excessively far reaching legal and financial consequences. Instead, it was replaced by a limited community of property which, in principle, only consists of assets that were joint property of spouses before marriage and all assets they acquire during marriage, although gifts and inheritances are excluded. As a consequence, spouses share less of their assets during and after divorce. Furthermore, it has always been possible for spouses to conclude a prenuptial agreement to deviate from the legal default system of the community of property. They can opt to limit the community of property or to expand it. It is also possible by Dutch law to opt for spouses to exclude any community of property, with or without a contractual obligation to divide any acquired gains during marriage, either periodically (yearly) or at the end of their marriage. The most recent data show that in around one in three prenuptial agreements, spouses opt not to share any assets (Schols and Hoens, 2012: 951).

As in many other continental European countries, in the Netherlands it is compulsory to conclude prenuptial agreements by notarial deed. Notaries are therefore the central leading figure. The role of the notary is to ensure legal certainty for third parties. First, the notary will formulate prenuptial agreements in accordance to law, and the usage of legal terms will make it easier for third parties to interpret and understand prenuptial agreements. Secondly, the involvement of a notary will ensure that prenuptial agreements will not be antedated. The notary also provides legal protection to spouses. The notary is obliged to inform spouses about the legal consequences of prenuptial agreements. A notary also advises spouses, given their wishes and objectives, about the suitable type of prenuptial agreement. Normally, spouses will have a meeting with the notary at the notary's office, where the notary will take stock of the assets and debts of spouses, the (future) presence of children, and whether one of the spouses owns a company. Then, based on the wishes of spouses, the notary will advise which prenuptial agreement spouses should choose, outlining possible alternatives and the legal consequences entailed. The notary has a legal duty to avoid one spouse taking advantage of the legal ignorance of the other spouse, or an uneven power balance. The spouses will receive a draft of their prenuptial agreement which, after approval, they sign in the presence of the notary. This process ensures that at the moment of concluding a prenuptial agreement, the spouses make a conscious and well-informed decision to enter into a particular type of prenuptial agreement.

This protection is especially relevant to spouses when they opt to exclude any solidarity by choosing the exclusion of any type of community of property without a contractual obligation to divide any acquired gains during marriage (periodically) or at the end of their marriage. The law assumes that spouses will remain aware of their conscious and well-informed decision and that they will behave accordingly. Without any form of solidarity, apart from maintenance, both spouses are themselves responsible for acquiring assets. In this situation, it is vital that spouses take a more professional attitude towards each other, especially concerning the division of paid and unpaid labour, for example taking care of the children: if they do not look after their own interests, they might risk an unequal accumulation of assets.

However, there is a tension between this view and the reality of having an affectionate relationship during marriage, which we will turn to in the next section. However, some notaries do take this into account. Recent research based on expert meetings and older participative research shows that some notaries for this reason advise, sometimes even in a compelling way, that spouses should include a contractual obligation in their prenuptial agreement to divide any acquired gains at the end of their marriage (Kocken, 1997: 89–90; Antokolskaia et al, 2011: 100). It shows that notaries take into account the reality that the behaviour of spouses may deviate from the arrangement in their prenuptial agreement during the (long) course of their marriage.

B. Behaviour in Relation to Societal Views

Approximately 35 per cent of spouses who opt for a prenuptial agreement choose the exclusion of any community of property, without a contractual obligation to divide acquired gains during marriage (periodically) or at the end of their marriage. These spouses are themselves responsible for accumulating assets. This would indicate that, based on their (well-informed) choice of this type of prenuptial agreement, both spouses should divide paid work and care for the children equally, because otherwise the chosen regime is clearly to the disadvantage of one of them. These spouses should take this very seriously, for one in three marriages in the Netherlands ends by divorce. However, it can prove to be difficult for spouses to remain aware of this during marriage: although spouses know about the high divorce rate, most expect that their own marriage will not be ended by divorce.

On the financial awareness of spouses, a few useful studies are available, mainly based on interviews with spouses. The findings are, in short, that the financially dependent partner, mostly the woman, is not well aware of the financial risks of a possible divorce. During marriage, the lack of a sufficient independent income for both partners is not seen as a priority. The income of the woman is often considered as an extra, not vital, contribution to the household or solely meant for personal expenditure (SCP (Social and Cultural Planning Bureau), 2018: 7). Both men and women find it important to have their own income, for the purpose of any impending risk of divorce, but they often do not consider that this needs to be enough to achieve self-sufficiency. Economic dependence is not experienced as such, and does not play a role in most marriages; the couple may divide labour unequally, with one spouse working more paid hours and the other spouse to a larger extent responsible for care duties and the household. During marriage people seldom take divorce into account, as this is considered to show a lack of faith in the marriage. This is in line with the limited ability of people to deal with financial risks during marriage (Schrama, Dijksterhuis and Spalter, 2020: 17–18; see also: SCP, 2018; Hoog and Van Egten, 2012; WRR, 2017). Even highly educated women have a low self-awareness of the financial risks to them of divorce.[6]

In addition, other norms also influence the behaviour and choices of spouses during marriage. Prenuptial agreements are not a regular contract and spouses are influenced in particular by societal views on marriage. The foremost societal view on marriage accepts a gendered division of labour for spouses. Research has shown the great impact of societal views (Ruitenberg, 2014a: 58; Ruitenberg and De Beer, 2014: 315; Ruitenberg, 2014b). Firstly, societal views on marriage are gendered because in the Netherlands women are still considered to be more suited than men to bringing up children. Two-yearly *Statistics Netherlands* reports to the Dutch government about the emancipation of women, in a '*Emancipatiemonitor*'. Many people still view women as better suited than men to raise children: 37 per cent of the fathers and 22 per cent of the mothers with children below the age of 12 years have this view (CBS, 2020: 79–80). Even though 62 per cent of Dutch parents, married or non-married, prefer that both spouses equally rear the children, still 24 per cent prefer women to take more responsibility for it. In the Netherlands, contrary to many other countries, formal child care is frowned upon ('outsourcing of children') and spouses or their relatives are expected to a large extent to raise their children themselves. Forty-one per cent of Dutch mothers who have a child between the age of 0 and 1 year think their child should go to childcare a few days a week, and 51 per cent of parents whose children go to school also hold the same view. These societal views, that women are better suited for child rearing and the preference not to send children to formal child care, at least not for four or five days a week, are an important reason why most spouses have a gendered division of labour. This is also referred to as the 'child penalty' which disproportionately affects mothers (CPB (Netherlands Bureau for Economic Policy Analysis), 2021).

Secondly, husbands are still expected to be the breadwinner of the family. This is partly because women are expected to be the primary caretaker of children in the family. In society people expect men to work 39 hours on average and women 29 hours on average (CBS, 2020: 32–33). This view is broadly shared, as 71 per cent of Dutch women themselves want to work part-time. When a family has young children, most people prefer that the husband works full-time (26 per cent) or four days a week (40 per cent), and when children are between the age of 4 years and 12 years the preferred number of working hours of husbands increases: 38 per cent prefer full-time employment and 42 per cent prefer four days a week. However, for women the expected amount

[6] www.womeninc.nl/actueel/hoger-opgeleide-vrouw-is-financieel-onbewust, accessed March 2022; this also applies to the other weblinks.

of paid work is dramatically less: when a couple, married or unmarried, has young children, 68 per cent of society prefers the woman not to work more than three days a week, 26 per cent prefers the woman to work four days a week and only 6 per cent expects the woman to work fulltime.

C. Financial Position

As discussed in the previous two sections, the societal views and norms of how spouses should divide paid and unpaid work are opposite to the way that spouses are expected to behave when they opt for a prenuptial agreement which consists of a total separation of property. Research shows, as do numerous court cases, that spouses with such prenuptial agreements tend to disregard the prenuptial agreement and behave in the same manner as other spouses. The division of labour is equal for spouses who married with and without a prenuptial agreement, which shows that prenuptial agreements are of little value to spouses in this respect (Giesen, 1999: 78–79; see also Poortman and Mills, 2012: 373–75).

However, this unequal division of labour could prove to be a risk for spouses who opted for a prenuptial agreement with total exclusion of property because they lack the protection and solidarity of the community of property. As a result of societal views on marriage and the role of spouses, men tend to work more paid hours than women. In the Netherlands men who are in a relationship and have children work 40 hours a week on average. Women with children who are in a relationship worked on average around 27 hours a week in 2017 (CBS, 2020: 90). This is a slight increase from 2007 when these women worked around 23 hours a week. Also, in conformity with social views, only 19 per cent of women with children work full-time, while 86 per cent of men with children work full-time (CBS, 2020: 85).

The difference in the amount of paid work hours between men and women leads to differences in average income. Income is of vital importance to enable a person to acquire assets and have the capacity to gain wealth (Glendon, 1981: 186). In 2019, for men with young children between the age of 0 and four years the average income was €64,300. For women in the same position this was only €37,400.[7] Because men work more hours a week, they are more likely to progress in their career and increase their income: in 2019 men with children between the age of 12 and 18 years have an average income of €78,000. The income of women on the contrary hardly seems to increase over the years, because in 2019 women who had children between the age of 12 and 18 years had an average income of €39,200, which is only very slightly more than the average income of women with very young children. Having children and working part-time has a negative effect on the earning capacity of women.

[7] See CBS 2020, *StatLine M/V, Inkomen en economische zelfstandigheid; persoonskenmerken*: mvstat.cbs.nl/#/MVstat/nl/dataset/26018NED/table?ts=1574871878239.

As a consequence of lower income, women are less able to acquire assets than men, which may lead to an unfair situation when spouses conclude a prenuptial agreement with a total separation of property. Although both spouses may work 40 or 50 hours a week on average, women tend to do most of the unpaid work, for which they are not compensated, also not when their marriage ends by divorce. Even though spouses are supposed to make a well-informed choice at the moment before they marry, during the marriage prenuptial agreements have a very static character because they can only be amended by notarial deed. Therefore, spouses run the risk that their prenuptial agreement becomes outdated because of changes of circumstances during marriage (Flos, 2018).

i. Division of Labour During the Covid-19 Pandemic

Due to the Covid-19 pandemic many people have been forced to work from home. This is especially the case for higher educated people who do less physical work that would require them to go to their work place. If both spouses work at home, it should be easier for them to take equal care of their children when schools and childcare settings such as nurseries are closed. However, preliminary research shows that the unequal division of labour has been persistent, even during the Covid-19 pandemic. During the first lockdown in the Netherlands, which started in March 2020, care for children was more equally divided between parents. During the second lockdown during the autumn of 2020 the division of care for children between parents was the same as before the pandemic.[8]

III. DIVORCE

A. Legislation on Maintenance and Underlying Assumptions

On 1 January 2020 a new law on maintenance came into force.[9] The duration of maintenance has been limited, apart from a few exceptions for specific situations, from 12 years to five years.[10] If a marriage has lasted less than 10 years, the maximum maintenance term is half the duration of the marriage. The exceptions are, first, for parents with children under 12 years with a maximum duration of 12 years; second, for older people around the age of 55 years and older who were

[8] www.uu.nl/nieuws/zorgen-voor-de-kinderen-tijdens-corona-de-rol-van-de-vader-wordt-weer-kleiner. Also see COVID Gender (In)equality Survey Netherlands, second policy: brief: www.uu.nl/sites/default/files/Policyletter%20COGIS%20juni%202020%20def.pdf.

[9] 'Wet van 18 juli 2019 tot wijziging van Boek 1 van het Burgerlijk Wetboek en van enige andere wetten in verband met de herziening van het stelsel van partneralimentatie (Wet herziening partneralimentatie), geldend van 01-01-2021.'

[10] If the former spouse who is entitled to receive maintenance, marries someone else or enters into a long-term relationship and lives with someone as if they were married, the right to receive maintenance ends.

in a marriage of long duration, who will receive maintenance until they reach the age of 67 years and will become entitled to a state pension (the 'AOW'); and, third, for people in the beginning of their 50s with a maximum duration of 10 years. But this last category is temporary and meant as a transition for the financially weaker partners who could not foresee this new legislation when they married and who would, according to the legislator,[11] perhaps have made different choices during their relationship if they had known. Lastly, there is a hardship clause, meant for individual cases, where the judge needs to weigh the different circumstances. When an appeal on the hardship clause is granted, the duration of maintenance is extended (Schrama, Dijksterhuis and Spalter, 2020: 62–83; see also Kolkman et al, 2021: 50–54).[12]

This is not the first time that the legislator has decided to limit the duration of maintenance; In 1994 maintenance was limited to 12 years duration, while before that year, the right to be supported by the former partner could last a life time (Dijksterhuis, 2008: chapter 2, also see Schrama, Dijksterhuis and Spalter, 2020: 25). When we look at these interventions by the legislator, we clearly see a pattern: the legislator has felt less urgency to protect the financially weaker party and has put the financial responsibility on the shoulders of the individual partners. It is important to stress that maintenance has always been an exception to the general rule that every adult is responsible for their own financial situation. However, as spouses generally depend on each other, including financially, they may make decisions that are not per se beneficial for their own financial situation, for example by taking a larger share of either paid work or care duties, or one of the partners may take an altruistic attitude (Maclean, 1991: 35; see also Gilligan, 1982), and maintenance has for many years provided a safety net. It has forced partners towards solidarity, by providing mandatory financial support to the financially weaker partner for a few years after divorce.

However, maintenance as a source of temporary financial support has received less and less political support in recent years. This is not only a typically Dutch situation: in many (Western) countries maintenance is almost non-existent or only provided under strict conditions, for example in Denmark, while in some others it can still be a lifetime obligation, as in England. Underlying the new Dutch legislation are many explicit and implicit assumptions about how people behave, make decisions in marriages, and furthermore about the influence of legislation on this process. First, it is assumed that, a duration of 12 years for maintenance does not match social reality.[13] Second, those who are obliged to pay maintenance, mainly men, are considered to be financially worse off than women after a divorce. In line with this, a long duration of maintenance

[11] But this is just an assumption of course, as this chapter shows.

[12] A hardship clause already existed, but under the new legislation it has been made easier to appeal to it. This amendment was a concession and meant to satisfy the more sceptical members of parliament.

[13] See the paragraph on societal views on marriage.

is considered to cause conflicts between, and dissatisfaction of, former spouses. Also, when looking at the many lawsuits on maintenance, it is the assumption of the initiators of the new legislation that the number of lawsuits will decrease because there are fewer feelings of injustice (regarding the former spouses who are obliged to pay maintenance) (Schrama, Dijksterhuis and Spalter, 2020: 30–31). Third, a maximum duration for maintenance of five years would encourage women to be economically self-sufficient during marriage; also women who work only part-time during marriage could work more hours after the divorce (Schrama, Dijksterhuis and Spalter, 2020: 24–27, 29–35). In other words: the legislation is, though ill-founded, presented as an act for the emancipation of women, encouraging them to perform more paid work both during and after marriage. Some quotes from a Minister and members of parliament from the entire political spectrum will illustrate these assumptions: the Minister of legal protection Sander Dekker (VVD; a conservative-liberal political party) stated that 'a long duration of maintenance does not further financial independence';[14] and 'a shorter duration of maintenance will stimulate women to become economically independent faster'.[15] Member of parliament Attje Kuiken (Labour party) stated during the parliamentary debate on the new law that 'our legislation on maintenance comes from a time when men earned the money and women stayed home to take care of the household. Fortunately, this era lies far behind us'.[16] Member of parliament Kathalijne Maria Buitenweg (Green party) put forward that 'the legislative proposal can contribute to a change in thinking, which is a step forward towards a greater economic independence of women, by emphasising that everyone needs to "be self-sufficient"'. It is significant that these assumptions are widely shared by parties on the left and right of the political spectrum and by both men and women (Dijksterhuis, 2019a).

The inadequacy of a maintenance system in not offering enough legal protection for the financially weaker partner is not only problematic with relation to determining maintenance, but also when looked at the failure to pay the due amount. Non-compliance with maintenance obligations is high; in 2017 between 67 per cent and 78 per cent of the cases where a judge awarded maintenance or child support[17] ended up at the National Office for the Collection of Maintenance Payments (LBIO)[18] because the (monthly) maintenance or child

[14] 'Een lange alimentatieduur bevordert de financiële onafhankelijkheid niet.'

[15] 'Een kortere alimentatieduur zal vrouwen die partneralimentatie ontvangen stimuleren om sneller economisch zelfstandig te worden.'

[16] 'Onze alimentatie-wetgeving stamt nog uit de tijd dat mannen het geld verdienden en vrouwen thuis voor het huishouden zorgden. Die tijd ligt gelukkig ver achter ons.' in 'Partneralimentatie: na een scheiding weer je eigen leven vormgeven', *Joop*, 10 June 2018.

[17] This can be either a maintenance or child support obligation that is determined by the judge, because parties could not agree on the amount or duration of maintenance or an agreement by former partners that is confirmed by the judge.

[18] This central authority was established because of the Convention on the international recovery of child support and other forms of maintenance of 23 November 2007 (Hague Convention on Recovery of Maintenance 2007).

support was not paid. In other words: in the majority of the cases where there is a judicial decision on maintenance or child support, there is non-compliance (Huitink et al, 2018: 17–35).[19] The general view is therefore that payments of maintenance in many cases are not made according to the awarded amount following the judicial decision (or agreement of former spouses).[20] Moreover, there is no insight into, or data on, what proportion of the total group of people who are entitled to receive maintenance appeal to the national office when maintenance is not paid (Huitink et al, 2018: 17, 33–35). Though there are other views on the severity of the non-compliance problem. Kolkman et al state on the basis of an exploratory survey[21] that the majority of the divorced partners receive the amount of maintenance they are entitled to, and that only 10–15 per cent do not pay the due amount (Kolkman et al, 2021: 10, 219–220, 283).

B. Financial Position, Wellbeing and Views of Divorcees

Contrary to some assumptions, men hardly seem to be the financial victims of divorce. A report from Statistic Netherlands 'CBS' on trends in the financial consequences of divorce for men and women (CBS, 2017a) shows that men's purchasing power after a divorce declines about 0.2 per cent and the purchasing power of women declines about 22 per cent.[22] For divorced mothers, who are in most (Dutch) families the primary carers of (young) children, the average purchasing power of divorced mothers with whom the children live is €17,000, which is about the level of social welfare for a single parent household. Women who received maintenance still had a decline in purchasing power of 38 per cent, because of the high joint income level of the spouses before divorce. Economically independent women had a large loss of purchasing power, also due to the high income of their former partner. The largest group at risk were the economically dependent women; about 36 per cent had to deal with the risk of poverty after divorce (Schrama, Dijksterhuis and Spalter, 2020: 15–16; Dijksterhuis, 2019a).

There are also empirical data available that give insight into the welfare and wellbeing of single parents, who are mainly mothers. These also highlight the financial problems of women after divorce. A significant proportion are single parents because of divorce. The report of Statistic Netherlands on the

[19] Unfortunately, the quantitative data make no distinction between child support and maintenance.

[20] According to an exploratory survey in 2012 we found some explanations for not paying, of which the divorcees' lack of understanding of the calculation and the rules on which it was based was an important factor (Dijksterhuis and Vels, 2012).

[21] Total: 776 respondents; 249 respondents were either entitled to receive or had an obligation to pay maintenance.

[22] More recent, additional research by the CBS shows that five years after divorce the purchasing power of divorced women, in comparison to divorced men, had improved slightly: www.cbs.nl/nl-nl/nieuws/2021/38/gemiddelde-koopkracht-vrouwen-5-jaar-na-scheiding-vijfde-lager-dan-mannen.

quality of life (CBS, 2017b) showed that single parents, especially mothers, with children under 12, have the lowest score on welfare and wellbeing: more than 40 per cent had a low score on these parameters. Single mothers easily run the risk of living below the poverty line and receiving state benefits. About a third of single parent families, are dependent on social welfare; and for the lower educated people this is true for half of this group. The bad financial position of single parents, especially mothers, has severe consequences for the wellbeing of children. In many cases these children grow up in poverty, dependent on welfare (Schrama, Dijksterhuis and Spalter, 2020: 16; Dijksterhuis, 2019a; Kolkman et al, 2021: 165–66).

According to a report on the self-reliance of people by the Scientific Council for Government Policy (WRR), divorce can be considered as a life event with a significant impact; in particular finances ask a lot of someone's mental ability to cope; making the right decisions in such life events was hard for people and they tended to make (financial) decisions that would not promote their wellbeing in the long term. This has also to do with the many sources of income of a single parent that require careful management. This is especially hard because this sudden life event causes stress which affects the ability to cope, even for people who are normally self-sufficient (WRR, 2017: 140–41).

How do divorcees look at their own financial position after divorce; what are their experiences with the settlement of finances? And what is the role of (legal) experts in this context? According to a recent survey of divorcees, women were most worried about housing (46 per cent), whether they could financially cope (36 per cent) and the emotional consequences for the children (35 per cent). Men were mostly worried about the emotional consequences for the children (36 per cent), followed by housing (32 per cent) and whether they would financially cope (28 per cent).

On the basis of research by Motivaction, at the request of the Dutch association of family lawyers and the insurance company Aegon,[23] it appears that about four in ten of divorcees regretted financial arrangements made during divorce (Lingsma et al, 2019: 26). Women especially were unprepared for the financial consequences of divorce. Fear of the financial consequences of divorce was the biggest concern for both spouses. Former spouses who made good financial arrangements (with or without professional help) were more positive about their divorce than those who let the court decide. This research was part of an initiative by Aegon and the Dutch association of family lawyers to offer a financial, educational service to (former) partners: a tool on the financial preview at divorce 'Financiële Vooruitblik bij Scheiden'.[24] Reliable information from

[23] Respondents = 525.

[24] M Sperling, 'In één klap wordt het financiële plaatje inzichtelijk, 1 March 2019: www.aegon.nl/blog/opinie/%E2%80%98-%C3%A9%C3%A9n-klap-wordt-het-financi%C3%ABle-plaatje-inzichtelijk%E2%80%99.

(legal) experts is important for the acceptance of child and spousal maintenance (Kolkman et al, 2021: 242). The amount of maintenance is calculated on the basis of open norms and judicial guidelines with the help of computer programs. Experts such as lawyers and mediators not only have to make calculations but also explain the calculation of the amount due to divorcees. But especially when it concerns entrepreneurs who should pay maintenance, it is a more complex and therefore less predictable task to determine the amount of maintenance (Dijksterhuis, 2008; Kolkman et al, 2021: 255–56). Since the new legislation on maintenance, there is a legal obligation to make the calculation transparent as part of the judicial decision (Schrama, Dijksterhuis and Spalter, 2020: 83–86). Online divorce tools leave more room for people to make their own arrangements. The impression is that it fulfils especially the need of self-reliant people in a divorce. It would be useful to find out in the future to what extent the choice of these online platforms influences financial arrangements regarding maintenance and matrimonial property aspects. According to an evaluative research on Rechtwijzer in 2015, researchers of the University of Twente found that divorce conflicts were often characterised by dependence asymmetry; women felt more dependent on their ex-partner and vice versa and many people had concerns about debts and especially an (impending) fall in income (Dijksterhuis 2019b: 199, 210–211; see also Bickel, Van Dijk and Giebels, 2015).

IV. CONCLUSION

The key question of this chapter was: should family justice systems reflect social behaviour in financial arrangements after divorce?' One of the aims of the Dutch family justice system has always been to regulate the finances of spouses during and after marriage. Matrimonial property law provides rules for spouses during marriage and on the (possible) division of assets if the marriage were to end. Maintenance protects spouses who do not have sufficient income to support themselves after divorce.

In recent years, the legal protection of the financially weaker partners, still mostly women, has been eroded. There is less emphasis on solidarity and more emphasis on self-sufficiency. The point of departure of the new matrimonial property law that came into force on 1 January 2018, is that, in principle, only the assets (and debts) accumulated since the start of the marriage are common property. Spouses can deviate from the legal default and conclude a prenuptial agreement, which they can customise to their needs and wishes. The role of the notary is to enable spouses to make a well-informed decision; even in some cases strongly advising them to share their assets to some extent, for example when a couple has children. This freedom of contract remains almost without any limits, and it allows spouses not to share any assets, during and after marriage.

The same tendency could be observed regarding the changes in the legislation on maintenance. New legislation on maintenance, which came into force on

1 January 2020, drastically shortened the duration of maintenance, with a few exceptions to increase support. The debate in Parliament shows that parties on the right and left of the political spectrum had strong views on the reality of the emancipation of both partners and how work and care should be divided. With regard to maintenance, in the process of or after divorce, former spouses can, in the run-up to divorce or during the divorce process, also deviate from the legal system, which places the responsibility to be legally well informed and aware of one's financial position and needs on oneself. The inadequacy of a maintenance system to offer enough legal protection for the financially weaker partner is not only problematic with regard to awarding maintenance, but also when considering the failure by many to pay the amount of maintenance due.

The legal rules on prenuptial agreements and maintenance have in common that the legislator has particular expectations regarding the behaviour of spouses. The law expects spouses who opt for a prenuptial agreement that excludes any community of property to behave in an almost professional manner towards each other in matters related to their financial position. Similarly, the law expects spouses to be financially self-sufficient up to a certain extent and strive for an equal division of labour in order to achieve this. The legislator has the same expectations on maintenance. One of the reasons for shortening the maximum duration of maintenance was to provide spouses with an incentive during marriage to be or to remain financially independent.

However, these expectations run counter to the actual behaviour of spouses during marriage. Our study shows that in real life, spouses tend to disregard the law and their prenuptial agreement. Other, non-legal norms are more compelling to them. The societal view on marriage is very influential; in the Netherlands, husbands are still expected to be the primary breadwinners and women to be the primary caretakers of children. The majority of Dutch women work part-time: on average, they work 27 hours a week, while most men work full-time. The consequence is that women are often still not financially independent, but even if they are, their purchasing power greatly diminishes after divorce. This makes the need for good financial advice from lawyers, mediators or other (legal) experts during marriage and in a divorce process more pressing. Spouses in hindsight often regret the (financial) choices they made when they faced divorce. Divorcees frequently emphasise the importance of better financial advice during the divorce. This conflict is insufficiently addressed by the family justice system.

This leads to an important mismatch in our family justice system between legal and non-legal norms, which results in financial asymmetry between former partners, as our case illustrates. Although both spouses contribute to the wellbeing and welfare of their family, upon divorce Mary will bear most of the financial inequities due to an uneven division of labour between spouses during the marriage. Also, her wellbeing will probably be lower as, in general, single parents after divorce have a lower score on these aspects due to financial problems. Therefore, it would be better if the legislation could be evidence-based, thus taking into account behavioural psychology. It is important that the effects of new legislation on the partner with the most care duties, in general still the woman, are taken into account. If a new law on maintenance drastically harms the financial position of women, alarm bells should go off and pressure groups for women's rights and members of the Parliament, and perhaps even academics and the legal professions, should take responsibility. Moreover, we need story-telling using real-life cases such as the one above. Data impresses members of parliament insufficiently when debating new legislation.

In addition, we need to consider which role the legal professions should have in this context. Perhaps they could be more active in ensuring a fairer system, in accordance with the behaviour of (former) spouses. As described, notaries have the possibility to advise spouses more proactively to choose a matrimonial property law that divides assets in accordance with their actual paid work and care division. The alternative is that we let the weaker financial partners cope on their own. This is unsatisfying, not only for the finally weaker spouse but also for the children who are likely to suffer the consequences. The middle way is education: the (legal) professions that assist people in a divorce, especially lawyers and mediators, might start initiatives to explain to married people what the financial consequences of their behaviour and decisions might be after divorce. The initiative by the insurance company Aegon and the Dutch association of family lawyers, vFAS, is illustrative. Still, this is unlikely to be enough to ensure a fair system for both partners, and commercial parties, such as insurance companies, may take over the role of the state. This commercial aspect is not necessarily a hindrance, but their focus is on making profit, while not following a professional code as lawyers do. In line with our study, it can be concluded that a family justice system should be designed to organise solidarity between (former) partners in order to respect their behaviour, choices and decisions. The state has a responsibility, because society's interest is at stake as this situation effects the financial situations of many (former) partners and their children.

REFERENCES

Antokolskaia, M, Breederveld, B, Hulst, J, Kolkman, J, Salomons, F and Verstappen, L (2011) *Koude Uitsluiting. Materiële problemen en onbillijkheden na scheiding van in koude uitsluiting gehuwde echtgenoten en na scheiding va ongehuwd samenlevende partners, alsmede instrumenten voor de overheid om deze tegen te gaan* (Den Haag, Boom Juridische uitgevers).

Bastard, B and Cardia-Vonèche, L (1988) *Les familles monoparentales face à leur situation économique* (Paris, COS, CNRS).

Bastard, B, Cardia-Vonèche, L and Maclean, M (1988) *Woman's Resources after Divorce, Cross National Studies No 5* (Birmingham, Aston University).

Bickel, E, Dijk, M Van and Giebels, E (2015) *Online legal advice and conflict support: A Dutch experience* (Twente, Department Psychology of Conflict, Risk & Safety, Faculty of Behavioural, Management and Social Sciences University of Twente).

CBS (Van den Brakel, M and Arts, K) (2017a), *Trends in de financiële gevolgen van een echtscheiding voor man en vrouw* (Den Haag, CBS).

CBS (2017b), *Kwaliteit van leven* (Den Haag, CBS).

CBS (Van den Brakel, M, Portegijs, W and Hermans, B) (2020) *Emancipatiemonitor 2020*, report CBS and SCP (Den Haag, CBS and SCP).

CPB (Rabaté, S, and Rellstab, S) (2021) *Discussion Paper. The Child Penalty in the Netherlands and its Determinants* (Den Haag, CPB).

Dijksterhuis, B (2008) *Rechters normeren de alimentatiehoogte, Een empirisch onderzoek naar rechterlijke samenwerking in de Werkgroep Alimentatienormen (1975-2007)* (Leiden, Leiden University Press).

Dijksterhuis, B (2019a) 'Het wetsvoorstel partneralimentatie: vooronderstellingen en feiten', *Tijdschrift voor Familie- en Jeugdrecht* 43, 200–04.

Dijksterhuis, B (2019b) 'The Online Divorce Resolution Tool Rechtwijzer uit Elkaar examined' in M Maclean and B Dijksterhuis (eds), *Digital Family Justice. From Alternative Dispute Resolution to Online Dispute Resolution?* (Oxford, Hart Publishing).

Dijksterhuis, B and Vels, N (2012) 'De mening van alimentatieplichtigen en alimentatiegerechtigden over de berekening van kinderalimentatie', *Tijdschrift voor Familie- en Jeugdrecht* 63, 178–83.

Eekelaar, J (1978) *Family Law and Social Policy* (London, Weidenfeld and Nicholson).

Flos, A (2018) 'Prenuptial and Tenancy Agreements as Relational Contracts' in L Ratti (ed), *Embedding the Principles of Life Time Contracts. A Research Agenda for Contract Law* (Utrecht, Eleven International Publishing).

Giesen, D (1999) 'Juridische arrangementen' in W Kalmijn, W Bernasco and J Weesie (eds), *Huwelijks- en samenwoonrelaties in Nederland. De organisatie van afhankelijkheid* (Assen, Van Gorcum).

Gilligan, G (1982) *In a different voice* (Cambridge, Mass, Harvard University Press).

Glendon, MA (1981) *The New Family and The New Property* (Toronto, Butterworth).

Hoog, S and Van Egten, C (2012) *Vrouwen en financiën: van roze wolk naar financieel bewustzijn* (Amsterdam, Aletta E-Quality).

Huitink, B, Reitsma, J, Schepers, R and Maas-Vos, G van der (2018) *Evaluatie Landelijk Bureau Inning Onderhoudsbijdragen* (Ministry of Justice and Security).

Kocken, C (1997) *De hand van de notaris. Een rechtssociologisch onderzoek naar de onpartijdigheid en invloed van de Nederlandse notaris* (Deventer, Kluwer).

Kolkman, W, et al (2021) *Alimentatie van nu. Acceptatie van alimentatie in het licht van de maatschappelijke ontwikkelingen* (Den Haag, WODC).

Lingsma, J, et al (2019) *Dag van de scheiding 2019* (Onderzoeksrapport, Motivaction & vFAS 30 augustus 2019).

Maclean, M (1991) *Surviving Divorce: Women's Resources after Separation* (London, Palgrave Macmillan).

Maclean, M and Eekelaar, J (2016) *Lawyers and Mediators: The Brave New World of Services for Separating Families* (Oxford, Hart Publishing).

Poortman, AR and Mills, M (2012) 'Investments in Marriage and Cohabitation: The Role of Legal and Interpersonal Commitment', *Journal of Marriage and Family* 74, 357–76.

Ruitenberg, J (2014a) 'A Typology of Dutch Mothers' Employment Narratives: Drifters, Privilegeds, Balancers, Ambitious', *Gender Issues* 31, 58–82.

Ruitenberg, J (2014b) *Socialized Choices: Labour Market Behaviour of Dutch Mothers* (Amsterdam, Pallas Publications).

Ruitenberg, J and De Beer, P (2014) 'Exploring the Social Origins of Dutch Mothers' Ideal Family Lives', *Sex Roles* 70, 315–28.

Scherpe, J (ed) (2012) *Marital Agreements and Private Autonomy In Comparative Perspective* (Oxford, Hart Publishing).

Schols, F and Hoens, F (2012) 'CNR-Huwelijksvoorwaardenonderzoek, deel I: algemeen en koude voorwaarden', *Weekblad voor Privaatrecht, Notariaat en Registratie* (6956), 943–53.

Schrama, W, Dijksterhuis, B and Spalter, N (2020) *Commentaar en Context Wet herziening partneralimentatie* (Den Haag, Boom Juridische Uitgevers).

SCP (Portegijs, W) (2018) *Ons geld. Vrouwen en mannen over het belang van inkomen en economische zelfstandigheid voor vrouwen* (Den Haag, SCP).

WRR (2017) *Weten is nog geen doen. Een realistisch perspectief op redzaamheid* (Den Haag, WRR).

4

Implementing Gender Equality as an Aim of the Swiss Family Justice System

MICHELLE COTTIER, BINDU SAHDEVA AND GAËLLE AEBY

I. INTRODUCTION

IN SWITZERLAND, AS in most countries today, the great majority of divorces are resolved through 'private ordering' and are based on mutual consent and a full agreement. According to the influential analysis by Mnookin and Kornhauser (1978–1979), the negotiation of divorce agreements takes place 'in the shadow of the law'. Therefore, the main role of the family justice system is to provide, together with the legislator, the normative framework or, according to Mnookin and Kornhauser, the 'bargaining chips' for the spouses' negotiation.

Previous research has been interested in the impact of the normative framework on the negotiation of private agreements from a gender perspective. According to some studies, the indeterminacy of divorce law might work to women's disadvantage because it sets few boundaries for negotiations, and women are less likely than men to exploit ambiguity to their own advantage (Rebouché, 2016; Wilkinson-Ryan and Small, 2008). A statutory legal framework with clear principles and guidelines, based on formal equality between husband and wife, has been shown to limit negotiations of private agreements to these formal-egalitarian arguments, making it more difficult to achieve agreements favouring the primary carer (Mair, Wasoff and Mackay, 2015).

In Switzerland, we observe that different interpretations of gender equality are currently competing in divorce law and sometimes contradicting each other, just as in other Western countries (see Bessière, Biland and Fillod-Chabaud, 2013; Boyd, 2015; Côté and Gaborean, 2015; Glennon, 2010; Scheiwe and Wersig, 2011; Smart, 2013; Wersig and Künzel, 2008). This reflects the coexistence of change, and the persistence of family-related gender norms in Western societies more generally (Maihofer, 2014). Indeed, in Switzerland, the predominant family arrangement is a gendered division of tasks. Due to the lack of childcare institutions, the wage gap between women and men, and the lack of policies for balancing work and family life, after becoming parents most couples adopt the model of the father as breadwinner and the mother working part-time in the labour market (Le Goff and Levy, 2016). In the event of divorce, the division of labour practiced during the marriage is in most cases continued. That means that, on the one hand, a majority of divorced fathers are at greater risk of seeing their children less often. On the other hand, a majority of divorced mothers have to shoulder day-to-day child-rearing responsibilities alone, which puts them into a difficult position in relation to labour market participation, economic security, old age provision and health (Cottier, Widmer, Tornare and Girardin, 2017).

In view of this predominantly still very gendered division of labour before and after divorce, the implementation of the guarantee of gender equality enshrined in article 8 section 3 of the Swiss Federal Constitution as well as in the UN Convention on the Elimination of All Forms of Discrimination Against Women (CEDAW), ratified by Switzerland in 1997, has an important function and task in the Swiss family justice system. However, in accordance with the ideal of 'divorce based on mutual agreement' an estimate of 90 per cent of all divorces in Switzerland are based on a full settlement agreed by the spouses.[1] The role of the family justice system is in these cases reduced on the one hand to providing the normative framework, or to quote Mnookin and Kornhauser (1978–1979) the 'bargaining chips' for the spouses' negotiation, and on the other hand to exercising judicial control of the final divorce agreement. After a brief overview of the main developments in divorce law in Switzerland since the turn of the twenty-first century, we will explore the different interpretations of gender equality in spousal and child maintenance law based on nine court decisions published by the Swiss Federal Supreme Court (SFSC). More precisely, we will investigate how and to what extent the SFSC fulfils its task of implementing gender equality in divorce law based on its interpretation of gender equality. Combining a legal and a sociological approach, we will do so by, first, uncovering how themes related to gender equality are interlinked with one another and, second, how the bargaining chips are distributed between parties regarding the issue of maintenance. This will allow us in conclusion to assess the prevailing interpretation of gender equality in divorce law.

[1] Statistics on the grounds for divorce collected by the Federal Statistical Office from cantonal civil courts, available only until 2010, show that every year around 90% of all divorces in Switzerland involved full agreement by the spouses. In 2010: 19,675 out of a total of 22,081 divorces, ie 89% (Federal Office of Statistics, 2021).

II. DIVORCE AND GENDER EQUALITY SINCE THE TURN OF THE TWENTY-FIRST CENTURY

A. 2000: The Reform of Divorce Law

In Switzerland, 2000 was a turning point for divorce law with a critical reform placing gender equality at the centre stage and abolishing fault-based divorce (Schwenzer, 2011; Federal Council, 1996). During the period of the reform discussions in the federal parliament in the late 1990s, a study was published that highlighted the fact that Swiss cantonal courts relied on different interpretations of gender equality in their divorce practice and that certain interpretations disadvantaged women in terms of the financial outcomes of divorce (Binkert and Wyss, 1997: 302). The authors identified three interpretations of gender equality. The *traditionalist* interpretation sees the gendered division of labour as given by nature, ensuring that the husband's economically privileged position is not questioned, meaning his interests generally prevail. The *formal-egalitarian* interpretation demands that the wife should speedily achieve financial independence, ignoring the reality of unequal distribution of childcare responsibilities after separation, and leads to low levels of spousal maintenance after divorce. In contrast, the *compensatory* interpretation sees mothers as the primary caregivers, who need to be compensated through generous maintenance payments for their care work, with the disadvantage of reinforcing their position as caregivers and mothers and therefore delaying their transition to financial independence. Binkert and Wyss recommended an approach close to the compensatory interpretation, based on *substantial (material) equality*, which aims at equalising economic advantages and disadvantages due to the division of roles between husband and wife, through adequate maintenance payments, but without fixing women in their gendered role as mothers. Namely, the authors suggested that post-marital maintenance payments should finance (continuing) education measures to improve the earning capacity of the spouse who has been (partly) absent from the labour market due to childcare (Binkert and Wyss, 1997: 295–96).

The reform of divorce law introduced no-fault divorce and the ideal of divorce based on mutual agreement into the Civil Code. As empirical research had shown, this corresponded to the living law applied by cantonal courts (Bastard, Cardia-Vonèche and Perrin, 1987). In the reform process, explicit reference was made to the constitutional obligation to implement substantial gender equality in the family. However, although the CEDAW Convention had been ratified by Switzerland in 1997, no reference was made to it in the reform process (Pfaffinger and Hofstetter, 2015: N 11).

In spite of the explicit aim of furthering substantial gender equality, the legislator did not follow Binkert and Wyss's recommendation of a spousal maintenance law based on substantial equality and favoured a financial 'clean break' at the moment of divorce, thereby stressing formal equality. The clean break in relation to post-divorce financial independence was made more viable by the new obligation to equalise pension rights accrued by husband and wife during the marriage, resulting in most cases in a transfer of pension assets from the husband's to the wife's pension fund at the moment of divorce. This was and still is of great importance, as in most Swiss divorces, pension assets are the only savings the couple has, since in Switzerland a majority of people rent their homes and do not own them.[2] However a subsequent evaluation showed that pension assets were not always correctly divided and that women often renounced their rights without courts intervening to protect them (Baumann and Lauterburg, 2004: 76). The reform finally introduced the possibility of joint parental responsibility after divorce, on request from both parents.

The strong focus on the clean break principle in maintenance law, and the problems with the implementation of the law on the equalisation of pension assets led to a reaction of the CEDAW Committee. In its Concluding Observations from 2009 concerning Switzerland's third periodic report on the measures adopted to give effect to the provisions of the CEDAW Convention,[3] it expressed concern at the inability of Switzerland's divorce law to adequately address gender-based economic disparities between spouses resulting from traditional work and family-life patterns.[4]

B. 2014: The Reform of the Law on Parental Responsibility

Following the implementation of the divorce law reform, an interdisciplinary study published in 2009 on post-divorce parental responsibility arrangements (Büchler et al, 2009), showed the persistence of unequal distribution of care work and low satisfaction of mothers in the case of joint parental responsibility. As parenting was only truly shared and, therefore, deemed satisfactory, in 5 per cent of cases, the authors recommended implementation of joint parental responsibility with very limited joint decision-making (Büchler et al, 2009).

However, the legislation again chose to disregard recommendations from socio-legal research. It adopted a reform of parental responsibility based on formal equality, that came into force on 1 July 2014. It declared joint parental responsibility (*autorité parentale conjointe/gemeinsame elterliche Sorge*) the rule, and sole parental responsibility the exception (Federal Council, 2011; Schwenzer and Keller, 2014). Differing from what had been recommended by

[2] According to the latest available statistics from 2017, only 38% of all residents of Switzerland own the property they live in, see Federal Office of Statistics (2019b).

[3] See art 18 CEDAW for the details of the reporting procedure. See also Freeman, Chinkin and Rudolf (2012).

[4] CEDAW, Concluding Observations Switzerland, no 3/2009 (UN Docs CEDAW/C/CHE/CO/3), para 41.

Büchler et al (2009), parliament adopted a strong consensus model (Scheiwe, 2019: 158), in which joint exercise of parental responsibility is the general rule for important decisions and for legal representation of the child, whereas the primary caretaker can act alone only exceptionally. The reform was strongly influenced by the political activism of father's rights groups who insisted on shared parenting, thereby advancing arguments of gender equality (Gisler, Steinert-Borella and Wiedmer, 2009).

The CEDAW Committee, in its Concluding Observations from 2016 concerning Switzerland's fourth and fifth periodic report expressed its concern that the default rule of joint parental authority and preference for shared custody might lead to a reduction in the number of child maintenance orders, with no mechanism to ensure that shared custody is indeed practised, and reflects the reality of time and cost allocation between parents.[5]

C. 2017: The Reform of Child Maintenance Law and of the Law on the Division of Pension Assets

A swing back to a stronger focus on compensation and substantive equality was brought about by the new law on child maintenance, that came into force on 1 January 2017 (Federal Council, 2014). The innovation in this reform is the introduction of a new component of child maintenance aimed at covering the 'indirect costs' of childcare, ie the loss of income of the primary parent caring for the child. This new component is called 'childcare maintenance' (Article 285 para 2 CC) (Federal Council, 2014). The approach is rather original and unique as it recognises the loss of income due to care work and the need for legal remedies to equalise these costs among the two parents. As a gendered division of roles prevails in Switzerland with mothers working part-time in the labour market and fathers full-time (Federal Office of Statistics, 2019a), mothers more often than fathers are entitled to this 'childcare maintenance'. The reform goes back to claims advanced by women's interest groups as well as legal scholars insisting on the need to compensate economic losses due to the division of labour among spouses and cohabiting partners (Schwenzer and Egli, 2010). In divorce law, the reform means that former components of spousal maintenance are now elements of child maintenance, which implies some advantages, such as protection against loss of maintenance rights in case of remarriage and the right to receive advance payments from the state, which are in most cantons only available for child maintenance. What is however quite surprising is that in the course of the reform process reference to gender equality has practically completely

[5] CEDAW, Concluding Observations Switzerland, no 4-5/2016 (UN Docs, CEDAW/C/CHE/CO/4-5), para 48.

disappeared from the argument, whereas the child's best interest has been stressed as a rationale for the reform (see Cottier and Muheim, 2019).

On 1 January 2017, a reform of the division of pension rights also came into force (Federal Council, 2013), which weakens, in the name of 'autonomy of the spouses', the original idea of equalising pension assets, but introduces, in a move in the opposite direction, the idea of compensation for post-divorce disadvantages into this area of the law. On the one hand, the strict principle of equal division of pension rights is eased, meaning that spouses can more easily renounce their rights; on the other hand, the possibility to confer more than half of pension rights to the parent who takes care of children after divorce is possible, thereby allowing for compensation of post-divorce disadvantages in terms of possibilities to save for old age, due to reduced activity in the labour market.

The CEDAW Committee is currently reviewing again the progress Switzerland has made in implementing the CEDAW Convention (Cottier, 2021). In its 'list of issues of questions prior to reporting' from November 2019,[6] divorce law has again been among the issues addressed.[7] On this basis, Switzerland has presented its sixth periodic report,[8] and the Concluding Observations by the Committee are expected in 2022.

III. METHODOLOGY AND DATA

A. Context of the Study

The results presented in this article are preliminary results from a four-year research project looking into gender equality in the Swiss family justice system. The project is entitled 'The negotiation of divorce agreements and gender (in) equality in Switzerland' (Cottier and Widmer, 2019–2023) and is funded by the Swiss National Science Foundation. This project encompasses three parts following a sequential explanatory design: (1) an analysis of written law; (2) a survey aimed at divorce lawyers; and (3) qualitative interviews with lawyers and divorcees. These preliminary results are based on the first part of this project dedicated to an extensive analysis of legislation, case law and legal writing.

[6] Since 2018, a simplified reporting procedure has been available on request of the State parties. Under the simplified reporting procedure, the Committee transmits a 'list of issues prior to reporting' (LOIPR) to the State party concerned prior to the submission of its report. The replies of the State party to the list of issues prior to reporting constitute its periodic report under art 18, para 1(b) CEDAW. See www.ohchr.org/EN/HRBodies/CEDAW/Pages/ReportingProcedures.aspx.

[7] CEDAW, LOIPR Switzerland, no 6/2019 (UN Docs CEDAW/C/CHE/QPR/6), para 24.

[8] CEDAW, Periodic Report Switzerland, no 6/2020 (UN Docs CEDAW/C/CHE/6), paras 181–87.

B. Body of Data: Decisions of the Swiss Federal Supreme Court in the Area of Maintenance

The data consists of nine decisions of the Swiss Federal Supreme Court (SFSC)[9] published on the official website (www.bger.ch) and freely accessible to the public (see Table 4.1 in section III.B below). In family law cases, the SFSC is the court of third instance, deciding on appeal by one of the parties, after the first instance cantonal civil court, and the cantonal appeals court. The selection of decisions is limited to cases on issues of child maintenance and/or post-divorce (spousal) maintenance. We selected fundamental rulings in areas sensitive to gender equality in divorce law, namely rulings which are notable for bringing changes in case law, clarifications of earlier case law or the confirmation of older case law after an extended period of time. Criteria also included how often a particular decision was cited in the legal literature; whether it summarised the case law on a topic; whether it was mentioned as important in the media communications of the SFSC; and whether it was exemplary for a particular topic or problem. On the basis of these criteria, we compiled a list of decisions. Using our expertise in the field of divorce law, from that list we made a selection of nine Federal Supreme Court decisions, numbered in Table 4.1 from no 1 to no 9 by year of publication. The length of the decisions varied from 1191 words to 6595. The nine decisions cover the years between 2006 and 2018. As previously mentioned, several important legislative reforms occurred during this period: in 2014, the reform on joint parental responsibility (Federal Council, 2011), and in 2017, the introduction of a provision favouring shared parenting (alternating residence of the child) (Federal Council, 2014) as well as the reform on equitable division of pensions (Federal Council, 2013).

Table 4.1 Summary of the Data

No	Decisions	Year	LG	Size (words)	Nbr codes	Main topic
1	BGE 132 III 593	2006	GE	1376	63	Child maintenance and spousal maintenance (with solvent debtor)
2	BGE 135 III 59	2008	GE	2468	61	Pre-marital cohabitation and qualification of a marriage as 'life-shaping'
3	BGE 135 III 66	2008	GE	4615	113	Rules on who bears the deficit in case of insufficient financial means

(continued)

[9] In German: Bundesgerichtsentscheide; in French: arrêts du Tribunal fédéral.

Table 4.1 *(Continued)*

No	Decisions	Year	LG	Size (words)	Nbr codes	Main topic
4	BGE 135 III 158	2008	GE	1191	42	Spousal maintenance calculation method (with old age provision)
5	BGE 137 III 102	2010	FR	4423	122	Principles applicable to the calculation of post-marital maintenance
6	BGer 5A_373/2015	2015	FR	3467	50	Suspension or termination of post-marital maintenance in case of former spouse cohabitating with a new partner
7	BGE 141 III 465	2015	GE	2222	94	Maintenance to ensure standard of living in case of earlier retirement of the creditor spouse
8	BGE 144 III 377	2018	FR	3974	84	Calculation method for covering indirect costs of childcare (new childcare maintenance)
9	BGE 144 III 481	2018	GE	6595	190	New rules on obligation of caregiver to re-enter the labour market based on child's school age
Total				30,331	819	

Notes: LG = language of decision; GE = German; FR = French; Nbr codes = number of codes attributed.

C. Methods: A Combination of a Legal and a Sociological Approach

To shed a new light on the recurring themes across the nine selected decisions, we combined a legal and a sociological approach in a 2-step process. First, we systematically coded the data using a computer-assisted qualitative data analysis (QDA) software drawn from a content analysis approach inspired by Mayring (2000). Content analysis consists of a bundle of techniques for systematic text analysis applied to empirical data of various types. The approach we developed for this analysis is based on a deductive application of predefined categories, but enriched through the data coding procedure. Three researchers discussed the categories and one main researcher coded the data line by line. At different stages, meetings were held with the two other researchers to ensure the reliability of the coding system. Within a feedback loop the codes were revised and eventually regrouped into main categories. When looking at the distribution of codes across decisions (see Table 4.1), there is a mean of 91 codes applied by decision with a minimum of 42 for the shortest (BGE 135 III 158) and a maximum of 190 for the largest (BGE 144 III 481).

Applying the coding procedure described above, we were able to identify 25 recurring themes that we grouped into eight main categories in Table 4.2. Standing out are the codes relating to the different types of maintenance existing in the Swiss system (post-divorce maintenance, child maintenance and childcare maintenance introduced in 2017) as well as situations where maintenance has to be reconsidered due to changing circumstances. In second position are the codes relating to children linked more specifically to childcare arrangements, children's age, and the principle of children's wellbeing. In third position, the situation of the 'creditor/recipient' parent (in all our cases women) appears and especially earning capacity and return to paid work. The situation of the 'debtor' parent (in all our cases men) is less prominent, but still emerges in relation to both earning capacity and risk of deficit. We created a code category exclusively for issues related to pension in old age after retirement. Similarly, a specific code category was created for the use of references to interdisciplinary knowledge stemming primarily from socioeconomic science and also to some extent from the field of child psychology. In the category 'gender principles', we grouped mentions of overarching principles related to different interpretations of gender equality, used as justifications to back up the arguments of the SFSC. Interestingly gender equality was not mentioned verbatim in any of the decisions, but was indirectly hinted at with principles such as clean break, post-divorce solidarity, etc. Finally, the last category of codes relates to the economic situation of the family, distinguishing low, medium and high income.

Table 4.2 Overview of the Coding System of 25 Main Codes

Different types of maintenance (n=239)	
Post-divorce maintenance (*MaintenancePostDivorce*)	102
Child maintenance (*MaintenanceChild*)	39
Childcare maintenance (*MaintenanceChildcare*)	39
Change in the maintenance amount (*MaintenanceChange*)	31
Termination of maintenance due to repartnering (*MaintenanceConcubinage*)	28
Children (n=165)	
Childcare arrangements (*ChildCare*)	91
Age of the child, minor and adult children (*ChildAge*)	43
Child wellbeing, child's best interest (*ChildWellbeing*)	31

(continued)

Table 4.2 *(Continued)*

Situation of the 'creditor/recipient' parent (n=123)	
Capacity to earn an income, also associated with hypothetical income *(CreditorCapacity)*	56
Return to paid work, also associated with 'school level system' *(CreditorActivity)*	44
Age *(CreditorAge)*	23
Situation of the 'debtor' parent (n=65)	
Capacity to earn an income, also associated with hypothetical income *(DebtorCapacity)*	29
Deficit, also associated with protection of debtor's subsistence minimum *(DebtorDeficit)*	20
Age *(DebtorAge)*	16
Pension in old age *(Pension)*	40
Interdisciplinary knowledge *(Expertise)*	35
Gender principles (n=115)	
Arguments related to clean break and self-sufficiency *(P_CleanBreak)*	33
Preservation of the living standard *(P_LifeStandard)*	24
Principle of trust *(P_Trust)*	23
Compensation of disadvantages *(P_Compensation)*	13
Post-divorce solidarity *(P_Solidarity)*	12
Right to the same living standard for both ex-spouses *(P_SameLife)*	10
Family socioeconomic situation (n=37)	
Low income *(SituationLow)*	20
High income *(SituationHigh)*	12
Medium income *(SituationMedium)*	5

Notes: Total number of applied codes = 798819. The shorter code names that will be used in the PCA analysis are shown in brackets and italics.

In a second step, we could use this coding system to conduct an analysis of the data at two levels. At the first level (see section IV.A), we followed a sociological approach and performed a principal component analysis (PCA), analysis technique for quantitative data,[10] to build up a bi-dimensional map, taking into account simultaneously various variables without assuming causal direction.

[10] All computations were made using the R statistical environment (R Development Core Team, 2020) and the package 'FactoMineR' for the principal component analysis (Lê, Josse and Husson, 2008).

The objective was to analyse the pattern of relationships between several variables simultaneously and, by doing so, to represent the underlying structures of a dataset. The PCA was performed on an individual/variable matrix, where the rows represented individuals (here the nine decisions) and the columns represented the variables (here the 25 thematic codes). With PCA, we obtained a bi-dimensional map on which it was possible to visualise proximities between variables in a geometric space. At a second level (see section IV.A), we conducted a legal analysis of the decisions.

IV. RESULTS

A. Interlinked Themes Related to Gender Equality: The Best Interest of the Child and Individualistic/Solidarity Value Considerations

Our first research question regarding gender equality in SFSC decisions concerned recurring themes across the nine selected decisions. In a first subsection, we describe and discuss the recurring themes, and, in a second subsection, we analyse how they relate to one another.

Moving beyond the number of occurrences (Table 4.2), it is important to look at how the different themes relate to one another with the help of the aforementioned PCA. Figure 4.1 shows the bi-dimensional map we obtained. The contributions of the variables to the map are indicated, as well as the tests indicating whether a variable contributes significantly to the definition of the axes. Concerning the first dimension represented by the horizontal axis, the main themes characterising it are located on the right side of the map and are related to children (*childcare*, *child wellbeing*, *child age*) and to both *childcare maintenance* and *return to work* of the creditor parent. Interestingly, the theme *expertise* (interdisciplinary knowledge) was also associated with this axis. In contrast, the theme *pension* was at the left side of the map. We interpreted this horizontal axis as that of considerations relating to the 'child's best interest' stretching from an absence of the topic (left side) to a high focus on the topic (right side). Concerning the second dimension represented by the vertical axis, the upper part was characterised by the situation of the debtor parent regarding their *earning capacity* and *deficit* and, to a lower extent, by the parallel issue of the *earning capacity* of the creditor parent as well as *child maintenance*, while the lower part was characterised by the themes *trust* and, to a lower extent, *compensation*. We interpreted this vertical axis as that of considerations relating to 'individualistic versus solidarity values' with topics related to individual needs and economic circumstances in the upper side and topics related to the commitment achieved during marriage in the lower side.

Figure 4.1 Map of the Themes, using PCA

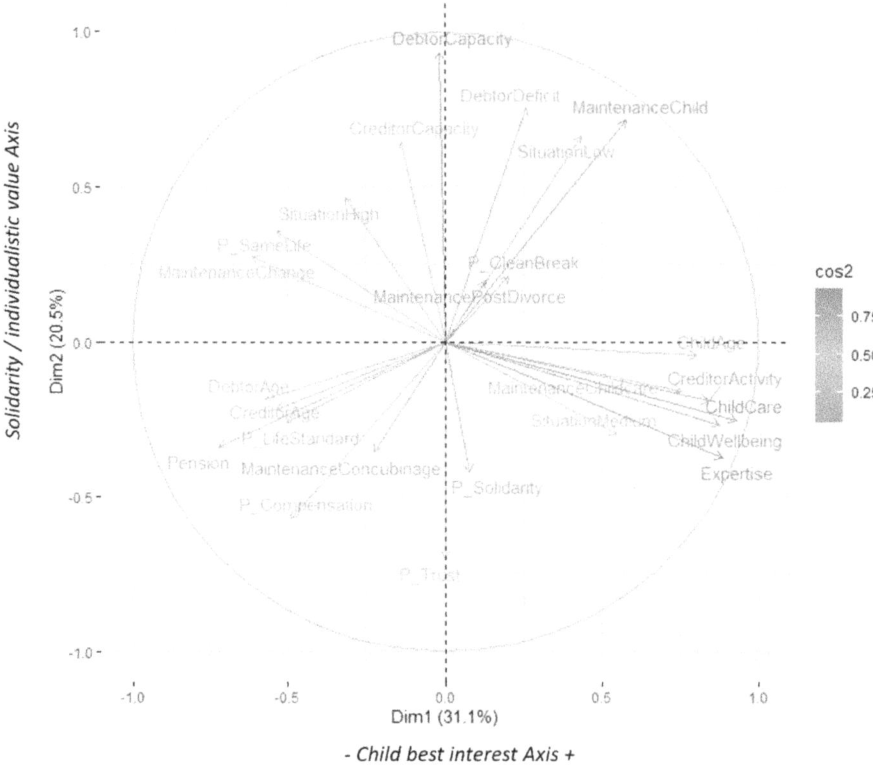

Regarding the organisation of themes on the map along these two axes, we can distinguish three subgroups. The first group (middle to lower right square of the map) shows an association between themes related to the creditor parent – here women – and to the child's best interest. It shows that the question of whether women return to work and become financially independent is directly linked to their role as primary care givers. This is clearly linked to the gender division of roles still prevailing in Swiss society and persisting after divorce. The second group (lower left square of the map) consists of themes such as life standard, pension in old age, the principle of compensation, and the age of the two parents (debtor and creditor). Those concerns seem to be related to situations without children, or more probably, situations where children are grown up and no longer represent a main concern. In those cases, also characterised by a long marriage and the development of trust, there is more concern for ensuring pension payments and the upholding of the wife's living standard. Finally, the third and last group of themes (middle upper part of the map) is about the situation of the debtor parent – here men – and also family situations with low income and the creditor parent's hypothetical ability to work to earn an income. It shows that men's situations are often considered on their own, as if they were disconnected from considerations other than financial ones. In Swiss law, this is reflected in the principle of the protection of the subsistence minimum for the debtor[11] which means that in most cases the economic consequences of a divorce lay on women's shoulders when means are scarce.

To sum up, this first analysis of the main themes related to gender equality shows that women are in a critical position as their position after divorce is bound up with that of their children, whereas the men's position is considered separately.

B. Controversial Issues of Maintenance and the Unequal Distribution of Bargaining Chips

We then conducted a classical in-depth legal analysis of the decisions regarding the three main controversial issues linked to the different types of maintenance. In particular, we focused on the presence in the SFSC decisions of the three interpretations identified by Binkert and Wyss (1997) (*traditionalist, formal-egalitarian, compensatory*) presented in the introduction (section I).

i. Spousal Maintenance: Trust in a Life-shaping Marriage, but with Multiple Hidden Conditions

Four of the decisions we selected for in-depth analysis touch on the issue of spousal maintenance. Two main themes are highlighted by the analysis: the importance of pre-marital and post-marital cohabitation (BGE 135 III 59 and BGer 5A_373/2015) and the calculation of maintenance in cases of a gap in old age provision (BGE 135 III 158 and BGE 141 III 465).

The Importance of Pre-marital and Post-marital Cohabitation

In the decisions addressing the subject of spousal maintenance, cohabitation plays a role in two out of three decisions. In the decision BGE 135 III 59, the period of cohabitation prior to the marriage was not considered sufficiently formative for the couple's relationship to qualify the following, relatively short marriage as 'life-shaping', and therefore the wife was not awarded higher spousal maintenance of longer duration (which is usually due in marriages that have a lasting impact on the spouse's economic situation).

In BGer 5A_373/2015 of 2 June 2016, the issue was the suspension or termination of spousal maintenance in the case of post-marital cohabitation of the

[11] In German: Schutz des Existenzminimums des Unterhaltsschuldners; in French: protection du minimum vital du débirentier.

spouse entitled to post-marital maintenance. As in most cases women are the maintenance creditors, the suspension or termination of spousal maintenance mainly affects women (Federal Office of Statistics, 2020). In this specific decision, the cohabitation of the wife with a new partner after the divorce was taken into account for the termination of spousal maintenance.

When comparing these two cases, we can observe contradictory argumentation. In the case BGE 135 III 59, the consideration of pre-marital cohabitation could have been a reason for a higher post-marital maintenance payment. This would have been advantageous for the economically weaker spouse (the wife), but the duration of cohabitation of 10 years was not considered long enough to establish sufficient trust in the support community of the subsequent marriage. In the other case, where consideration of post-marital cohabitation disadvantaged the economically weaker spouse (the wife), five years of cohabitation were considered sufficient to justify the termination of spousal maintenance after a life-shaping marriage. The SFSC's interpretation is each time disadvantageous for the economically weaker spouse, ie usually the wife (Cottier and Muheim, 2019: 65). This practice weighs all the more heavily when one considers that cohabitation in Switzerland offers no legally regulated protection for the economically weaker partner, ie cohabitants have no legal obligation to support their partners during or after the relationship (cf Diezi, 2014: 259). In summary, the Federal Court's reasoning on the legal basis for the maintenance claim seems to be not the marriage per se but rather post-marital solidarity (Schwenzer and Büchler, 2017). This interpretation of the SFSC distributes the bargaining chips to the disadvantage of the economically weaker maintenance creditors, who then have to consider whether they can 'afford' cohabitation at all.

Maintenance in Cases of Gaps in Old Age Provision

In the area of spousal maintenance, the issue of the method of calculating the maintenance pension to cover the gaps in old age provision that arise *after* the divorce due to childcare (Geiser, 2012: 356) came up in the decision BGE 135 III 158. The SFSC enumerated the various methods of calculation and took the spouses' standard of living as the basis for calculating the pension. The rationale for awarding the wife a contribution to the build-up of her old-age pension lies in a compensatory idea. The wife, who foregoes gainful employment to raise the children and run the household, is to be placed largely on a substantially equal footing with the husband through contributions to the pension. The wife entitled to maintenance has a claim to continuation of the standard of living during the marriage if the financial means allow it.

In BGE 141 III 465, the SFSC had to review the question of whether the wife, who was 10 years older than the husband, was protected in her trust in the community of care of their life-shaping marriage beyond her retirement age even if there was a temporary ability to provide for herself during her active years. The SFSC ruled that for the time the wife was temporarily capable of providing for herself, the maintenance payments could be suspended, but that there was no reason to terminate the maintenance obligation permanently. Thus, the wife was entitled to maintenance payments after reaching retirement age. For the SFSC the fact that at the time of the wedding, the couple was aware of their age difference of 10 years, was significant in this context. As the couple had no children, the main argument was not a compensatory, but a conservative one: the trust in a long-lasting marriage as a support community for the economically weaker spouse must be protected.

ii. Childcare Maintenance: Stripping a Compensatory Idea to the Strict Minimum

Following the reform of child maintenance (see section II.C), the two decisions on childcare maintenance in our sample (BGE 144 III 377 and BGE 144 III 481) were issued shortly after each other and clarified the calculation basis for the new component of child maintenance (Federal Council, 2014).

In the first decision, BGE 144 III 377, the SFSC clarified that the so-called 'cost of living method' is the method of choice to calculate the new childcare maintenance. This means that it is not calculated on the basis of the loss of income of the parent who mainly cares for the child(ren), which would mean a calculation on the basis of the actual salary. Rather, the childcare maintenance owed by the other parent is only supposed to supplement the amount the caregiver is not able to cover with their own income in order to meet the minimum subsistence level. So-called 'childcare maintenance' is thereby interpreted in the most restrictive way possible, benefiting only caregivers in low wage occupations who cannot cover their subsistence level by part-time employment. Carers with higher qualifications do not benefit from this new instrument. The idea of compensation for income loss due to childcare is reduced to the minimum impact. In essence, this new form of maintenance primarily relieves the burden on social assistance, which does not have to be paid to the main caregiver who cannot provide for their own maintenance, since social assistance is subsidiary to maintenance obligations under family law (CSIAS, 2020).

In the other decision, BGE 144 III 481, the SFSC goes a step further and establishes new rules regarding the primary caregiver's obligation to re-enter the job market. Whereas under the older '10/16 rule', the divorced primary caregiver could ask for maintenance payments to allow them to take care of their youngest child until the age of 10 and only work in a part-time, 50 per cent occupation until this child's sixteenth birthday, a faster reintegration into the job market is now expected: The standard percentage of gainful employment since then is: 50 per cent from compulsory schooling of the youngest child (from age four, depending on the cantonal legislation); 80 per cent from the date of transition to lower secondary education (usually at age 12); and 100 per cent from age 16.

Both the calculation method and the introduction of the new system of 'school levels' mean that the primary caregivers, mostly women, have to return to work earlier and, on balance, receive less maintenance. The original compensatory approach has been transformed into a formal-egalitarian rule through case law. In terms of the 'bargaining chips' at the parties' disposal, it will be difficult for the party who suffers financial losses due to childcare to adopt a compensatory argument in divorce negotiations in the area of childcare maintenance.

iii. The Interdependency between Child and Spousal Maintenance: The Importance of the Economic Situation

In our sample, child maintenance was systematically discussed in direct relation to spousal maintenance. This seems logical, given the need to align the claims of various maintenance creditors. The hierarchy among maintenance creditors is particularly important: where the resources available to the maintenance debtor are insufficient, not all maintenance contributions can be fully funded. There are big differences between cases where the economic situation is very good and those where there is just enough money to cover the maintenance debtor's subsistence minimum. The three decisions BGE 132 III 593, BGE 135 III 66 and BGE 137 III 102 illustrate this in an exemplary manner.

The two decisions BGE 132 III 593 and BGE 137 III 102 deal with cases in which the economic situation is very good. Thus, the maintenance claims can be covered without further ado, even if the rules on the limitation or graduation of spousal maintenance apply, which expect the creditor spouse's to be fully or partially self-supporting after a certain period of time (BGE 137 III 2, cons 4.1.2). Both cases involve marriages with a traditional role division. Typically, women in marriages with traditional role division can often only maintain their standard of living after divorce if they receive spousal maintenance. However, the rather generous case law should be read in conjunction with the aforementioned case law on termination of spousal maintenance when in cohabitation with a new partner. After a long marriage with a traditional division of roles, the temporary suspension and annulment of spousal maintenance can be particularly drastic. This means that when choosing to cohabitate with a new partner, there is a risk that spousal support will cease after three or five years, which in turn can result in a significant reduction in the standard of living. Even if the new partner lives in tight economic circumstances, there is no entitlement to preservation of the marital standard (Hofmann and Mordasini-Rohner, 2018). Which may lead to a situation where a woman has to choose between preserving a good standard of living – the loss of which would also affect their children – or taking up and remaining in a cohabitating relationship.

The problem is quite different in low-income situations. In the decision BGE 135 III 66, with the least favourable economic situation, the SFSC dealt with the various arguments of legal doctrine concerning the question of how maintenance payments should be determined when the means of the debtor are not sufficient to cover the subsistence level of all family members after the divorce. The practice to date has been to leave the debtors with enough of their income not to rely on welfare, thereby putting the burden of welfare dependency entirely on the economically weaker parties, ie the primary carer and the children. Several authors had argued that it constituted indirect gender discrimination to proceed in this way, since the primary caregivers were mostly women (Bigler-Eggenberger, 2002; Freivogel, 2007). They had suggested a new rule, according to which the shortcoming of financial means would be shared between debtor and creditor(s). The SFSC agreed that the unequal treatment of the debtor and the creditor of maintenance payments in cases of insufficient means was problematic, but denied a problem of discrimination based on gender. The SFSC argued that men and women were submitted to the same rules if they were maintenance creditors, thereby demonstrating a lack of awareness of the concept of indirect discrimination and reducing gender equality to the formal-egalitarian interpretation, leading to criticism from the CEDAW Committee in 2016.[12] In terms of bargaining chips, as the minimum subsistence level of the maintenance debtor is protected in any case (see BGE 135 III 66), this makes it impossible for the party demanding higher maintenance to negotiate a divorce agreement which would result in both parties bearing the deficit (and both parties depending on social welfare).

V. CONCLUSION: INTERPRETATIONS OF GENDER EQUALITY AND (STILL) LIMITED IMPLEMENTATION OF THE CONSTITUTIONAL MANDATE

After this in-depth analysis, we can return to our research questions of the extent to which the SFSC fulfils its task of implementing gender equality in divorce law based on its interpretations of the principle. The interpretations of gender equality are reflected in the decisions of the SFSC in various forms. In the interplay of doctrines, court practice, facts of the cases and arguments, the SFCS's stance on gender equality is not directly discernible. It was only through the analysis of several cases that regularities became apparent, and patterns emerged (Gilgun, 2005).

During the period of the SFSC rulings we examined, Swiss divorce law was reformed and changed in many ways (see section II). The case law reflects this change in the legal foundations, just as it reflects changing social values in the areas of marriage, family and divorce. Among the arguments present in the legislative process, in legal doctrine and in society at large, however, it makes a selection and thereby narrows down the possible acceptable arguments in the day-to-day resolution of divorces.

We have uncovered that in many cases arguments made by doctrine for a compensatory interpretation of spousal and child maintenance were listed, but

[12] CEDAW, Concluding observations Switzerland, no 4-5/2016 (UN Docs CEDAW/C/CHE/CO/4-5), para 48.

in the end the decision in the specific case was not motivated by these arguments and a less compensatory direction was chosen (BGE 135 III 59, BGE 135 III 66, BGE 137 III 102, BGer 5A_373/2015, BGE 144 III 377; see section IV.B.i) which in our sample led to men winning the appeal to the Federal Supreme Court more often than women. The arguments of practical feasibility (BGE 135 III 66, cons 7), legal certainty and social views are cited by the SFSC as arguments against a change in practice towards more substantive equality. In some cases, procedural reasons were the key factor in the decisions. This demonstrates the ongoing tension between social change and 'institution' stability (in legal terms 'legal certainty'). With regard to gender equality, even though the SFSC acknowledges existing problems of substantive inequality due to the unequal division of care and prevailing societal structures of gender inequality in general, it does not take the lead in bringing about possible changes in the current legal system, but rather passes the responsibility to the legislator (BGE 135 III 66, cons 7 *in fine*).

We argue that in the context of the negotiation of an agreement concerning maintenance payments upon divorce, the normative framework provided by the SFSC seriously restricts the 'bargaining chips' available to spouses who have reduced their income in the labour market due to childcare, ie mostly mothers. Indeed, in all analysed maintenance situations (spousal and child), the bargaining chips were to the disadvantage of the creditor party, and this was specially the case for less favourable economic situations. Here, women will not be able to back up their claims based on arguments of substantive gender equality by reference to the SFSC case law but must rely on other sources of legal authority, such as the recommendations of the CEDAW Committee, which are, however, seldom referred to even by specialist lawyers. Finally, we noticed that since the reform of marriage law in 2000, the discussion has shifted away from the issue of gender equality towards the principle of child wellbeing, especially strikingly in the discussion of the new component of childcare maintenance introduced in 2017 (Federal Council, 2014). This 'tossing aside' strategy may be cause for concern given the aim of implementing gender equality of the Swiss family justice system.

Further research is needed to understand better the implications of these findings. In the currently ongoing project 'The negotiation of divorce agreements and gender (in)equality in Switzerland' (Cottier and Widmer, 2019–2023), we will further explore how the different concepts of gender equality found in written law are interpreted by lawyers specialised in divorce law. We expect that their understanding of gender equality is closely related to their professional style, which in turn influences the process of negotiating divorce agreements with their clients. In the next step, divorcees' personal life trajectories will be examined. Taken together, the three sets of analyses will allow us to understand better the configuration of cooperation and tension among actors in which divorce agreements are framed in terms of gender equality.

REFERENCES

Bastard, B, Cardia-Vonèche, L and Perrin, JF (1987) *Pratiques judiciaires du divorce: Approche sociologique et perspectives de réforme* (Lausanne, Réalités sociales).

Baumann, K and Lauterburg, M (2004) *Evaluation Vorsorgeausgleich. Eine empirische Untersuchung an sieben Scheidungsgerichten* (Bern, Stämpfli).

Bessière, C, Biland, E and Fillod-Chabaud, A (2013) 'Résidence alternée: La justice face aux rapports sociaux de sexe et de classe', *Lien social et Politiques* 69, 125–43.

Bigler-Eggenberger, M (2002) 'Überschuss und Manko bei Ehetrennung und Ehescheidung – ein Problem rechtlicher und tatsächlicher Gleichstellung von Frau und Mann?' in T Geiser, T Koller, R Reusser, HP Walter and W Wiegand (eds), *Festschrift für Professor Heinz Hausheer zum 65. Geburtstag* (Berne, Stämpfli).

Binkert, M and Wyss, K (1997) *Die Gleichstellung von Frau und Mann im Ehescheidungsrecht: Eine empirische Untersuchung an sechs erstinstanzlichen Gerichten* (Basel, Helbing Lichtenhahn).

Boyd, SB (2015) 'Equality: An uncomfortable fit in parenting law' in R Leckey (ed), *After Legal Equality. Family, Sex, Kinship* (Abingdon and New York, Routledge).

Büchler, A, Simoni, H, Cantieni, L, Trost-Melchert, T and Rusch, M (2009) *Kinder und Scheidung: Der Einfluss der Rechtspraxis auf familiale Übergänge* (Zurich and Chur, Rüegger).

Côté, D and Gaborean, F (2015) 'Nouvelles normativités de la famille: La garde partagée au Québec, en France et en Belgique', *Canadian Journal of Women and the Law* 27(1), 22–46.

Cottier, M (2021) 'Impulsions des instruments de protection des droits humains de l'ONU en matière d'égalité et de protection contre les discriminations pour le droit de la famille suisse', *Revue de droit suisse* 2, 119–89.

Cottier, M and Muheim, J (2019) 'Travail de "care" non rémunéré et égalité de genre en droit de la famille suisse: une évaluation critique du nouveau droit de l'entretien de l'enfant', *Revue de droit suisse* 138(1), 61–88.

Cottier, M and Widmer, ED (2019–2023) *The negotiation of divorce agreements and gender (in)equality in Switzerland* (research project funded by the Swiss National Science Foundation, no 100011_182364).

Cottier, M, Widmer, ED, Tornare, S and Girardin, M (2017) *Etude interdisciplinaire sur la garde alternée* (Geneva, University of Geneva).

CSIAS – Conférence suisse des institutions d'action sociale (2020) *Normes CSIAS*: rl.skos.ch/lexoverview-home/lex-RL_A_1.

Diezi, D (2014) *Nachlebensgemeinschaftlicher Unterhalt; Grundlagen und Rechtfertigung vor dem Hintergrund der rechtlichen Erfassung der Lebensgemeinschaft* (Berne: Stämpfli).

Federal Council (1979) 'Message concernant la révision du code civil suisse (Effets généraux du mariage, régimes matrimoniaux et successions) du 11 juillet 1979', *Feuille fédérale* 1979, 1179–405.

Federal Council (1996) 'Message concernant la révision du code civil suisse (état civil, conclusion du mariage, divorce, droit de la filiation, etc.) du 15 novembre 1995', *Feuille fédérale* 1996, 1–231.

Federal Council (2011) 'Message concernant une modification du Code civil suisse (Autorité parentale) du 16 novembre 2011', *Feuille fédérale* 2011, 8315–50.

Federal Council (2013) 'Message concernant la révision du code civil suisse (Partage de la prévoyance professionnelle en cas de divorce) du 29 mai 2013', *Feuille fédérale* 2013, 4341–408.

Federal Council (2014) 'Message concernant la révision du code civil suisse (Entretien de l'enfant), du 29 novembre 2013', *Feuille fédérale* 2014, 511–76.

Federal Office of Statistics (2019a) *Enquête sur les familles et les générations 2018. Premiers résultats* (Neuchâtel).

Federal Office of Statistics (2019b) *Strukturerhebung. Gebäude- und Wohnungsstatistik* (Neuchâtel).

Federal Office of Statistics (2020) *Schweizerische Arbeitskräfteerhebung (SAKE), Erwerbsbeteiligung der Frauen 2010–2019* (Neuchâtel).

Federal Office of Statistics (2021) *Divorces et divortialité depuis 1876*, download from: STAT-TAB – the FSO's interactive database: www.pxweb.bfs.admin.ch.

Freeman, MA, Chinkin, C and Rudolf, B (2012) 'Article 18' in MA Freeman, C Chinkin and B Rudolf (eds), *The UN Convention on the Elimination of All Forms of Discrimination Against Women: A Commentary* (Oxford, Oxford University Press).

Freivogel, E (2007) 'Nachehelicher Unterhalt – Verwandtenunterstützung – Sozialhilfe', *FamPra.ch* 8(3), 497–525.

Geiser, T (2012) 'Aufbau einer angemessenen Altersvorsorge und Dauer des nachehelichen Unterhalts', *FamPra.ch*, 353–68.

Gilgun, J F (2005) 'Qualitative research and family psychology', *Journal of Family Psychology* 19(1), 40–50.

Gisler, P, Steinert-Borella, S and Wiedmer, C (2009) 'Double lives, double narratives: Tracing the story of the family in Rousseau, the Swiss Civil Code and the fathers' rights debates', *Feminist Legal Studies* 17(2), 185–204.

Glennon, L (2010) 'The limitations of equality discourses on the contours of intimate obligations' in J Herring, S Choudhry and J Wallbank (eds), *Rights, Gender and Family Law* (New York, Routledge).

Lê, S, Josse, J and Husson, F (2008) 'FactoMineR: An R package for multivariate analysis', *Journal of Statistical Software* 25(1), 1–18.

Le Goff, J-M and Levy, R (eds) (2016) *Devenir parents, devenir inégaux: Transition à la parentalité et inégalités de genre* (Zurich, Seismo).

Hofmann, R and Mordasini-Rohner, CM (2018) 'Nachehelicher Unterhalt in sehr guten Verhältnissen' in R Fankhauser and A Büchler (eds), *Neunte Schweizer Familienrecht§Tage: 18./19. Januar 2018 in Basel* (Berne, Stämpfli).

Maihofer, A. (2014) 'Familiale Lebensformen zwischen Wandel und Persistenz: Eine zeitdiagnostische Zwischenbetrachtung' in C Behnke, D Lengersdorf and S Scholz (eds), *Wissen – Methode – Geschlecht: Erfassen des fraglos Gegebenen* (Wiesbaden, Springer VS).

Mair, J, Wasoff, F and Mackay, K (2015) 'Family Justice Without Courts: Property Settlement on Separation Using Contracts in Scotland' in M Maclean, J Eekelaar and B Bastard (eds), *Delivering Family Justice in the 21st Century* (Oxford and Portland OR, Hart Publishing).

Mayring, P (2000) 'Qualitative Content Analysis', *Forum: Qualitative Social Research* 1(2), doi.org/10.17169/fqs-1.2.1089.

Mnookin, RH and Kornhauser, L (1978–1979) 'Bargaining in the shadow of the law: The case of divorce', *The Yale Law Journal* 88, 950–97.

Pfaffinger M and Hofstetter, D (2015) 'Art. 16. Umsetzung Schweiz' in E Schläppi, S Ulrich and J Wyttenbach (eds), *CEDAW. Kommentar zum Übereinkommen der Vereinten Nationen zur Beseitigung jeder Form von Diskriminierung der Frau* (Berne, Stämpfli).

Rebouché, R (2016) 'A Case Against Collaboration', *Maryland Law Review* 76(3), 547.

Scheiwe K (2019) 'Parental conflicts over the exercise of joint parental responsibility from a comparative perspective: From daily matters to relocation' in H Willekens, K Scheiwe, T Richarz and E Schumann (eds), *Motherhood and the Law* (Göttingen, Universitätsverlag Göttingen).

Scheiwe, K and Wersig, M (2011) *Cash und Care – Kindesunterhaltsrecht und Geschlechter(un)gleichheit* (Göttingen, V&Runipress).

Schwenzer, I (2011) 'Ten years divorce reform in Switzerland' in B Atkin and F Banda (eds), *The International Survey of Family Law* (Bristol, Jordan Publishing).

Schwenzer, I and Büchler, A (2017) 'Art. 125' in I Schwenzer and R Fankhauser (eds), *Familienrechts-Kommentar Scheidung*, Band I: ZGB, 3rd edn (Berne, Stämpfli).

Schwenzer, I and Egli, I (2010) 'Betreuungsunterhalt – Gretchenfrage des Unterhaltsrechts', *FamPra.ch*, 18–32.

Schwenzer, I and Keller, T (2014) 'New rules on parental responsibility in Switzerland' in B Atkin (ed), *The International Survey of Family Law 2014 Edition* (Bristol, Jordan Publishing).

Smart, C (2013) 'Sharing the Children: Brave New World or the same old gender wars?' in B Bannwart et al (eds), *Keine Zeit für Utopien? Perspektiven der Lebensformenpolitik im Recht* (Zurich and St Gallen, Dike).

Wersig, M and Künzel, A (2008) 'Ehegattenunterhalt als Bremse des Wandels der Geschlechterverhältnisse – Beispiel Deutschland' in K Arioli et al (eds), *Wandel der Geschlechterverhältnisse durch Recht?* (Zurich and St Gallen, Dike).

Wilkinson-Ryan, T and Small, D (2008) 'Negotiating Divorce: Gender and the Behavioral Economics of Divorce Bargaining', *Law & Inequality* 26, 109–32.

Part B

Participants

5

Reforms and Reorganisation of Family Justice in France: What Are the Current Responses to the Needs of Divorcees?

BENOIT BASTARD

IN THIS CHAPTER, I propose to draw up a sociological inventory of the system for handling family matters in France, limiting myself to the part which is concerned with separations, divorces and their consequences. The question I would like to answer is the following: how is this system organised today? And, knowing how diverse and lively expectations and needs are in this respect I ask: to which demands does the system respond well? For which litigants? And for which clients is it less likely to respond – or unable to respond?

These questions will be addressed in three stages. First, I will describe the meaning of the reforms undertaken in recent decades: how did the legislator (ie the state), previously propose to respond to the needs of litigants in this field and how does it do so today? Second, I will describe the system for the treatment of separation and divorce: how do the 'providers' organise themselves? What is available for candidates seeking separation or divorce? Finally, in the third part, I will raise the question of the adequacy of the proposals – both the services proposed and the demand, ie the needs of the litigants.

For this analysis, I rely on research I have carried out – the most recent of which concerns the implementation of divorce without a judge (Bastard, 2018) – as well as on the data available on these questions.

I. PRIVATISATION AND THE SEARCH FOR EFFICIENCY

Since 1975, the reforms undertaken in the French system for dealing with family breakdown have gone further and further in the same direction. The legislator – with the help of the judges, who have often been at the forefront of this movement – has adopted a constant line of approach. The reforms carried out have been based on two interrelated principles.

The first is the 'privatisation' of family matters. This trend is present, specifically in divorce cases, with the idea that the best decision is the one that comes from the parties themselves because, being elaborated by them, it will be better adapted and therefore better applied. This conception is in line with the transformations that have affected the family and the organisation of the private sphere in recent decades. In the vision that continues to assert itself, the idea prevails of a family that should be autonomous, capable of making space for the individuals who make it up, and of governing itself, even in the event of conflict, and also capable of maintaining relations between children and parents, even in the event of separation. In this perspective, what has been put forward legally, in reform after reform, is the need for children to see their parents agree about the arrangements for their care, and to show themselves capable of being cooperating parents at the same time as separated spouses.

The other trend that runs through the justice system, as well as society as a whole, in the same period, is the search for efficiency. The concept of 'managerialisation' has reached the family jurisdiction as well as the judicial institution and the whole of society (Bastard, 2015). It has had a profound effect on family law and the way judges work. From this point of view, the best decision is the one that will ensure the greatest speed for the judicial process and that will have the lowest impact in terms of workload for the magistrates and the clerks (*les greffes*). The predominance of this way of thinking, which makes speed the main criterion for evaluating quality, is due to the fact that the main concern is to preserve the image of a justice system which is capable of responding to the demands of litigants and of 'getting the job done' in a timely manner – even though the courts are short of judges, clerks and resources.

The two trends, privatisation and managerialisation, are very strongly linked: having decisions made 'elsewhere' than in the courtroom, without the need for judicial intervention, and having the judge's role limited to encouraging spouses to self-regulate and to endorse the decisions made, is not only of benefit for litigants and their children, but also, at the same time, a significant time-saver and a success for justice.

I will briefly recall here the main stages of the reforms based on these ideas. Divorce by mutual consent was introduced into family law in 1975.[1] After that, the question of parental authority was formulated differently. Joint parental authority became the normal mode of taking care of children. In 2002, the concept of co-parenting was adopted by the legislator. Alternating residence, which had previously been prohibited, became the norm, and the idea that parents had to maintain relations with each other in the interest of their children, even when they were separated, was further reinforced.[2] Finally, more recently, in 2016–2017, a shift occurred in the direction of privatising divorce with the

[1] Loi no 75-617 du 11 juillet 1975 portant réforme du divorce.

[2] Loi no 2002-305 du 4 mars 2002 sur l'autorité parentale.

introduction of divorce without a judge.[3] This is a new path that has been opened: since 1 January 2017, the processing of divorce by mutual consent has been entrusted to lawyers (*avocats*), without any intervention by the court. Each of the parties must be assisted by a lawyer. The agreement protocol signed by both parties is then kept by a notary. Finally, the latest reform, which came into force in 2021, aims at simplifying judicial divorce – in other words, cases where there is conflict.[4] The conciliation hearing before the judge has been suppressed. A lawyer must represent each party from the beginning of the proceedings. After the lawyers have ascertained that no conciliation is possible, the procedure is directly introduced before the judge. A hearing, called the 'orientation hearing', is used to determine the provisional measures if necessary and to define the calendar of the procedure. Everything is done, once again, so that agreements can be reached. The preparation of the case is then carried out by the lawyers. The divorce can be pronounced without the need for a new hearing.

Everything fits together and is moving in the same direction, ie these reforms aim, at the same time, to simplify procedures in order to relieve the courts and to give more responsibility to the parties in decisions relating to their separation.

The question of meeting the expectations of litigants is not absent from these reforms, but it is considered in a over simplistic way. The changes in the law that go in the direction of simplifying the procedure are based on the idea that the main need of litigants is for divorces to be granted quickly – which may be true in some cases, but which is not necessarily an expectation shared by all the parties. In the same way, the changes that go in the direction of privatisation make it seem as if the litigants were necessarily eager to make their own decisions, whereas we know that this is not always the case – by going to court, are some couples not trying to avoid but instead seeking for solutions to be imposed on them?

Through these changes, what is most apparent is the search for solutions that allow the legal institution, no matter what, to respond to the requests that are made to it. The question then arises as to how the professionals in charge of the legal systems set up in this way have reorganised their interventions to deal with these requests.

II. THE REDISTRIBUTION OF PROFESSIONAL ROLES

We can now review the positions that the actors of the family justice system have been placed in as a result of these different reforms – judges, family mediators and lawyers.

[3] Loi no 2016-1547 du 18 novembre 2016 de modernisation de la justice du XXIe siècle. Décret no 2016-1907 du 28 décembre 2016 'relatif au divorce prévu à l'article 229-1 du code civil et à diverses dispositions en matière successorale'.

[4] Loi no 2019-22 du 23 mars 2019 de programmation 2018-2022 et de réforme pour la justice.

A. Judges 'Refocused' and Entrenched

Long ago, the position of judges in this system could be described as both dominant – because they were the ones who imposed, against all odds, the 'privatisation' of decisions – and powerless – because they found themselves unable to bring about, on their own, the negotiated solutions they were calling for (Cardia-Vonèche, Liziard and Bastard, 1996: 277–98). Now, the position of judges has changed. They are supposedly refocused on what is, or should be, the core of their function as judges: to state the law, and to settle disputes.

This has been done through the successive reforms mentioned earlier. In 2017, the introduction of divorce without a judge freed judges from all non-contentious cases. The paradox is that they had previously been very much opposed to this reform because, they said, their presence in these proceedings was a guarantee for the support of the weakest litigants. The reform was carried out in spite of their views and they gained by being relieved of a whole set of procedures – even if those had been the easiest to handle.

In 2021, the reform of the judicial treatment of divorce removed from the judges the preliminary phase of the treatment of the cases (*audience de non-conciliation*) – which is replaced by a compulsory attempt at mediation before any procedure before the judge – and also relieves judges by providing that any contentious request must be brought before the court with the presence of lawyers for each of the parties. The presence of the lawyers ensures a preliminary shaping of the cases in such a way as to simplify the task of the judge.

This double movement has the explicit objective of refocusing the judge on his adjudicative role. It leads to giving him an entrenched position in the system. Through these successive reforms, has the family court judge become more and more of an Olympian figure (Ost, 1991: 241–72)? The role of the judge seems to be limited to the treatment of legal points in the proceedings. Thus, it is unclear if judges are able to maintain something of their role as coach ('*juge entraîneur*' (Ost, 1983)) – in other words, with their concern, in all proceedings being to push the parties towards a consensus. It should be added that the Covid-19 pandemic has only accentuated this trend by reinforcing developments that were already apparent. Judges were already tending, in order to save time, to reduce the oral dimension of cases. At the hearing, they limited the interventions of the lawyers by refocusing their pleadings on the points to be decided. As soon as the health crisis began, hearings were abolished, except for those concerning situations of great urgency, such as domestic violence. Judges then continued to work through the ongoing cases on file, which confirmed the pattern described here.

Family judges remain convinced of the merits of seeking agreement in all cases where this is possible. However, the reforms that have taken place have placed them in the background – they have ceased to review and control every situation. They are still essentially the judges of intractable situations – those in which parents are continuing their conflicts over their children.

> Society becomes violent in its reactions and parents even more so. It is a society where relationships between individuals are based on violence and immediacy. The family judge is more and more confronted with power relationships: children taken as hostages, violent separation for the children. It is a failure of parental responsibility. The judge is seized for everything: the choice of the school, the choice of the professional orientation of the child ... The parents are unable to decide that. They make the judges go into areas where they should not go. This is where our role is perverted. So I will decide – I am a judge, it is my job – but I will say things at the hearing. (Interview with a family judge, April 2020)

B. Family Mediators Ousted – And Disappointed

Family mediators gained great institutional recognition by becoming a profession in the 2010s, via the creation of the state diploma of mediator. However, this recognition has not been followed by any effect as regards their activity. Indeed, even though the reforms of family law followed, in principle, the direction of what they were advocating – noticeably the sharing of parental authority – it turns out that the successive rearrangements of the divorce 'market' have been unfavourable to them.

The reform that came into effect in January 2017 was a blow to mediators. By entrusting the handling of consent divorce to lawyers, it took away their access to the greatest number of situations in which their intervention would have found its place. Of course, it is always possible to call upon a family mediator in such situations, but who is going to consult a mediator when two lawyers and a notary are already involved, with a cost higher than that of divorce in the previous configuration?

Another reform project, which occurred shortly before, may have seemed promising for mediation. It consisted in introducing in the whole civil sector, including family courts, a requirement for an extrajudicial compulsory mediation attempt before starting any contentious action.[5] This project was launched for an experimental period, in 11 courts, with the idea that it could be generalised after its evaluation. Paradoxically, it could be described as a sweetness containing a deadly poison. It turned out that family mediators holding the state diploma were not the only ones entitled to practise in this framework – it can also be done by other registered professionals such as lawyers, notaries and bailiffs (*huissiers*). Moreover, the fact that the attempt is 'compulsory' does not fit well with the ethics of the group of family mediators, and research shows that imposed mediation is very burdensome for a whole group of those who are obliged to do it and who see it as a waste of time or as a punishment (Boussard, 2020). Finally, the limits of family mediation are very apparent

[5] Loi no 2016-1547 du 18 novembre 2016 de modernisation de la justice du XXIe siècle.

in this context, especially with regard to the situations of the poorest, the marginalised or women caught up in relationships of dependence or control. In fact, this measure, which in principle aims at preventing conflicts and pacifying participants, can sometimes have the effect of dissuading the parties from pursuing their legal action (Boussard, 2020).

Compulsory family mediation was abandoned when the new rules of judicial divorce were adopted and came into force on 1 January 2021. To simplify the procedure, the conciliation hearing before the judge was also abandoned. The initial conciliation still exists, but it is now in the hands of the lawyers – each party being required to be represented by a counsel before initiating any legal action. It is therefore up to them to seek any amicable solution before directly initiating legal proceedings.

Consequently, it is difficult to see what place and what specific action remains for family mediation. It is, in my opinion, the greatest loser in the current reorganisations.

C. The Winners: Lawyers

In contrast to family mediators, lawyers (*avocats*) have come out of the reorganisation stronger.

First, since 2017, they have been in charge of most divorces by mutual consent, ie almost half of the situations of marital breakdown that were submitted to courts. Here we find the same paradox as for judges: lawyers did not want this reform, and they had opposed it vigorously, on several occasions, because they feared that it would be to their detriment by reducing their presence and, perhaps, by favouring mediators. However, they could not but rejoice in it afterwards – even if they did not like the brutality with which it was decided. The result for them was a mechanical increase in the number of clients in this matter since the law prescribes that each party, even in the case of an agreement, must be accompanied by a counsel. This has certainly also meant more responsibility and more work for lawyers in dealing with these cases – it is the lawyers, and no longer the judge, who are responsible for guaranteeing the authenticity of the consents and validating the decisions made by the divorcees. Despite this increasing responsibility, lawyers emphasise their satisfaction that these tasks have been given to them.

The entry into force of this new divorce without a judge has not been accompanied by any of the difficulties that its detractors predicted. This undoubtedly reflects the fact that it corresponds to an expectation – and one can only wonder if it does not have unexpected effects, as far as litigants are concerned, in terms of delays and costs.

Second, the reform of the judicial part of divorce – in other words, contentious divorces – gives lawyers yet another role. Here again, their presence is reinforced, since the litigants who are in the position of defendant in a case must now be systematically assisted by a lawyer as soon as the case is introduced.

If this measure goes in the direction of protecting the interests of the parties, it also aims to 'protect' the judges, who often find themselves helpless in situations where the parties address them in terms that are at a distance from the law, which implies additional work by the judge to unravel the case and to push the parties to reformulate their demand in legal terms. It is now through the lawyers that justice passes and it will be interesting to observe how the implementation of this reform impacts their work in the near future.

Lawyers are therefore active on all fronts in family matters, in a way that has been entirely renewed and refreshed. They were, of course, the first intermediaries for divorce candidates a few decades ago, but they were then often seen as troublemakers who would stir up conflict in difficult family situations by taking advantage of the divorcees' desire for revenge. Now 'converted', they have become the vectors of the search for agreements in the whole field of consensual divorce and they remain simultaneously present in their traditional role of defender of their client's interests in judicial divorce.

III. WHAT HAS BEEN THE RESPONSE TO THE NEEDS AND EXPECTATIONS OF LITIGANTS?

The successive reforms of family law have brought about, as we have just seen, a new configuration of professional interventions in the treatment of family break-ups. Having described these changes, the question now arises as to whether these reorganisations meet the needs and expectations of litigants. In practice, once we notice that these needs and expectations are not uniform among divorce candidates, we come to identify major distinctions and strong inequalities between the populations of litigants concerned. These gaps are particularly evident in the difference between divorcees who are ready to embark on the path opened up by the privatisation of decisions and those who refuse to do so for various reasons.

A. A Perfect Fit for Those Who 'Know How to Do It' by Themselves

For spouses who 'play the game' and accept the need to go beyond their differences to reach an agreement in the interest of their children, the existing care system meets their 'needs' well. This is not to say that passage through this system is easy, without tension and without suffering, since they have to carry out the operations expected of them and mentioned above (getting along when they are in conflict; maintaining parental relations when they are separated). However, when they do so, they obtain resources to accompany them and a certain satisfaction is derived from this. In fact, the negotiation of divorce in the presence of lawyers in the context of mutual consent brings the parties, according to the lawyers, some benefits. There is, for example, the fact that they are not constrained by the dates set by the court, nor are they obliged to appear at a hearing before an institution that the divorcees do not see as useful. In the same way, for certain situations, which are certainly limited in number, the negotiation with the mediators who intervened during the *tentative de médiation familiale préalable obligatoire* (TMFPO) – nowadays-abandoned – could prove to be beneficial. These were well-intentioned spouses who, thanks to the availability of this mediation service, engaged in a process of seeking to make arrangements (Boussard, 2020). The study cited also provides precise information on the characteristics of the small group of divorce candidates who have such a perspective: they belong to the most affluent categories and are not opposed to the idea of negotiation. It thus seems to be diametrically opposed to the needs of those among the divorce candidates who fail to conform to the prevailing prescriptions.

B. What Can Be Done for Divorcees Who Do Not Conform to the Ambient Norms?

There remains a heterogeneous group of litigants who have difficulty in meeting the expectations of the socio-legal system. And here again, the recent analysis of the TMFPO cited above is a good indicator of the difficulties they face.

Generally speaking, these are litigants who are waiting for the justice system to recognise the harm that has been done to them or the fact that they have not obtained what they consider to be their due at the end of the period of cohabitation. It is also about the recognition, for some women, of the fact that they are dependent on or under the influence of a difficult spouse.

Their characteristics are in contrast to those of the first group described (still relying on Boussard 2020): they are the divorcees who are among the poorest, the most marginal and the foreigners.

For all of these, the socio-judicial care system turns out to be ill-equipped and unwelcoming because it is above all concerned with consensus, or concerned with privileging the dimension of the best interests of the children – rather than giving the adults what they expect. Thus, for example, the 'emotional' and psychological dimension is perceived by the judge as a disturbance. Similarly, when expectations of recognition are expressed through excessive demands (eg in relation to visitation rights, in particular to prevent these when one of the parents is considered by the applicant to be problematic or abusive), this may be seen by professional actors as unreasonable or even contrary to the interests of the children.

IV. CONCLUSION

It can be debated why some of the divorce candidates succeed in achieving what is expected of them, while others do not. This is undoubtedly due to the characteristics of the couples, the available resources and to the existence of a prior practice of negotiation – but this is not the place to develop this aspect further.

One might also wonder whether the needs that are taken into account are only those of the litigants, or whether, for good or bad reasons, the reforms undertaken have not, in certain cases, given priority to the needs expressed by the professionals involved. We are thinking here as much of the protection of family judges, who are subject to all sorts of pressures due in particular to the number of cases they are expected to deal with, and of the consideration of the economic interests of lawyers – undoubtedly largely privileged in the recent reforms for institutional and political reasons.

Moreover, it may be thought that the reforms, the main aim of which was the pursuit of efficiency and privatisation mentioned earlier, have not always had the expected effects. In fact, the solutions adopted are often more expensive than those that existed before – in particular divorce without a judge, the cost of which is much higher than that of divorce by mutual consent in the period before the reforms. And they are also slower, contrary to the announcements made – this is true as much for divorce by mutual consent as for the experimental compulsory mediation in the context of judicial divorce, which appeared, as has been said, to form an additional barrier. The latter also occasionally led to the withdrawal and the exclusion of certain litigants.

Recent studies from a feminist perspective also show that the way cases are handled according to these logics does nothing to correct the inequalities that arise from marriage (Collectif Onze, 2014). Moreover, it must be emphasised that the trend towards privatisation and the insistence on immediate efficiency leave family judges rather ill-equipped to deal with situations of violence. Family judges, having been so attached, for several decades, to the objective of seeking agreements and cooperation from parents, have had difficulty in moving to a 'penal' rationale (Jouanneau, 2019). Still, things are now taking a different turn. The programmes and reforms that have taken place over the past decade have certainly brought the issue of violence against women to the forefront of the public agenda in France, as in many other countries. Measures have been created and judges have been made aware of the issue (especially during their studies at the National School of Magistrates), and these situations can now be followed by strong interventions. One thinks in particular of protective orders (*ordonnances de protection*)[6] and of innovative devices to alert or prevent close proximity (eg dedicated phones – *téléphone grand danger, TGD*).

In short, the socio-legal system for dealing with marital breakdowns has undergone multiple reforms that have profoundly modified its configuration: we are now witnessing the development of a dual system, each part of which has

[6] See *Rapport d'activité du Comité national de l'ordonnance de protection 2020-2021*, Ministère de la Justice, 2021. The number of protective orders increased by 11% in 2018. See www.vie-publique.fr/sites/default/files/rapport/pdf/280560.pdf.

entirely contrasting characteristics: one operates on the basis of private wishes, in a liberal mode; the other continues to rely on the presentation of opposing claims and on the appeal to the imperium of the judge. The whole is the result of strong tensions and bears the mark of this. The reform that allowed for the delegation of a whole section of the cases to lawyers was a success, but it came at the price of a backtrack by the state, which, after having been attached for a time to the development of another approach to family matters, preferred the security provided by the recourse to the legal profession. The prevailing logic is that of the lesser evil – to push divorcees to negotiate and to become associated parents – but this is achieved by leaving by the wayside those couples who show themselves incapable of adopting such a perspective.

The French legislator would like to eradicate entirely the conflicts linked to divorce, to spare the children and relieve the judges. This is unrealistic. Therefore, even if a part of these conflicts is dictated by resentment and marked by bad faith, it is important to continue to imagine mechanisms of justice that permit a voice to be given to these divorcees and to debate their conflicts, keeping the children as far as possible from the effects that result for them.

REFERENCES

Bastard, B (2018) 'Divorce without a judge in France', *International Working Group on Legal Professions*, Andorra, 10–13 July.

Bastard, B, Delvaux, D, Mouhanna, C and Schoenaers, F (2015) 'Controlling Time? Speeding up Divorce Proceedings in France and Belgium' in M Maclean, J Eekelaar and B Bastard (eds), *Delivering Family Justice in the 21st Century* (Oxford, Hart Publishing).

Boussard, V (ed) (2020) *L'évaluation de la tentative de médiation familiale préalable obligatoire (TMFPO). Quand médier n'est pas remédier* (Paris, Mission de recherche droit et justice).

Cardia-Vonèche, L, Liziard, S and Bastard, B (1996) 'Juge dominant, juge démuni. La redéfinition du rôle du juge en matière de divorce', *Droit et Société* 33, 277.

Collectif Onze (2014) *Au tribunal des couples. Enquêtes sur des affaires familiales* (Paris, Odile Jacob).

Jouanneau, S (ed) (2019) *Violences conjugales – Protection des victimes. Usages et conditions d'application dans les tribunaux français des mesures de protection des victimes de violences au sein du couple* (Paris, Mission de recherche droit et justice).

Ost, F (1983) 'Juge pacificateur, juge arbitre, juge entraîneur. Trois modèles de justice' in Ph Gérard, F Ost and M Van de Kerchove (eds), *Fonction et juger et pouvoir judiciaire. Transformation et déplacement* (Facultés universitaires Saint-Louis).

Ost, F (1991) 'Jupiter, Hermès, Hercule; trois modèles du juge' in P Bouretz, *La force du droit, Panorama des débats contemporains* (Paris, Editions Esprit).

6

Family Matters in the Polish Court: Law and Public Opinion

MALGORZATA FUSZARA AND JACEK KURCZEWSKI

THIS CHAPTER DEALS with public readiness to mobilise courts to settle family disputes, while previous research has demonstrated a general tendency to avoid the courts and to keep family life private (Kurczewski and Fuszara, 2017a, b).

Using courts for settling difficult cases and disputes in family matters is of utmost interest for sociologists of law. On the one hand, some cases must be dealt with by the court as this is mandated by the law, including for example the allocation of parental authority after divorce. On the other, it is well known that people arrange their private life as they wish in the best way possible independently of judicial decisions. Leon Petrażycki, the farsighted forerunner of the sociology of law (Podgórecki, 1980–1981) in his theory of law (Petrażycki 1907/1959, 1961) observed that family life is mainly ruled by internal law – rights and correlated duties (*obligatio*) – considered as binding for family members independently of official law and justice. He also observed that cases that are brought before the courts are just the tip of the iceberg, while the rest are settled by the mechanisms of unofficial private law with the meaning described above. This theoretical inspiration explains why, for decades, we have been studying the question of which intra-family conflicts people consider fit for judicial settlement and which cases they believe should never appear before the courts.

The second important question concerns social change in opinions on the subject. Legal regulations are changing as well as the ideologies which underpin them. For instance, the scope of private agreements concerning family matters recognised by the official courts is widening. Society at large is undergoing change – secularisation is increasing, attitudes towards physical coercion and punishment are changing, and the forms of family life are changing also. So one question is compelling: how are these choices reflected in attitudes towards the use of courts to settle family problems? This is why we have continued ever since the period of communist rule in Poland to study public opinion and the practice of judicial intervention in family life and the mobilisation of courts to settle family issues. This chapter draws on the findings of the survey we completed in February 2020, referred to as 'The 2020 study of public opinion in Poland on Families and Courts' with an all-Polish representative random sample of 956 people who were asked about a detailed list of family issues and the respective willingness to have such issues settled by the judiciary. The list included 13 hypothetical issues involving disagreements between spouses who are parents about the education of children, household maintenance, financial independence, post-divorce parental custody, mutual violence, reproductive and gender identity autonomy, as well as violence between parents and children. Before presenting these more recent findings we would like, however, to briefly refer to our earlier 2014 study of the various attitudes towards the judicialisation of family problems.

I. THE 2014 STUDY OF PUBLIC OPINION IN POLAND

The questions which follow were asked in our earlier survey study of Polish legal opinion of a representative random sample (n = 1,059) by CBOS in 2014 (Kurczewski and Fuszara, 2017a) to deal with this issue directly (see Table 6.1).

Table 6.1 Judicialisation of family disputes in general (Poland 2014: n = 1,059)

Do you agree or disagree with the opinion that in the case of a dispute, there are different approaches for people we are close to from approaches for other people. Please tell us which of the opinions is closest to how you feel?	Number	Percent
If a dispute takes place within a family, you can never take it to an institution, but if the opponent is not a family member, it is OK to go to an institution, eg a court.	172	16.2
It does not matter whether a dispute is within a family or not. If your interest is at risk, you have to go to an institution (eg a court), even if the other person is a family member.	228	21.5
Generally when there is a dispute in a family, you shouldn't go to court or another institution, but sometimes if a dispute is about something very important (eg assault, reputation, major assets) you have to go to court or another appropriate institution.	615	58.0

Table 6.2 presents results of the logistic regression analysis carried out using a standard set of socio-demographic variables to check whether there is a statistically significant relationship between any of them and declarations of support for bringing family disputes before the court. Our assumption following our previous studies was that a better social position on this or another dimension would make people feel more secure about the official state machinery of law

and justice, and such was indeed the general outcome of the 2014 survey of Polish popular legal culture (Kurczewski and Fuszara, 2017a, b).

Table 6.2 Socio-Demographic Variables Predicting the Approval of Approaching of the Court in a Family Dispute (Poland 2014, n = 1,059)

The use of a family court allowed as a reference category.

	Beta	Standard error	Chi2	Df	Significance	Exp(bB)
GENDER_R (1 – men)	0.078	0.180	0.187	1	0.665	1.081
AGE–RR (1 – up to 50 yrs)	0.138	0.189	0.532	1	0.466	1.148
EDUCATION_R (1 – higher)	0.493	0.236	4.366	1	0.037	0.611
EMPLOYMENT_R (1 – employed)	0.080	0.221	0.132	1	0.716	1.084
LIVING STANDARD_R (1 – good and very good)	0.071	0.193	0.136	1	0.712	0.931
URBANISATION (1 – above 20,000 inhabitants)	0.077	0.178	0.190	1	0.003	1.081
const	−1.773	0.367	23.392	1	0.000	0.170

Of the socio-demographic variables included in the multivariate logistic regression analysis – gender, age, education, employment, self-assessment of living standard, and level of urbanisation of the place of residence – only one, education, was significantly ($p<0.01$) associated with support for family privacy. Higher education increased the likelihood of bringing a family conflict to the court. Other components of social position (as well as the summary index of social position) were not significantly related (at $p<0.01$ level) with attitudes towards family privacy. These details are important as we had also discovered that when all legal consciousness variables in the questionnaire were used, including family secretiveness, the latter showed a significant association ($Exp(B)=0.49$, $p<0.01$) with preference for using the court rather than mediation as a means to satisfy one's claims. Even more importantly, family secretiveness is a better predictor (to a small degree) of the choice of the court than personal experience of a court, knowledge of unjust verdicts, or the general sense of uneasiness related to being in a court described above (Kurczewski and Fuszara, 2017a: 110–11).

II. THE 2020 STUDY OF PUBLIC OPINION IN POLAND ON FAMILIES AND COURTS

In February 2020 we asked a much more detailed question concerning judicialisation of family matters of a national random sample (n = 956) in our latest research using the same methodology and the same polling center (CBOS) as in 2014 on behalf of the Institute of Applied Social Sciences, University of Warsaw. Thirteen questions were asked, each containing a shorthand description of a hypothetical intra-family conflict:

Shorthand description of problematic cases: which of these cases should be decided by the courts?

1. The parents disagree over the child's school.
2. The parents disagree over parental authority after divorce.
3. A parent punishes the child with a slap.
4. The child is beaten by a parent.
5. Spouses argue over how the household costs are shared.
6. The husband argues with the wife as she has inherited €5,000 and kept it for herself.
7. Family members argue over the division of inheritance.
8. One of the spouses in a couple with a child wishes to change sex.
9. Someone in the family drinks and behaves aggressively.
10. The husband beats the wife.
11. The wife beats the husband.
12. The adult child beats the parents.
13. A woman aborts a pregnancy because she simply does not wish to have a child.

The respondent could choose from the following list of answers:

1. Such a case should always go before the court.
2. Such cases should always go to the court if the other methods like mediation or compromise fail.
3. Don't know.
4. Such cases should end in the court only in exceptional circumstances.
5. Such cases should never be brought before the court.

We began our analysis of the responses by preparing a general judicialisation scale, adding the values of replies to the 13 questions listed and then carrying out multiple linear regression analysis performed on the aggregate scale (see Table 6.3).

Table 6.3 Multiple linear regression analysis with judicialisation of family issues in general as the dependent variable and socio-demographic independent variables

Cases of violence in general should always go to the court		Nonstandardised coefficients		Standardised coefficients		
		B	Standard error	Beta	t	Significance level
1	(constant)	10.883	.409		26.629	.000
	Gender	−.276	.529	−.016	−.521	.603
	Age	4.261	.584	.255	7.295	.000
	Education	−1.243	.567	−.074	−2.192	.029
	Employment	−.345	.585	−.021	−.590	.555
	Living standard	−.810	.550	−.047	−1.472	.141
	Social habitat	−2.000	.532	−.119	−3.761	.000

a. Dependent variable: judicialisation.

The result of the linear regression analysis was that judicialisation in general was significantly related to three social background variables – age, education and residential area; those who were younger, better educated and urban were more likely to advise the use of courts in the family issues whatever the matter at stake. These 2020 findings corroborate the 2014 finding that education is related to secretiveness about family life although the socio-ecological factor had not been found to be (significantly) related in the previous research. It seems reasonable, though, that this result is spurious, as it will be seen in the forthcoming analysis that all three factors had been related to the judicialisation of *all physical violence* cases.

Homogeneity of the overall judicialisation scale is doubtful. As Table 6.5 shows, the 13 items of our scale do not form a homogenous whole and the first factor had the top ratings on four of the five domestic violence questions (9.4, 9.10, 9.11, 9.12) plus aggressive drunken behaviour at home (9.9) while being low on spanking (9.3), a matter to which we shall return below. The second factor rated highest on two questions concerning financial disputes within the family (9.5 and 9.6); the third concerned relations with a child (9.1 and 9.3); the fourth concerned a household's 'moral controversies' such as change of gender (9.8) and abortion (9.13); and the fifth concerned post-divorce parenting arrangements as to parental custody (9.2).

A more restricted calculation using only the five main components showed the same factor, ie violence, explaining about 23 per cent of variance; the economic differences factor (9.5, 9.6, 9.7) explaining around 12 per cent of variance; and the other factors (9.1, 9.3, 9.8 and 9.13) explaining around 11 per cent. All three together explained around 47 per cent of variance and were followed on the judicialisation scale by factors of less explanatory power.

Table 6.4 Bartlett's test of homoscedasticity

		.796
Bartlett's test of homoscedasticity	Chi square approx	3197.398
	Df	78
	Significance	.000

Table 6.5 Matrix of five rotated components

	Components				
	1	2	3	4	5
m91			.698		
m92			.271		.800
m93a	.220		.738		
m94	.509		.402		
m95		.714	.314		
m96		.833			
m97	.205	.522	−.207		.564
m98				.718	.312
m99	.545				.331
m910	.910				
m911	.897				
m912	.816				
m913				.791	
Varimax rotation with Kaiser's normalisation achieved in 6 iterations.			]		

The next step in the analysis was to construct a specific scale of judicialisation of family violence including only the five questions in our survey (9.3, 9.4, 9.10, 9.11 and 9.12) directly related to this subject. When this was done age, education, being employed and self-assessment on living standard clearly emerged as significantly related (see Table 6.6). The multiple linear regression analysis then reduced the significant relationships to only one independent variable: age, ie the younger respondents were less inclined to keep violence in the family closet.

Table 6.6 Multiple linear regression analysis with judicialisation of family violence as the dependent variable and socio-demographic independent variables

		Nonstandardised coefficients		Standardised coefficients		
Cases of violence in general to the court		**B**	**Standard error**	**Beta**	**T**	**Significance**
1	(constant)	10.883	.409		26.629	.000
	Gender	−.037	.273	−.004	−.137	.891
	Age	1.831	.302	.209	6.073	.000
	Education	−.998	.293	−.114	−3.404	.001
	Employment	−.168	.302	−.019	−.555	.579
	Living standard	−.398	.283	−.044	−1.405	.160
	Social habitat	−1.546	.275	−.176	−5.631	.000

a. dependent variable: judicialisation of family violence.

The results of this factor analysis support further discussion of the findings divided into, first, the question of the domestic or family (these terms are used interchangeably in Polish law) violence and, second, all the other aspects of family disputes that may be brought before the courts to seek settlement.

III. WHAT IS FAMILY VIOLENCE?

Polish law is statute based, as in typical Continental systems. The judge applies the words of the legislation and precedent has no officially recognised position in judicial argument, except for rulings of the Supreme Court on matters which are not clearly regulated. Not only criminal law but also other areas of law such as civil law or family law are codified and supplemented by specific legislation.

Family violence became the focus of public debate in Poland as late as 1990, ie after the breakdown of the communist regime. Its existence and high frequency earlier had not been denied as part of 'obvious' common knowledge about everyday social life but it was taboo within official discourse. Moreover, it was seen as 'someone else's problem' and thus marginalised as a problem affecting only some specific social groups, such as alcoholics and the uneducated, and viewed as being the part of their social situation. Family violence was nevertheless penalised. In the Criminal Code of 1970 it had been defined as 'mistreatment of a family member'. This crime is also penalised in the more recent Criminal Code of 1997:

> Article 207. § 1. Whoever mentally or physically mistreats a person close to him, or another person being in a permanent or temporary state of dependence to the perpetrator, a minor or a person who is vulnerable because of his mental or physical condition, shall be subject to the penalty of deprivation of liberty for a term of between 3 months and 5 years.
>
> § 2. If the act specified in § 1 is compounded with a particular cruelty, the perpetrator shall be subject to the penalty of deprivation of liberty for a term of between 1 and 10 years.
>
> § 3. If the consequence of the act specified in § 1 or 2 is a suicide attempt by the injured person on his or her life, the perpetrator shall be subject to the penalty of deprivation of liberty for a term of between 2 and 12 years.

This definition has been criticised as providing insufficient grounds for prosecuting and punishing family violence for two reasons. First, the 'mistreatment' in criminal jurisprudence is interpreted as recurring. It must occur for some time and be composed either of many individual acts or one action extended over time. A single beating might therefore be prosecuted on the grounds of the general clauses in the criminal code but not as family violence. It can happen that courts decide to consider a single action of intense psychological and physical brutality as 'mistreatment' but such cases are extremely rare.[1] The definition not only hampers prosecution but also lays on the victim the need to prove that violent actions have been repetitive and recurrent. The second weakness of the statutory definition is the particular intensity of the acts or action as a condition for recognising the harmful effects as 'mistreatment'. If a court does not recognise the effects as particularly harmful, humiliating and intense, even recurrent, frequent and long-term actions will not be considered as 'mistreatment'.[2]

So much for the Criminal Code. 'Family violence' is, however, defined differently in the 'Law on counteracting family violence' of 2005, especially after the 2010 amendments. The Law defines family violence as 'the one-off or recurrent intended action or omission abusing personal rights or goods [...] in particular exposing these persons to the danger of losing life, health, abusing their dignity, bodily integrity, or freedom, including sexual freedom, resulting in damage to their physical or psychological health and also suffering and moral harm for the victims.'[3] The Law imposes several duties on state administrative bodies at various levels in order to provide assistance to the victims of violence and in prosecuting the perpetrators; it also orders the government to carry out systematic

[1] For instance, judgment of District Court in Siedlce of 12-08-2014 (II Ka 388/14).

[2] Judgment of Supreme Court of 09-01-2001 (WA 43/00 LEX nr 550460).

[3] Art 2, p 2 ustawy z dnia z dnia 29 lipca 2005 roku o przeciwdziałaniu przemocy w rodzinie, Dz U 2005 nr 180 poz 1493, tekst jednolity po nowelizacji Dz U 2020r, nr 218, poz 956.

monitoring of anti-violence activities and to enact annual National Programs for Preventing Family Violence. In the debate that accompanied the introduction of this law most of the controversy was focused on the introductions of the new practice of judicial injunctions requiring the perpetrator to leave the common residence and/or to keep a distance from the victim(s).

In 2020 the law on policing was amended giving civil and military police the right to order a person suspected of using violence within the family to immediately leave the common residence and keep a distance away.

The list above should be supplemented by the ratification by Poland in 2015 of the Council of Europe Convention on preventing and combating violence against women and domestic violence, better known as the Istanbul Convention of 2011. This ratification was accompanied by fierce parliamentary debate in which one of the authors (Fuszara) took part as rapporteur on behalf of the then liberal-democratic government and later as the advisor. The main controversy concerned the term 'gender' instead of the biologically understood 'sex' as well as the sources of the violence. The political right is of the opinion that violence results above all from the abuse of alcohol, and they specifically attack Art 12.5 which states that 'Parties shall ensure that culture, custom, religion, tradition or so-called "honour" shall not be considered as justification for any acts of violence covered by the scope of this Convention' as putting religion in the frame for accusation. The controversy continues and the recent government of the 'Unified Right' coalition has promised to withdraw from the Convention following such a decision made in Turkey.

IV. FAMILY VIOLENCE IN REALITY

It is extremely hard to assess the amount of family violence. The only full 'hard' data at our disposal are the number of proceedings initiated by the official bodies obliged by law to prosecute such cases. In 2020, 28,912 proceedings under Art 207 of the Criminal Code were initiated – close to the 2018 figure and slightly less than in 2019. According to the police, of 85,575 people suspected of being victims of family violence in 2020, 73 per cent were adult women, 14 per cent were minors, and 13 per cent were adult men. Amongst the 73,228 suspected perpetrators, the ratios are the reverse: 90 per cent adult men, almost 9 per cent adult women and less than 1 per cent minors.[4]

Another way to assess the volume of family violence is to investigate representative samples within Polish society. Such research has been conducted since 2002 and points to an almost stable frequency of people reporting battery by a partner, the figures hovering around 10 per cent. In 2019, 10 per cent of those

[4] 'Sprawozdania z realizacji procedury 'Niebieskie Karty' – Przemoc w rodzinie – Statystyka' (policja.pl), accessed 14 July 2021.

surveyed said that they had been victims of such act. In the last 17 years the figures ranged from 9 per cent in 2020 to 13 per cent in 2003.[5] Women report being victims of such an event more often than men, and more often declare it to be recurrent. It is, nevertheless, widely assumed that there is a strong bias against talking about such experiences even under conditions of anonymity. This may be illustrated by a recent survey of the inhabitants of Warsaw in which 95 per cent of the sample said they had not observed a rise in family violence in their milieu in 2020–2021 during the Covid-19 pandemic while 44 per cent reported experiencing a personal crisis such as the deterioration of mental health or experiencing violence against them.[6]

In the case of violence, a significant element is the extent to which it is tolerated. The findings of our public opinion research point to puzzling differences in how condemnation of a 'he-partner' for violence relates to the gender of the victim. As many as 83 per cent of respondents were unequivocal in condemnation of violence against women described in the questionnaire as 'battering in anger one's wife'. But 8 per cent still claimed this might in some circumstances be justified. There was more tolerance of the inverse case of women who in anger had battered their 'husband'. This might be justified according to 30 per cent of the respondents. Notably, these attitudes were not related to the gender of the respondents.

In our research, however, the gender of the perpetrator is not related to the opinion of the respondents about whether such a case should be referred to the court.

Table 6.7 Q 9.10: Which of these cases should be decided by the courts? Husband has beaten the wife

	Number	Percentage
Such cases should always go before the court	564	59.0
Such cases should always go to the court if other methods like mediation or compromise fail	243	25.4
Such cases should end in the court only in exceptional circumstances	102	10.6
Such cases should never be brought before the court	23	2.4
Don't know	22	2.3
No answer	3	0.3
Total	956	100.0

[5] 'Przemoc i konflikty w domu. Komunikat z badań'. CBOS 48/2019.

[6] www.um.warszawa.pl/sites/all/files/download_file.php?file=/sites/default/files/attach/aktualnosci/sytuacja_rodzinna_i_osobista_mieszkancow_warszawy_w_czasie_epidemii_-_kobiety_1.pdf, accessed 22 July 2021.

Table 6.8 Q 9.11: Which of these cases should be decided by the courts? Wife has beaten the husband

	Number	Percentage
Such cases should always go before the court	534	55.9
Such cases should always go to the court if other methods like mediation or compromise fail	243	25.4
Such cases should end in the court only in exceptional circumstances	108	11.3
Such cases should never be brought before the court	44	4.6
Don't know	26	2.7
No answer	1	0.1
Total	956	100.0

In both hypothetical cases a similar majority is of the opinion that the issue should always be brought before the court, independent of the gender of those involved in physical violence in the family. However, about one quarter of the sample is of the opinion that mediation or negotiation should be attempted first. Such an opinion in fact means support for hiding the incidence of physical abuse within the confines of family.

As for social demographics, the multiple linear regression analysis revealed age, level of education achieved and social habitat (size of the place of residence ranging from a village to a city with a population of more than one million) as significantly related to judicialisation of beating in two cases, with older, less educated respondents living in smaller communities less in favour of bringing the case before the court.

Finally, we should include in this chapter the results of questions concerning an aggressive member of the household:

Table 6.9 Q 9.9: Which of these cases should be decided by the courts? Someone in the family gets drunk regularly, starts arguments, and is aggressive

	Number	Percentage
Such cases should always go before the court;	397	41.6
Such cases should always go to the court if other methods like mediation or compromise fail	370	38.7
Such cases should end in the court only in the exceptional circumstances	136	14.2
Such cases should never be brought before the court	35	3.6
Do not know	15	1.6
No answer	3	0.4
Total	956	100.0

Respondents most often suggested unconditional reference to the court of such cases, followed by those who supported first trying to accommodate the problem in an informal way. In the set of significantly related independent socio-demographic variables, this time apart from age and social habitat, it was the women who more often demanded judicialisation. This might be explained by the gender differential in the experience of victimhood in this kind of intra-family violent behaviour.

V. VIOLENCE AGAINST ELDERS

Violence against elderly people is studied much less often than violence against women or children. It may take a variety of forms. Apart from physical violence, older people may encounter psychological violence, not only obvious bullying, but also 'softer' versions though similarly cruel behaviour such as denigration, humiliation, ridicule and insults. To this can be added sexual violence and frequently economic violence.

The specific vulnerability of elderly people to violence is due to the fact that it is often committed precisely by those on whom the victims are dependent for their survival.[7] Common residence, poor health, physical and mental dependence and the need for nurture put old people at risk. One thinks usually about violence as a physical act, but in the case of the elderly it can also take the form of omission and neglect, especially for those who rely on others in their everyday life, not to mention dealing with external contacts in administration and business. The appropriation of pensions and other old age benefits, that are often the elderly person's only means of existence, on the pretext of the need to provide care is the paramount type of economic violence against the elderly. Another peculiarity of violence against the elderly is often their limited opportunity to look for assistance; limited not only by deterioration in health but also through – often manipulated by close others – ignorance of the places and ways that may offer the necessary assistance.

Another aspect is the 'symbolic abuse' of the elderly that is manifested above all through treating old people as of lesser value, through neglecting the achievements of the older generation, making out there is a 'proper elderly person' by enforcing or persuading stereotyped 'proper' dress, idiom and behaviour, or through treating the elderly as incompetent and helpless like a child (Kwiatkowski, 2015). The contemporary culture that highly values youth

[7] WHO, 'European report on preventing elder maltreatment', edited by Dinesh Sethi, Sara Wood, Francesco Mitis, Mark Bellis, Bridget Penhale, Isabel Iborra Marmolejo, Ariela Lowenstein, Gillian Manthorpe and Freja Ulvestad Kärki, WHO Europe, 2011, p. VIII https://apps.who.int/iris/bitstream/handle/10665/107293/e95110.pdf?sequence=1&isAllowed=y.

reinforces 'ageism' and 'gerontophobia'.[8] This is illustrated by the image of the elderly in the media:

> Still, it is the mass media, especially television, which promote the stereotype of old people as always tired, slow, sick, forgetful, uninformed, lonely, inefficient, passive, anti-social, quarrelsome and poor. The focus is on youth, even the so-called cult of youth, in which old age is undesirable, and its signs must be hidden, e.g. through using special cosmetics, hair transplants, plastic surgery, etc. (Zwoliński 2105: 30)

All this facilitates the use of various forms of violence against the elderly.

Widely hidden, the violence against the elderly is nevertheless present in the statistics, even if particular indicators may contradict each other. According to WHO: 'Around 1 in 6 people 60 years and older experienced some form of abuse in community settings during the past year.' A comparative study of 28 countries had shown:

> The pooled prevalence rate for overall elder abuse was 15.7% (95% CI 12.8–19.3). The pooled prevalence estimate was 11.6% (8.1–16.3) for psychological abuse, 6.8% (5.0–9.2) for financial abuse, 4.2% (2.1–8.1) for neglect, 2.6% (1.6–4.4) for physical abuse, and 0.9% (0.6–1.4) for sexual abuse.

In Europe,

> about 2.7% of older people have experienced maltreatment in the form of physical abuse – equivalent to 4 million people aged 60 years and older in the Region. For sexual abuse, the proportion is lower at 0.7%, equivalent to 1 million older people; for mental abuse, this is far higher at 19.4%, equivalent to 29 million older people; and 3.8% have been subjected to financial abuse, equivalent to 6 million older people.

Other meta-analyses provide higher indicators of suspected violence against the elderly. The highest level was reported from Spain with 44.6 per cent overall prevalence of suspicion of abuse, and lower in the developing countries – from 13.5 per cent to 28.8 per cent. In research carried out in 2011 in Poland, 5.9 per cent of old people reported violent experiences, women significantly more often (6.8 per cent) than men (5 per cent). Most frequently victims reported insults, ridiculing, and being despised by others (5.4 per cent of the whole sample) while physical violence was mentioned by 1.5 per cent of the respondents (Halicka, Halicki and Ślusarczyk, 2012: 497). A survey of women over 65 years of age in Cracow gave more results – more than 14 per cent reported experience with physical or psychological violence, amongst whom 60 per cent reported physical battery or psychological bullying.

Our survey included only physical violence, as the relevant question concerned a hypothetical case of beating parents by an adult child (Q 9.12).

[8] 'Ageing in the Digital Era', UNECE Policy Brief on Ageing No. 26 July 2021, Policy Briefs – UNECE.

Table 6.10 Q 9.12: Which of these cases should be decided by the courts? An adult child has beaten their parents

	Number	Percentage
Such cases should always go before the court	556	58.2
Such cases should always go to the court if other methods like mediation or compromise fail	238	24.9
Such cases should end in the court only in exceptional circumstances	106	11.1
Such cases should never be brought before the court	27	2.8
Don't know	26	2.8
No answer	2	0.2
Total	956	100.0

The distribution of answers is similar to cases of violence between spouses, with a majority opinion that cases of physical violence against parents should always be referred to the courts while one quarter of the sample were willing first to attempt mediation or mutual reconciliation. As in the case of beating a spouse, judicialisation is significantly related to (lower) age, (better) education and (larger) site of residence.

VI. VIOLENCE AGAINST CHILDREN

To begin we would like to quote one of many definitions that deals with violence against children in general: 'Maltreatment (including violent punishment) involves physical, sexual and psychological/emotional violence; and neglect of infants, children and adolescents by parents, caregivers and other authority figures, most often in the home but also in settings such as schools and orphanages.'[9] So, violence against children also assumes a variety of forms but in our study we have asked only about sending to the court cases involving physical violence.

The specific and most widely discussed aspect of such a violence is the question of whether some forms of punishment for children which have been traditionally allowed should be included in the statutory meaning of 'violence' or not. The specific and most controversial issue raised in that context concerns some forms of violence such as spanking or face slapping, traditionally considered in many countries as legitimate forms of punishment for children by adults. The answer is of decisive significance for attempts to assess the volume of the violence as well as for the prosecuting and penal policy. Debate continues not

[9] WHO Fact sheets 'Violence against children' (who.int).

only in Poland but elsewhere in the world with the side effect of rendering unclear any comparative study of violence against children in different countries.

This can be well illustrated by a comparative study that was based upon 112 research projects made in 96 countries around the world. As the authors wrote:

> Definitions vary on the measurement of exposure to any given type of violent victimization. Definitions vary particularly in whether they include hitting with bare hands, or spanking, as a form of violence. For example, in the WorldSafe, MICS, and survey adaptations using CTS, 'moderate physical violence' includes 'slapping, hitting with bare hands, hitting with an object, shaking, or spanking'; in contrast, the NatSCEV and VACS exclude spanking from their measures. (Hillis et al, 2016)

In Poland this dilemma was settled in 2010 by a new Law on family violence that amended Art 2 of the Family and Guardianship Code of 1964 adding the new article 961: 'Persons who execute parental authority and custody and care over a minor are forbidden from using corporal punishment'.[10] Change in law does not mean, of course, automatic change in views, attitudes and even the reactions of the prosecuting authorities. The Polish Ombudsman for Children, concerned about lack of initiative on the part of prosecutors concerning violence against children, asked the relevant authorities about this in 2014. The answer by the then Minister of Justice points to the unequivocal official stand against the practice of waiving such actions:

> The Minister of Justice also stated that he had taken a clear position with respect to extra-statutory 'scolding countertype', indicating that the 'Act of 10 June 2010 amending the Act on Counteracting Domestic Violence and some other acts (Dz. U., Journal of Laws No. 125, Item 842) introduced a very important change into the Family and Guardianship Code in the form of a ban on the application of corporal punishment by persons who execute parental authority and custody and care over a minor. The change, though it was not equipped with a direct sanction in the case of violation, results in factual dismissal of the extra statutory countertype (exclusion of criminal liability) in the form of the currently applied procedure of departing from the prosecution of persons who, for example violated the bodily integrity of the child, pointing to the right to execute parental authority and educational purposes of scolding. Now that the change has been introduced, the prosecutor cannot make reference to this countertype and refuse to prosecute such persons.'[11]

At the same time the minister acknowledged that statistics do not differentiate such cases so it is not possible to know whether this is a wide issue or just a few individual cases.

[10] Ustawa z dnia 10 czerwca 2010 r o zmianie ustawy o przeciwdziałaniu przemocy w rodzinie oraz niektórych innych ustaw, DzU z 2010 r, nr 125, poz 842.

[11] 'Report on the activity of the ombudsman for children for 2015 with comments on the observance of the rights of the child', Warsaw 2016, str 199-200 brpd.gov.pl/sites/default/files/informacja_o_dzialanosci_rpd_2015_en_-_ebook.pdf.

A public opinion survey made in 2019 nine years after the new legislation brought ambivalent results. On the one hand, there was a sharp rise (10 per cent) up to 61 per cent of respondents who are against physical punishment. On the other hand, a majority (61 per cent) still consider slapping a child necessary under some circumstances; 25 per cent agreed that 'thrashing never spoiled anybody!' Changes in attitudes are evolving in the expected direction but rather slowly.[12] Most symptomatic as to the problems with public opinion is the conspicuous gap between the law that prohibits corporal punishment and acceptance by the majority of society of those forms of violence that until recently had been considered as the obvious implementation of the right (if not duty) to punish misbehaving children.

Public opinion research also points to symptomatic difference in assessing the frequency of violence according to who is asked. In the above quoted 2019 public opinion survey of an adult sample only 12 per cent of those with children under 20 acknowledged punishing them physically. Diametrically opposite findings were made when school children aged 11 to 17 had been asked. This time two separate questions were posed – as in our own 2020 survey, one about beating, another about spanking.[13] In sum, 33 per cent of the surveyed pupils reported being subject to some form of physical violence from a close adult. This included those who had been slapped or spanked at least few times in a year. Altogether as many as 48 per cent declared they had been spanked, though half of them claim it happened 'only once a year or less often'. The optimistic finding is that only 2 per cent of pupils reported being spanked several times a week, while 4 per cent that it had happened in the year preceding the study. Against the stereotype, girls are more often victims of violence, including physical violence, than boys. To a lesser degree such a difference is also present in the official statistical data on violence against youths under 21 years of age. The table below also shows a slight rise in the volume of registered victims, both women and men.

Table 6.11 Registered victims of domestic violence under age of 21 years: 2016–2019

Year	Men	Women
2016	1722	1833
2017	2002	2141
2018	1954	2107
2019	2154	2201

Source: Calculated using Main Statistical Office (GUS) data (https://stat.gov.pl/obszary-tematyczne/wymiar-sprawiedliwosci/wymiar-sprawiedliwosci/ofiary-gwaltu-i-przemocy-domowej,1,1.html).

12 'Przemoc domowa wobec dzieci', CBOS Komunikat z badań nr 49/2019.

13 Report by Foundation Dajemy Dzieciom Siłę: 'Ogólnopolska diagnoza skali i uwarunkowań krzywdzenia dzieci' based on representative survey of 1155 school students aged 11–17.

Also, in our survey a difference between attitudes towards 'beating' and 'spanking' was evident.

Table 6.12 Q 9.3: Which of these cases should be decided by the courts? The child is punished by a parental slap

	Number	Percentage
Such cases should always go before the court	71	7.4
Such cases should always go to the court if other methods like mediation or compromise fail	170	17.8
Such cases should end in the court only in exceptional circumstances	240	25.1
Such cases should never be brought before the court	452	47.3
Don't know	22	2.3
No answer	1	0.1
Total	956	100.0

Table 6.13 Q 9.4: Which of these cases should be decided by the courts? A child has been beaten by the parents

	Number	Percentage
Such cases should always go before the court	576	60.2
Such cases should always go to the court if other methods like mediation or compromise fail	176	18.4
Such cases should end in the court only in exceptional circumstances	136	14.2
Such cases should never be brought before the court	52	5.4
Don't know	14	1.5
No answer	2	0.2
Total	956	100.0

The attitudes of Polish public opinion towards the use of force against offspring differ drastically according to the classification of the physical act. Spanking is tolerated by a majority while beating is considered by the majority unconditionally to be brought before the court. Use of Polish terms 'klaps' and 'pobicie' (similar to English 'spank' and 'beating') suggest not only the difference in purpose (pedagogical instrument versus expressive aggression) but also level of the pain, though empirically the scope of both semantic fields cross over. As for the socio-demographic variables, the set of significant relationships as revealed in the multiple linear regression remains the same as in other physical violence cases: (elder) age, (lower) education and (smaller) site of residence related with (less frequent) judicialisation. In the case of beating, this set extends to include also (lower) self-assessment of living conditions of respondent's household.

VII. PARENTAL AUTHORITY

When considering domestic violence against children we have entered the wider area of parental authority. The relationship between parents and children are regulated in detail in Polish statutory law and the Code of Family and Guardianship of 1964 with later amendments referring to all rights and duties of parents towards children under the notion of 'parental authority' and that the principle should be executed for the 'child's welfare'.

The relatively detailed normative description of the *iuris nexus* between parents and children in the Code deserves quotation:[14]

> Article 87. Parents and children are obliged to respect each other and to support each other ... Article 92. The child remains under parental authority until the age of majority [which in Poland is 18 years for both sexes]. Article 93. § 1. Parental authority is vested in both parents ... Article 95. § 1. Parental authority includes, in particular, the duty and right of parents to exercise custody of the child's person and property and to raise the child, while respecting his or her dignity and rights .... § 3. Parental authority should be exercised as required by the best interests of the child and the public interest. § 4. Parents should listen to them before taking decisions on more important matters concerning the child's person or property if the child's mental development, state of health and maturity so allow, and take into account, as far as possible, his or her reasonable wishes. Article 96. § 1. Parents raise and direct a child under their parental authority. They are obliged to care for the physical and spiritual development of the child and prepare them properly for work for the good of society according to his or her abilities.

As a correlative duty and right on the part of a child, the Code states in Art 95 § 2:

> A child under parental authority should obey his or her parents and, in cases where he or she can make decisions and make declarations of intent himself or herself, should listen to the opinions and recommendations of the parents for his or her benefit.

Parental authority resides thus with both parents who should jointly take all decisions concerning the child. In situations when such consensus on the 'essential child's problems' is not obtained. the Code delegates the decision to the guardianship court (Art 97 § 2). The concept of 'essential child's problems' is not defined in the Code and the legal literature – which is unauthoritatively filling the gap – mentions, for example, giving a name or changing the surname, travel, especially if abroad, citizenship, medical treatment and choice of school or of profession (Słyk, 2013). Some authors are of the opinion, however, that subjective assessment is decisive here and any application to the court for decision in a matter on which the parents disagree should be considered as concerning the 'essential problem' that the court must settle (Stojanowska, 1985). Lack of

[14] Ustawa z dnia 25 lutego 1964 r. Kodeks rodzinny i opiekuńczy (Dz.U.2012.788).

decision and leaving the issue open would, according to this opinion, be disadvantageous for a child and thus contradictory to the principle of the child's welfare as the supreme rule of conduct of parents and institutions.

Judicial practice has been the subject of a few studies in Poland made of official written court files in 1979 and 2011 (Słyk, 2013). Though not revealing the point of view of the parties to the dispute, these studies allow us to describe who applies for settlement by the Guardianship Court, and under what circumstances they do so. First, they draw attention to the fact that these cases are often brought in situations where both parents have parental responsibility, but do not have a relationship. In a recent study of 166 randomly described cases (2011), those with a divorced parent (44 per cent) were the most likely to apply to the court, followed by those where parents had never been married (32.5 per cent). What is particularly important to emphasise is that the other parent is often completely absent from the child's life in these cases, is not interested in the child and often does not even have any contact with the child, and yet that parent's consent is necessary for various official activities. In 28 per cent of cases, despite attempts, the parent looking after the child was not able to establish contact with the child's other parent. These complications are often not provided for by parents consenting to shared responsibility after divorce who after many years need to return to the courts while the co-parent, almost always the father of the child, cannot be even located (Fuszara, 1994).

In the cases examined in 2011, we most often encountered those related to the issue of an ID card or passport to a child (59 per cent). It is worth noting that such cases have, in a sense, 'replaced' the numerous cases earlier for permission for a child to travel abroad. Now that Poland has entered the Schengen free travel area, having such a document allows a child to travel without the other parent's consent. The second most common reason for bringing cases was the desire to change the name of the child (19 per cent), which often meant seeking to fully integrate the child into a new family and avoid any marking out that might result from having a different name from other family members.

Polish public opinion was asked about parental authority for the first time as early as 1960 by Adam Podgórecki (1964). In our recent survey the topic was raised only in a limited way. The first occasion concerned seemingly common disputes, which nevertheless rarely reach the court, where parents cannot agree on an everyday life matter – such as the question of which school a child should attend. Judgments in such cases are recorded in the literature. Among the case files examined in 2011 as a 'case study' was a case brought by a father with whom the children did not live and who objected to the mother changing the children's kindergarten. The case was probably the result of a wider more complicated conflict, because another objection of the father was related to the change of religion by the children. The father accused the mother of obstructing his contact with the children, and the mother accused the father of exploiting the children while pretending they were under his care. The court files study points out that the case is brought to the court either if parents are not in contact or in the case of complex conflicts between them. This may not be known to our respondents where the majority answered that such cases should never be brought before a court (see Table 6.14).

Table 6.14 Q 9.1: Which of these cases should be decided by the courts? Parents disagree on the child's school

	Number	Percentage
Such cases should always go before the court	16	1.6
Such cases should always go to the court if other methods like mediation or compromise fail	167	17.4
Such cases should end in the court only in exceptional circumstances	175	18.3
Such cases should never be brought before the court	576	60.3
Don't know	22	2.3
Total	956	100.0

In contrast to the previously analysed questions in case of parental disagreement about the education of the child, the majority in the sample is categorically against bringing the controversy before the court even if attempts at compromise fail. Of the socio-demographic variables in our set only age is related to judicialisation, with younger people more prone to use the court in such situation.

The second question in our questionnaire, relating to parental authority, described situations of importance more frequently encountered in court, as it referred to possible misunderstandings about authority over the child after the parents' divorce. Judicial decision in this case is mandatory, as the Family and Guardianship Code states: 'In the divorce judgment, the court decides on parental authority over the joint minor child of both spouses and on the parents' contact with the child' (Art 58). In recent decades there were symptomatic changes in the settling of such cases. It seems that changes advancing the parental authority of both parents probably result at least from the two factors.

First, to an increasing extent, especially since the revision of the Code in 2008, the courts are required to take into account the written agreements concluded by parents. Agreements may concern both entrusting of authority over the child and the contacts of the parents and the child if such an agreement is, in the opinion of the court, in the interests of the child. Thus, the role of the court has changed over recent decades. Initially it had full power to rule on such cases. Over time, parents' agreements have been allowed, and it is now mandatory for the court to take such an agreement into account. The second change, which has been slow but very noticeable, concerns entrusting parental authority to both parents to an increasing extent. For many years, it was rather the opinion that a child should be brought up in one environment. This fostered consistency, including in education, and also took into account the realities in which in fact the 'main' parent was one person. Over time, however, the belief that the child should have constant care by both parents began to take shape, and that it is therefore more appropriate to entrust parental authority to both parents (Fuszara, 1994). This can be seen very clearly in the judicial statistics relating to the entrustment of parental responsibility after divorce.

Table 6.15 Allocation of parental authority in divorce proceedings in Poland: 2005–2019

Year	Number of cases	Parental authority granted to mother (%)	Parental authority granted to father (%)	Parental authority granted to both parents (%)	Other (%)
2005	45,695	64	3	31	2
2010	36,298	60	4	33	3
2015	39,144	59	4	35	2
2016	37,288	44	2	53	1
2017	38,214	41	3	55	1
2018	37,144	38	2	59	1
2019	37,144	35	2	61	2

Source: Own calculations based on data from the Ministry of Justice: isws.ms.gov.pl/pl/baza-statystyczna/opracowania-wieloletnie.

The change was therefore present in 2015, and was linked to another amendment to the Family and Guardianship Code, giving the courts a wider opportunity to grant joint parental authority to both parents, even if they did not reach an agreement on the matter. First, there is the evident increase of participation by fathers in raising children and widening the scope of the care they offer. With this change, attitudes towards parental authority of parents after divorce or in other situations where they do not constitute marriage have also changed.

Secondly, the granting of parental authority solely to mothers has often been criticised, in particular, by fathers' associations. It should be stressed, however, that when seeking divorce, not only mothers but also fathers often indicate the mother's place of residence as the place where the child will be raised. They rarely apply for equal participation in education themselves, but rather that, without acting as a 'primary parent', they are able to have contact with the child.

Research conducted in Poland both years ago and now shows that women are more likely to apply for divorce and childcare, and men are more likely to have more contact with a child living with their mother on a daily basis (Fuszara, 1994; Report by Kantar Polska for RPO, 2020). Polish law thus allows increasing room for agreements as to the decisions on post-divorce parental authority, and the majority of our 2020 respondents agreed with such a tendency (see Table 6.16).

Table 6.16 Q 9.2: Which of these cases should be decided by the courts? Parents disagree on parental authority after divorce

	Number	Percentage
Such cases should always go before the court	161	16.9
Such cases should go always to the court if other methods like mediation or compromise fail	471	49.2
Such cases should end in the court only in exceptional circumstances	207	21.6
Such cases should never be brought before the court	91	9.5
Don't know	27	2.8
Total	956	100.0

A majority of respondents considered the courts as the proper place to decide parental authority in divorce proceedings in the case of controversy, followed by almost one quarter who agree that such decisions should be made only in exceptional circumstances. All this amounts to rejection of the lack of autonomy of the parents who – hopefully – agree between themselves as to who is going to have the parental authority in future. Age and size of site of residence – but not education – are, as in case of the previously analysed questions, related to judicialisation in this context.

VIII. HOUSEHOLD ECONOMY

Our survey also included three questions related to household economy. The first dealt with disputes between spouses concerning the costs of living. Although such disputes erupt most often during or after the divorce, it sometimes happens that the respective claims are brought to the court for settlement when a request for divorce has not been made. Article 27 of the Code of family and guardianship states that '[b]oth spouses are obliged, each according to their strength and their earning and financial capacity, to contribute to meeting the needs of the family they have set up through their relationship' and some parents apply to the court for enforcing the respective duties of the co-spouse, which may include caring for the children or household duties.

In practice, such disputes, however, are more often seen when child maintenance costs are being established and, then usually in situations where the maintenance is not being paid. It is estimated that in Poland this group numbers around one million cases (Chełstowska, 2016). It needs to be mentioned that in Poland the maintenance system is based upon judicial decisions and – as in the UK – the work of a specialised agency (the Child Support Agency). In our survey we asked, however, about the less frequent case of the maintenance of a common household. That such cases exist has been revealed in the research on divorce (Fuszara, 1994) in which many women complained that husbands are not providing the means for maintenance of the family, which meant that all the financial costs as well as the caring obligations were falling on the shoulders of the women (Fuszara, 1994). If the marriage continues it is possible for both to apply for financial support using a simple procedurę to apply to court for securing the needs of the family, which can be implemented through a judicial injunction obliging the employer to send the pay of the negligent spouse directly to the co-spouse. Our question dealt then with the opinion of whether such disputes should be brought before the court (see Table 6.17).

Table 6.17 Q 9.5: Which of these cases should be decided by the courts? Spouses argue over the sharing of the costs of maintaining the household

	Number	Percentage
Such cases should always go before the court	58	6.0
Such cases should always go to the court if other methods like mediation or compromise fail	368	38.5
Such cases should end in the court only in exceptional circumstances	248	25.9
Such cases should never be brought before the court	259	27.1
Don't know	22	2.3
No answer	1	0.1
Total	956	100.0

In this case the sample interviewed was divided almost equally between three groups: those who think that the court should be approached only after negotiations and mediation have failed; those who consider that this should happen only in some exceptional circumstances; and those who think this never should happen. Almost everybody rejected judicial settlement of household economy disputes as a standard procedure. The only significant relationship that emerged from the multiple regression was between being employed, with judicialisation as the dependent variable.

The next question concerned the issue that, in practice, seemingly is not – to our knowledge – brought before the court, although it certainly might lead to severe conflict inside the family. This is when one of the spouses inherits assets and puts them aside on their own account and does not add them to the common pool of the household. This is exactly as Polish law says should happen unless the testator decided differently (Art 33 of the Code of Family and Guardianship Law). Although what the spouse does with the inheritance is legal, common knowledge provides cases of domestic conflict that arise in such circumstances. A relative majority of respondents said that such a case should never be brought before the court (see Table 6.18).

Table 6.18 Q 9.6: Which of these cases should be decided by the courts? Argument between spouses as the wife inherited 5,000 euros and kept it on her own account and was unwilling to share in the joint household budget

	Number	Percentage
Such cases should always go before the court	38	4.0
Such cases should always go to the court if other methods like mediation or compromise fail	239	25.0
Such cases should end in the court only in exceptional circumstances	230	24.0
Such cases should never be brought before the court	416	43.5
Don't know	33	3.5
Total	956	100.0

In this case no significant relationship was found through the multilinear regression analysis using the standard set of socio-demographic independent variables.

The approach to a court was advised more often in the third hypothetical case related to household economy that involves the dispute within a family concerning the partition of inheritance. The majority of inheritance cases are decided by courts in Poland in non-adversarial proceedings. The rarity of disputes might be corroborated by the huge gap between number of cases concerning judicial validation of the rights to inheritance (above 135,000 in 2019) and cases concerning partition of inheritance (14,000 in 2019). On the other hand, the partition might also be made before a notary of Continental type, unless there is a disagreement between inheritors. As for the contested partition of inheritance, there has been no recent research in Poland at all, to our knowledge, concerning this matter but we learned of the emergence of such disputes while studying different type of conflicts appearing before the courts such as, for example, cases concerning insult and slander often resulting from economic conflict about the partition of inheritance (Fuszara and Kurczewski, 2017a, b).

Table 6.19 Q 9.7: Which of these cases should be decided by the courts? Family members argue over partition of an inherited estate

	Number	Percentage
Such cases should always go before the court	193	20.2
Such cases should always go to the court if other methods like mediation or compromise fail	396	41.4
Such cases should end in the court only in exceptional circumstances	242	25.3
Such cases should never be brought before the court	109	11.4
Don't know	16	1.7
Total	956	100.0

For the first time in our multivariable regression only analysis, self-assessment of the material standard of living in one's household was found have a significant relationship with judicialisation, with those with better self-assessment opting more often for the use of courts in the case of an inheritance dispute. One may suspect this to be related to the possibly higher value of the assets to be partitioned.

As we compare these three tables there is a visible difference in the frequency of those who consider that such cases should never be brought before the court, the lowest being (11.4 per cent) when the inherited property has to be divided, through conflict over sharing the costs of household economy (27.1 per cent) up to almost half (43.5 per cent) in a case where a wife keeps for herself the inherited money.

As with family violence, an additive scale of the choice of judicial settlement of the family household economy disputes has been constructed. Age, education, employment, social ecology of residence and self-assessment of living standard taken separately as the independent variable are significantly related with judicialisation of economic issues; however, taking all the socio-demographic variables, including gender, as a set of independent variables in the multivariate linear regression, the three significant relationships – with age, education and social habitat – hold. There is also a significant relationship between overall index of social status and judicialisation of the household economy.

Table 6.20 Multiple linear regression analysis with judicialisation of household economy disputes as dependent variable and socio-demographic independent variables

Intra-family household economy disputes to the court		Nonstandardised coefficients		Standardised coefficients		
		B	Standard error	Beta	t	significance
1	(constant)	8.896	.254		35.022	.000
	Gender	−.067	.170	−.013	−.397	.692
	Age	.410	.187	.079	2.185	.029
	Education	−.178	.182	−.034	−.976	.330
	Employment	−.378	.188	−.075	−2.061	.040
	Living standard	−.326	.176	−.061	−1.851	.064
	Social habitat	−.185	.171	−.036	−1.084	.278

. dependent variable: judicialisation of household economy

IX. THE MORAL SOVEREIGNTY ISSUES

In 2011 the first transgender person was elected to a parliament in Europe: Anna Grodzka, a Pole who was born as a man, had been married and had begotten a son. She decided to change her sex when her son was adult. This process in her case ended in 2010. Her personal story illustrates the problems surrounding such a process in Poland. Not only did she wait until her son became adult but the legal necessity to sue her own parents had been decisive for her. This was because it was only when she was beginning the process, which necessitates initiating a case against the parents to change the birth certificate, did she discover that she had been adopted as an infant. All this is related to the state of the law, or rather to the lack of relevant legislation in Poland.

Despite many draft proposals Polish law still has no clear statutory rules on changing or harmonising sex. In these circumstances, the burden of filling the legal gap falls on the judiciary. At the beginning (the first verdict was made in 1964) courts had been authorising the correction of the birth certificates of those who had already undergone a change of sex. The Supreme Court decided that such correction might even be made before the whole medical operation of transsexualisation had been completed. A basic change was made in 1989 when the Supreme Court decided that such correction is legally impossible,[15] as only errors may be corrected and the birth certificates had not been wrong when made. It had been pointed out that change of the birth certificate is possible only on basis of Art 189 of the Code of Civil Procedure stating that '[t]he claimant may require the court to establish the existence or non-existence of a legal relationship or right where he has an interest in bringing proceedings'. As the transgender person has a legal interest in changing the data inscribed in the birth certificate that person may apply for it as 'additional information'. What seems a minor detail in the decision of the Supreme Court was, in fact, a far reaching change. Correction was made before this in a non-adversarial procedure, without any opposing addressee of the claim. Now, the need for an opponent has been created. The registered parents of the claimant are to be mentioned as defendants; a condition that, as in Anna Grodzka's case, may lead to unexpected outcomes such as discovering that one's parents are not the biological parents, which had been hidden behind the legal principle of adoptive secrecy. In no judicial decisions in such cases had the civil status of the applicant or other official characteristics like the medical correction of sex been considered as a necessary condition, although in a draft law being single had been proposed as such a limiting criterion (Urbanowicz and Bętkowska, 2018).

Other than parents, close relatives of the transgender person – namely the spouse and their offspring – appeared for the first time in the verdict of Supreme Court of 2013. The transgender person was undergoing medical change of sex, and the common court agreed with the demand for the alteration of the birth certificate. This decision had, however, been appealed by the prosecutor as the plaintiff had kept secret the fact that the plaintiff was married and had children.

[15] Uchwała Sądu Najwyższego z dnia 22 VI 1989, III CZP 37/89; sip.lex.pl/orzeczenia-i-pisma-urzedowe/orzeczenia-sadow/iii-czp-37-89-uchwala-sadu-najwyzszego-520097198.

In its 2013 verdict the Supreme Court decided that, in such a case, the spouse and children of a transgender person should appear as defendants. This was different from the verdict of the Supreme Court in 2019. In this complex case the transgender person was the father of six children, all but one of whom were adult. In 2014 the couple had divorced and parental authority had been granted by the court to the father. In its 2019 verdict the Supreme Court found that children are not the defendants as 'they have no legal interest' in the change of sex. Relations between parents and children are independent of their sex and in the birth certificate of a parent, children are not mentioned (!) The change in the birth documents of a parent thus has no influence on the legal situation or the legal documents of their children. As the Supreme Court stated, children may have a factual interest in the matter but not a legal interest.[16]

The complexity of such cases inclined us to question public opinion on the matter. On the other hand, such complexity resulted in an unusually low response rate on the part of the respondents, as shown in Table 6.21.

Table 6.21 Q 9.8: Which of these cases should be decided by the courts? One of the spouses, who have a child, wishes to change sex

	Number	Percentage
Such cases should always go before the court	196	20.5
Such cases should always go to the court if other methods like mediation or compromise fail	158	16.5
Such cases should end in the court only in exceptional circumstances	136	14.2
Such cases should never be brought before the court	262	27.5
Don't know	198	20.7
No answer	6	0.6
Total	956	100.0

The views of the sample were spread over all possible options including an unusually high frequency of no answer being given (20 per cent). There was no dominant tendency and the (younger) age group were only slightly associated with judicialisation.

Legal regulation of abortion has become a hot topic of heated disputes in Poland in recent years. This discussion has been going on since 1989, when, for the first time in many years, a proposal was sent to parliament to tighten abortion law. It is worth recalling that in Poland before 1989, the law allowed abortion not only in case of danger to the health or life of a pregnant woman,

[16] Sygn. akt II CSK 371/18 Wyrok w imieniu Rzeczypospolitej Polskiej, Dnia 10 stycznia 2019 r Wyrok SN w sprawie postępowania o ustalenie płci.pdf (brpo.gov.pl).

pregnancy resulting from a crime, irreversible foetal defect, and in the case of 'difficult living conditions of a woman'. In theory, there has never been an 'abortion on demand' in Poland, but the literature stresses that the latter condition actually served such a function (Fuszara 1991a, b).

Proposals for change had already been met with very strong public opposition in 1989. Demonstrations involving many thousands of participants, the collection of signatures for a referendum, and numerous petitions are just some of the actions taken as a result of a proposal to parliament which would drastically restrict women's rights to decide on abortion The initial draft was relaxed and finally passed by parliament in 1993. Abortion has become acceptable in four situations: threat to a woman's life; threat to a woman's health; irreversible foetal defect; and removal of pregnancy resulting from a crime (Fuszara, 1993).

On several occasions, attempts have been made both to relax and alternatively to strengthen abortion law. Attempts to tighten up have always provoked huge opposition and street demonstrations. The 'black protest' became famous, during which crowds of many thousand demonstrated in 2016 in both large cities and small towns against the referral to the *Sejm* of a draft restrictive abortion law. The protests have led to plans to tighten abortion laws, but also to changes in the strategy of advocates for tightening the law. Instead of an impossible legal tightening of abortion law, the question was asked of the Constitutional Court whether the right to abortion due to irreversible foetal defects is in line with the constitutional principle of the protection of life. The Constitutional Court has ruled that this provision is contrary to the Constitution, which means that abortion law has been strengthened.[17] Although these events took place during the Covid-19 pandemic, the decision of the Constitutional Court sparked many thousand street protests across Poland. Despite these protests, the decision came into force, restricting women's reproductive rights.

Poland's restrictive legal regulation contains however a very important element, which is the non-penalisation of aborting women. People who help or perform abortions (eg doctors) may be punished, but not the woman who undergoes the procedure. This, on the one hand, paves the way for an increasingly popular drug-induced medical not surgical abortion and certainly limits the strength of opposition. This also makes it difficult to answer the question we put in the questionnaire. On the one hand, abortion on demand is not legally permissible in Poland but, on the other hand, a woman cannot be punished for it. However, our question was not intended to verify respondents' knowledge of the law and their views on how to address such matters to court.

[17] Judgment by Constitutional Tribunal of 22nd October 2020 sygn akt K 1/20: Dziennik Ustaw – rok 2021 poz 175 – INFOR.PL.

Table 6.22 Q 9.13: Which of these cases should be decided by the courts? A woman had an abortion simply because she was unwilling to have a child

	Number	Percentage
Such cases should always go before the court	209	21.9
Such cases should always go to the court if other methods like mediation or compromise fail	131	13.7
Such cases should end in the court only in exceptional circumstances	214	22.4
Such cases should never be brought before the court	292	30.5
Don't know	102	10.7
No answer	8	0.8
Total	956	100.0

(Male) gender and (elder) age are related with judicialisation of such the decision of those who say that this case should never be brought before a court. The unconditional freedom to abort as in this hypothetical case has never been accepted by most of the Polish public, in contrast to the acceptance of abortion in the presence of several conditions like issues related to the health of the foetus rendered illegal under the recent conservative Catholic legislation. The question had also been directly asked in another part of our 2020 survey and showed that 32.6 per cent accept unconditional freedom of abortion (we do not discuss here the length of pregnancy as a condition), 49.5 per cent reject and 16.4 per cent do not have an opinion on the matter. Judicialisation is significantly related to the rejection of the women's right to abort at will. Interestingly, attitudes towards abortion at will are not (in contrast to judicialisation) related to the gender of the respondents. Women tend to take such decisions out of the court even if they are against abortion.

X. CONCLUSIONS

The following social characteristics were found in our 2020 small public opinion surveys to be related to readiness to approach the courts for judicial decision making, or judicialisation.

- Age was the characteristic most often related to judicialisation; the younger the respondent, the more likely they were to accept court intervention in all cases except financial disputes.
- Social habitat as indicated by level of urbanisation was related in cases involving physical aggression, and in questions of parental authority after divorce, with those living in larger communities being more favourable to approaching the courts.

- Education was always a factor when physical aggression was involved; the higher the level of education, the more willingness to use the courts.
- Gender was related to judicialisation in disputes about abortion and aggression in a family member.
- Employment was related positively to judicialisation of disputes about sharing household costs.
- Self-assessment of standard of living of one's household was only related to judicialisation of disputes about sharing inheritance; the higher the standard of living, the more willingness to approach the courts.
- Willingness to approach the courts about disputes about a spouse's right to share inherited property was unrelated to any of the social variables under consideration.

There was also evidence of the impact of religious and political beliefs on willingness to approach the courts. In our representative sample of adult Poles, 48 per cent declared their participation in religious services at least once a week ('dominicantes' in terms of Catholic church statistics), 13 per cent once a month, 22 per cent once or a few times a year, 14 per cent did not participate in religious services at all, and 2 per cent refrained from answering this question.

The frequency of religious participation[18] was inversely related (at .05 level of statistical significance) to the judicialisation of most family issues, except for the beating of a woman by her husband or parents by their adult child, aggressive alcoholism in the family, or a change of sex by a spouse. Our findings on the relationship between the judicialisation of family issues and subjective self-assessment of religiosity on a scale from the 'deeply believing' through 'believing' to 'rather unbelieving' and 'fully unbelieving' are also similar. In this case also most of the items were significantly (at .05 level of significance) related to judicialisation, except for controversy about the education of a child, sharing household costs, or an aggressive alcoholic in the family.

As for political orientation as measured on a right to left continuum, this was significantly (at .05 level) related with judicialisation of all family violence cases except for beating parents, economic issues except for partition of an inheritance, and change of sex and abortion at will. Political orientation was also significantly related with religiosity.

[18] These are declarations on participating in services. The statistics of the Catholic Church that refer to approximately 82% obliged from 7 years of age to participate in Sunday Mass amongst 85.6% of Poles who are registered in the Church provide lower figures (36.9% in 2019, 38.2 in 2018, 38.3 % in 2017) established through annual observation in all parochial churches in Poland(ISKK: praktyki religijne Polaków na stałym poziomie | Konferencja Episkopatu Polski; episkopat.pl/; instytut-statystyki-kosciola-katolickiego-opublikowal-raport-za-2019-rok; episkopat.pl. NB our survey of adults include also people of other Christian denominations being minority in Poland (mostly Eastern Orthodox and Evangelicals).

The Pearson correlation analysis of the two aggregate scales, the first composed of five items measuring readiness to approach the courts in cases of physical violence within the family, and the second composed of three items measuring readiness to approach the courts in cases of economic disputes within the family, revealed slightly different patterns of relationship. The mobilisation of courts against physical violence in general was significantly related to political attitudes, while mobilisation to resolve economic differences was not. Neither of the two scales was significantly correlated with religiosity in either subjective (strength of own beliefs) or objective (frequency of participation in services) measures. Finally, as for the *aggregate social position* index it is significantly (at .05 level) related to judicialisation of intra-family violence disputes and not related to the index of household economy disputes.

Overall social position was significantly related to political orientation, the left being better placed but – despite common expectations – unrelated to objective or subjective religiosity.

So the resulting picture is complex. On the one hand, degree of religiosity and right–left political orientation are associated, but political orientation is related to social position while religiosity is not. As all these variables are in some way related to judicialisation, slightly more detailed analysis is still needed.

First, we used social position, then religiosity and political orientation as the control variables and checked the relationships between the remaining variables of interest – religiosity, political orientation and two types of judicialisation. The results are clear: the relationship between both scales of judicialisation holds as significant independently of each of these control variables. The relationship between judicialisation of violence and social status holds independently of political orientation and both kinds of religiosity, while the lack of a relationship between the judicialisation of economic intra-family disputes and social status remains independent of these three control variables.

Second, the reader might have expected the analysis to compare the internal demography of a respondents' family household with judicialisation. Indeed, almost all the questions asked revealed a significant correlation between household size and readiness to bring an issue before the courts. But when we controlled for whether this finding is spurious by introducing family size into the set of socio-demographic independent variables in linear regression analysis, both in case of the judicialisation of family violence and of the household economy, size of household was not significantly related, while the relationship of judicialisation with *age, education and social habitat* in the first case of violence and *age and employment* in the second of economic issues continued to be statistically significant. When the presence of minor offspring with family living in the household is introduced in the same way, the same effect is obtained as for the judicialisation of violence in family, while the *presence of minors within a family is significantly related to judicialisation of economic household disputes, quite apart from the age of respondent and self-assessed standard of family living*. This might be interpreted as willingness to keep minors under official state protection with regard to their economic interests, although further inquiry on this line would be needed.

In general, Polish public opinion advocates *bringing to the court all cases of physical violence in the family except for 'slapping'*. In the latter case, as well as in the case of controversy about the child's educational career, and the financial and moral (abortion at wish) autonomy of the spouse, the use of the courts is likely to be rejected. As for post-divorce parental authority and two of the economic issues, the dominant response was in favour of trying first to reach a compromise, and to go to the court only if this failed. But it seems fair to describe the climate of opinion as generally favouring the referral of family conflicts that do not involve the physical violence (besides the 'slapping'!) to courts only as the exception, or in the case of failure to negotiate settlement. In Petrażycki's terms, we may say that the average contemporary Polish family still lives by its own unofficial self-governing legal order *unless an act considered as physical violence* within the family tears down the curtain of privacy and opens the path to official public law and the justice of the state. We should consider the impact on these attitudes of the legislation and policy of the executive branch, especially the Ministry of Justice which since 2015 has been systematically limiting the independence of the judiciary. Readiness to use the courts since these changes had until recently fallen slightly: in 2014, 52 per cent of the representative sample were choosing courts and 38 per cent informal mediation as the best way to settle disputes in general, while in the 2020 study 44 per cent chose the courts and 43 per cent chose mediation (Kurczewski, 2020). But in the case of physical violence *the threat of state justice is considered as legitimate by most people*. The results of the statistical analysis point to a *civilizational developmental lag* which seems to be correlated with advanced age, less education and more isolated living, and is manifested in less willingness to support the use of courts against family violence before attempting other private attempts to resolve the problem. This lag is slowing down the change from despotic family autocracy to free open family relationships.

REFERENCES

Literature

Chełstowska, A (2016) *Alimenty na dzieci – diagnoza polskiego systemu i przegląd praktyk zagranicznych* (Warszawa, Instytut Spraw Publicznych): bip.brpo.gov.pl/sites/default/files/Agata%20Che%c5%82stowska%20Alimenty%20-%20diagnoza.%20Raport%20ISP.pdf.

Fuszara, M (1991a) 'Will abortion issue give birth to feminism in Poland?' in M Maclean and D Groves (eds), *Women's Issues in Social Policy* (London, Routledge) 205–28.

Fuszara, M (1991b) 'Legal Regulation of Abortion in Poland', *Signs: Journal of Women in Culture and Society*, Autumn.

Fuszara, M (1993) 'Abortion and the Formation of the Public Sphere in Poland' in N Funk and M Mueller (ed) *Gender, Politics and Post-communism* (London, Routledge).
Fuszara, M (1994) *Rodzina w sądzie* (Family in the Court) (Warszaw, ISNS UW).
Halicka, M, Halicki, J and Ślusarczyk, P (2012) 'Przemoc w stosunku do osób starszych' in P Błędowski, M Mossakowska and AWięcek (eds), *PolSenior: Aspekty medyczne, psychologiczne, socjologiczne i ekonomiczne starzenia się ludzi w Polsce* (Poznań, Wydawnictwo Lekarskie PZWL).
Hillis, S, Mercy, J, Amobi, A and Kress, H (2016) 'Global Prevalence of Past-year Violence Against Children: A Systematic Review and Minimum Estimates', *Pediatrics* January 2016, peds.2015-4079; DOI: https://doi.org/10.1542/peds.2015-4079.
Kurczewski, JM (2020) *Spór i sądy* (Cracow, Nomos).
Kurczewski, JM and Fuszara, M (2017a) *How People Use the Courts. The Disputes and Courts in Poland* (Peter Lang: International Academic Publishers).
Kurczewski, JM and Fuszara, M (2017b) 'Patterns of Preference for Dispute Resolution in Poland', *Polish Sociological Review*, 505.
Kwiatkowski, S (2015) 'Role of Research on Elder Abuse: Introducing Main Issue' in K Jagielska, J Łukasik and N Pikuła (ed), *Violence Against the Elderly. Challenges – Research – Actions* (Toronto, European Association of Schools of Social Work: EASSW).
Petrażycki, L (1907/1959, 1961) *Teoria prawa i państwa w związku z teoria moralności*, vol 1 and vol 2 (Warsaw, PWN). Polish translation.
Podgórecki, A (1964) *Zjawiska prawne w pinii publicznej* (Warsaw, Wydawnictwo Prawnicze).
Podgórecki, A (1980–1981), 'Unrecognized Father of Sociology of Law: Leon Petrażycki', *Law and Society Review* 15(1), 183.
Słyk, J (2013) Rozstrzyganie o istotnych sprawach dziecka w przypadku braku porozumienia rodziców (art 97 § 2 k.r.o.) Prawo W Działaniu Sprawy Cywilne 14/2013: iws.gov.pl/wp-content/uploads/2018/08/Rozstrzyganie-o-istotnych-sprawach-dziecka-w-przypadku-braku-porozumienia-rodzic%C3%B3w-art-97-par.-2-kro.pdf.
Stojanowska, W (1985) Rozstrzyganie przez sąd na podstawie art. 24 i 97 § 2 k.r.o. o istotnych sprawach rodziny w braku porozumienia między małżonkami lub rodzicami, 'Nowe Prawo' 1985/7–8, s 81–82.
Urbanowicz, K and Bętkowska, M (2018) Prawne aspekty zmiany płci – uwagi na gruncie prawa polskiego oraz wybranych krajów europejskich DOI: 10.32055/mw.2018.10.9: nil.org.pl/uploaded_files/1579518421_09-urbanowicz-beetkowska.pdf.
Zwoliński, A (2015) 'Cultural Basis of Violence against the Elderly' in K Jagielska, J Łukasik and N Pikuła (ed), *Violence Against the Elderly. Challenges – Research – Actions* (Toronto, European Association of Schools of Social Work: EASSW).

Reports

'Ageing in the Digital Era' UNECE Policy Brief on Ageing No 26 July 2021, Policy Briefs – UNECE.
'European report on preventing elder maltreatment', Edited by D Sethi, S Wood, F Mitis, M Bellis, B Penhale, I Iborra Marmolejo, A Lowenstein, G Manthorpe and F Ulvestad Kärki, WHO Europe, 2011, p VIII apps.who.int/iris/bitstream/handle/10665/107293/e95110.pdf?sequence=1&isAllowed=y.

Ofiary gwałtu i przemocy domowej: stat.gov.pl/obszary-tematyczne/wymiar-sprawiedliwosci/wymiar-sprawiedliwosci/ofiary-gwaltu-i-przemocy-domowej,1,1.html.

Praktyki religijne Polaków: ISKK: praktyki religijne Polaków na stałym poziomie | Konferencja Episkopatu Polski; episkopat.pl/; instytut-statystyki-kosciola-katolickiego-opublikowal-raport-za-2019-rok; episkopat.pl.

'Przemoc domowa wobec dzieci', CBOS Komunikat z badań nr 49/2019.

'Przemoc i konflikty w domu. Komunikat z badań'. CBOS 48/2019.

Report by Foundation Dajemy Dzieciom Siłę: 'Ogólnopolska diagnoza skali i uwarunkowań krzywdzenia dzieci' based on representative survey of 1155 school students aged 11–17.

Report by Kantar Polska for Office of Spokesperson for Civil Rights 'Równe traktowanie matek i ojców w trakcie postępowań sądowych dotyczących opieki nad dziećmi – w doświadczeniu i w opiniach matek, ojców oraz pełnomocników i sędziów. Raport z badania jakościowego' (Warsaw, December 2020, unpublished).

Report on the Activity of the Ombudsman for Children for 2015 with Comments on the Observance of the Rights of the Child, Warsaw 2016, str 199-200 brpd.gov.pl/sites/default/files/informacja_o_dzialanosci_rpd_2015_en_-_ebook.pdf.

'Sprawozdania z realizacji procedury "Niebieskie Karty" – Przemoc w rodzinie – Statystyka' (policja.pl) accessed 14 July 2021.

Sytuacja rodzinna i osobista mieszkańców Warszawy w czasie Pandemii, 2021: www.um.warszawa.pl/sites/all/files/download_file.php?file=/sites/default/files/attach/aktualnosci/sytuacja_rodzinna_i_osobista_mieszkancow_warszawy_w_czasie_epidemii_-_kobiety_1.pdf, retrieved 22-07-2021.

WHO Fact sheets Violence against children (who.int).

Legal Regulation and Judgments

Judgment by Constitutional Tribunal of 22nd October 2020 sygn. akt K 1/20 Dziennik Ustaw – rok 2021 poz. 175 – INFOR.PL.

Judgment of District Court in Siedlce of 12-08-2014 (II Ka 388/14).

Judgment of Supreme Court of 09-01-2001 (WA 43/00 LEX nr 550460).

Judgment of Supreme Court of 2019 sygn akt II CSK 371/18 Wyrok w imieniu Rzeczypospolitej Polskiej Dnia 10 stycznia 2019 r Wyrok SN w sprawie postępowania o ustalenie płci.pdf (brpo.gov.pl).

Uchwała Sądu Najwyższego z dnia 22 VI 1989, III CZP 37/89 https://sip.lex.pl/orzeczenia-i-pisma-urzedowe/orzeczenia-sadow/iii-czp-37-89-uchwala-sadu-najwyzszego-520097198.

Ustawa z dnia 25 lutego 1964 r Kodeks rodzinny i opiekuńczy, Dz U 2012. 788.

Ustawa z dnia 6 czerwca 1997 r Kodeks karny. Dz U 1997 nr. 88 poz 553.

Ustawa z dnia z dnia 29 lipca 2005 roku o przeciwdziałaniu przemocy w rodzinie, Dz. U 2005 nr 180 poz 1493, tekst jednolity po nowelizacji Dz U 2020r, nr. 218, poz 956.

Ustawa z dnia 10 czerwca 2010 r o zmianie ustawy o przeciwdziałaniu przemocy w rodzinie oraz niektórych innych ustaw, Dz U z 2010 r, nr 125, poz. 842.

7

The Current Situation for Mediation and Other Forms of ADR in Spain with Special Reference to the Consequences of the Covid-19 Health Crisis

TERESA PICONTÓ AND ELENA LAUROBA*

I. INTRODUCTION

IN THIS CHAPTER we examine the current situation regarding the forms of Alternative Dispute Resolution (ADR) available in Spain together with family mediation and the introduction of the figure of the Parental Coordinator. Family mediation is more highly developed in some Autonomous communities, for example the País Vasco, Cataluña and Valencia, than in others, such as Aragón, where family mediation is only possible within the context of the judicial process. The Parental Coordinator is currently a controversial figure. In some Autonomous communities the role is being introduced with relative success (eg Cataluña, Navarra, Madrid), while in other communities it is not accepted (País Vasco) or pilot experiments have come to a standstill (Aragón). The aforementioned initiatives were completed, with the recent draft law (2021) aimed at the effective implementation of ADR, which goes beyond mediation.

In cases of separation and divorce for couples with children who are minors, mediation is available, but any agreements reached must be approved by a judge who has the responsibility for protecting the best interests of the child. However, cases of separation and divorce involving domestic or gender violence must be referred to the special Gender Violence Court, which has both civil and penal

* This chapter was written within the framework of the Project RTI2018-095843-B-I00: Analysis, evaluation and visualization for legislative argumentation: towards an applied theory of parliamentary justification of laws (AEVAL).

This chapter forms part of the DER 2017-82129-P and the 2017 SGR 151.

competencies. Mediation in such cases is prohibited. This prohibition also applies to cases of gender or domestic violence where the couple have children. This chapter outlines the various legal reforms relating to the protection of children in the context of domestic or gender violence implemented since 2015.

We will also discuss in general terms the changes in the family justice system which have taken place in Spain as a result of the Covid-19 health crisis. We close by offering some reflections with the purpose of inviting further discussion.

II. FAMILY MEDIATION AND THE PARENTING COORDINATOR IN SPAIN

A. Statewide Mediation Initiatives

Spain is a good example of the 'European Mediation Paradox'. Everyone is convinced of the advantages of the mediation methodology, but few conflicts are solved. Compared to the situation in other European countries, mediation in Spain is not used very often. The 2019 Report of the General Council for the Judiciary[1] concluded that the difficulties faced by mediation are related to the following factors: the lack of effort by the public administration in implementing ADR; the lack of uniformity in implementing mediation services in the different Autonomous Regions; the lack of consistent criteria for recruiting professional mediators and the need for better training; and the lack of incentives for the use of mediation by the courts, professionals and the public. This was the reason for a Draft Bill to promote mediation (approved by the Council of Ministers on 10 January 2019) (García Sánchez, 2019: 287–98; Saavedra 2019), which was analysed in strenuous detail at that stage, before possible approval. It proposed in certain areas a mitigated form of mandatory mediation.

The arrival of the Covid-19 pandemic has changed the coordinates. It supposed a paradigm shift. For instance, and even if experts disagree, the Bill to promote mediation has been forgotten. On 8 June 2020 a Green Paper on *Procedural, Technological Measures and the Implementation of Dispute Resolution Measures*[2] appeared. This was a consultation document inviting citizens, organisations and associations potentially affected by ADR to comment on the subject. The goal was to promote mediation and other forms of ADR because of the increase in claims resulting from the Covid-19 crisis. It is about establishing and promoting mediation and other ADR processes without excessive bureaucracy. Part of the aim was to reduce the burden on the courts, in addition to promoting solutions through dialogue.

[1] See www.poderjudicial.es/cgpj/es/Poder-Judicial/Consejo-General-del-Poder-Judicial/Actividad-del-CGPJ/Informes/Informe-al-Anteproyecto-de-ley-de-impulso-a-la-mediacion.

[2] See: ficheros.mjusticia.gob.es/Consulta_publica_APL_MEDIDAS_PROCESALES_solucion_diferencias.pdf.

The latest step is constituted in the Draft Law on Procedural Efficiency Measures of the Public Justice Service (APLMEP 2021).[3] Article 1 fixes the concept of ADR in Spain (known in Spain as *MASC*, the acronym of Adequate Means of Dispute Resolution). In general, the aim – after the pandemic episode is over – is to transform justice into becoming based on three pillars. The first pillar addresses the implementation of ADR. Chapter III of the APLMEP considers 'The different modalities of negotiation prior to judicial process', and lists the following: mediation, which will be governed by law 5/2012; private conciliation (arts 12 and 13); the confidential binding offer (art 14) and the opinion of an independent expert (art 15). It is a generic presentation, focused on the notion of *negotiation*, which incorporates commercial disputes as well as contract, property or family conflicts. The APLMEP does not make any mention of two relevant forms of family ADR: parenting coordination and collaborative law. In order to promote the use of these forms of ADR, the draft law establishes that the parties that go to court have to present a document proving that they have previously tried to resolve the conflict using ADR. This document is a procedural requirement in order to make the claim. The agreement derived from the use of ADR closes the conflict (ie the parties cannot later go to the courts). To be considered as an executive title, the agreement must be elevated to a public deed or be judicially approved.

Meanwhile, as we wait for the evolution of the APLMEP, mediation in Spain is voluntary (art 6.1 of the Civil and Commercial Mediation Act – Law 5/2012[4]). Law 5/2012 allows the parties to apply for mediation and consequently to suspend civil proceedings, but there must be mutual agreement to do so. However, the parties are free to decide whether to proceed with mediation at any stage. But, during the pandemic period, and thinking of the future, many voices are demanding it should become mandatory (Magro Servet, 2020).

B. The Initiatives of the Autonomous Communities

At the same time, the Autonomous Communities are paying special attention to mediation in relation to family conflicts. These Communities are now considering the task of consolidating mediation with the approval and development of specific regulations and by developing public policies.[5] The will to extend mediation beyond private law has been made clear in two regional laws: the Cantabria law (2011), and more recently, the Valencian Community mediation

[3] www.mjusticia.gob.es/es/AreaTematica/ActividadLegislativa/Documents/APL%20Eficiencia%20Procesal.pdf.

[4] See www.boe.es/buscar/pdf/2012/BOE-A-2012-9112-consolidado.pdf. A complete analysis of the law can be found in García Villaluenga, Rogel Vide and, Fernández Canales (2012); Castillejo Manzanares, Alonso Salgado and Rodríguez Alvarez (2013).

[5] A useful overview, despite the existence of later laws, is provided in Duplà (2012).

law (2018). There is a belief that bringing mediation to other conflicts in private law, and even public law, will benefit the use of mediation in family conflicts; it will be a closer option, with more taken into account. Both Laws constitute a model that other autonomous communities are now keeping in mind.

We want to highlight the Law 9/2020 of July 31, modifying Book II of the Civil Code of Catalonia and Law 15/2009 on Mediation in the field of private law (Lauroba, 2020a; Ortuño, 2020: 1–6). This law is apparently a minimal reform, but it could provide a real boost for mediation and ADR in Catalonia. In the Preamble of the Law (§ 4), it is recognised that:

> Knowledge of mediation remains scarce and information does not reach potential parties or stakeholders, legal professionals, which negatively affects the effectiveness of mediation services. Not even information available on the websites, nor the information brochures, nor the informative events, nor the visits to jurisdictional bodies have proven to be sufficient practices to motivate the parties, the legal professionals and jurisdictional personnel to use mediation.

First, the law introduces the mandatory nature of the pre-mediation briefing in two cases: either as previously agreed by the parties or pursuant to a court order. In point of fact, the Basque legislator had already introduced the mandatory informative session in family conflicts in the Family Relations Act in cases of separation or divorce (Ley 7/2015).[6] What is really new in the Catalan law is that the mandatory briefing transcends the merely informative component on the advantages and format of mediation. It includes an exploratory element, focused on evaluating its suitability for the dispute at hand (before the process as such). In brief, the defining element here is the concatenation between the strictly informative session and the properly exploratory session, once the parties have learned how the process works. To emphasise the importance of the sequence, the second part can take place immediately after the first. As the Preamble (§ 8) develops:

> In this previous session, the parties are informed of the characteristics and benefits of mediation, so that they can analyse freely and in an informed way and decide if they want to start the mediation process. Likewise, the possibility that the preliminary session can continue with an exploration of the conflict, if so agreed by the parties, after being heard, an option that can save time and paperwork and bring people even closer to mediation. In particular, the initiative also aims to protect children affected by conflict, their best interests and their right to maintain personal relationships with their parents and with other family members. It becomes, therefore, a manifestation of Article 3 of the Convention on the Rights of the Child, adopted by the United Nations in 1989, which obliges States to adopt all appropriate legislative and administrative measures to ensure to children the protection and care necessary for their well-being, taking into account the rights and parental responsibilities.

[6] Ley 7/2015, de 30 de junio, de relaciones familiares en supuestos de separación o ruptura de los progenitores (BOE núm 176, 24 July 2015).

Therefore, for the legislator, this measure has the best protection of minors as a priority objective.

Second, the reform attributes a greater role to lawyers in order to involve them in the mediation process. The Catalonian legislator knows that it is necessary to overcome the reluctance of legal professionals, who still feel that they are looked down upon by the parties choosing mediation.

The Law 9/2020 prescribes – in its article on mediation principles of impartiality and neutrality – that mediators must integrate the gender perspective in their actions (an aspect to be integrated in mediation training too, as a guarantee to overcome mistrust). Moreover, the Law introduces for the first time a mention of other forms of ADR, in a general way. In article 233-2 Civil code of Catalonia, about the pacts that married couples agree when they divorce (the regulatory agreement, 'convenio regulador'), the legislator adds a new paragraph: '7. The regulatory agreement may include submission to mediation and other alternative dispute resolution mechanisms'. This expression seeks to open the door to collaborative law, which is a welcome commitment of the Catalonian Generalitat, although the number of lawyers who already have a 'homologated' training in this form of ADR is limited for the moment. To assist this effort in this direction, the law changes the name of the Private Law Mediation Center. It has been renamed as the Mediation Center for Catalonia, with the aim of extending its scope beyond private law disputes and even, as the law indicates, to integrate other forms of ADR. Consequently, Law 9/2020 imposes on the government the duty to send a bill to the Parliament within a year for 'the prevention, management and resolution of conflicts' (in sum, going beyond mediation).

C. The Controversial Figure of the Parenting Coordinator

Although mediation continues to be the ADR par excellence for family conflicts, other forms are emerging strongly as parenting coordination. But parenting coordination is a very controversial idea. There are problems linked both to its conceptualisation and to the opposition that its use provokes in some sectors, notably from feminists. For a sector of feminist lawyers, the process is thought to actually benefit the father's relationship with their children (consolidating the father's parental power), to the detriment of the mother. At the same time, some experts think that parenting coordination should be relocated to social services and others see it as a juridical process, ie an institutional way to assist judges.

In Catalonia, parenting coordination is much more accepted; its role being to assist the courts (Lauroba, 2018: 2–69): in fact, it was introduced by the courts[7] without any explicit legislative support. This is a common factor for

[7] It was contested, but the Superior Court of Justice of Catalonia (26 February 2015) determined its validity and its utility to benefit minors, with the help of comparative law.

initiatives in Spanish territory: the lack of any legal norm that regulates the figure. In Aragon, attempts have been made since 2019-to implement the office of parenting coordinator, but the experts do not agree about its potential role. The Spanish government is aware of these initiatives and in 2018 the Minister presented in the Justice Commission – a place for convergence between the state administration and the Autonomous Communities – a proposal to implement parenting coordination as a resource to support families who have suffered difficult separation processes and for the sake of the protection of minors. For the moment there is no general approach, but other territories, such as Navarra, are now implementing the process in the courts.[8]

Despite these suspicions, we think that the parenting coordinator is becoming gradually incorporated into family practice. Today it generates greater interest among specialists. This is shown by the document supported by GEMME and CUEMYC (University Conference for the Study of Mediation and Conflict): *Base Document for the Development of Parenting Coordination* (September 2019[9]). In fact, the figure of the parental coordinator is nowadays becoming the subject of detailed studies in numerous training courses on mediation, despite the notable differences between these forms of ADR. And we also want to emphasise that as parenting coordination is not yet classified as a specific profession, each coordinator practitioner is subject to the deontological code linked to their degree / profession. We can affirm that parenting coordination will be one of the axes of debate in relation to finding the best way to manage family conflicts in the future.

III. GENDER VIOLENCE CASES, AND CASES OF CHILDREN INVOLVED IN DOMESTIC AND GENDER VIOLENCE

In cases where divorcing or separating couples have children who are minors or otherwise dependent on the parents, mediation is possible. However, any agreement must be ratified by the court. This is because the best interest of the child must be ratified by a judge.

But it is important to emphasise that there are some cases which have to go to court and for which mediation is forbidden. These include cases of gender violence and cases of children involved in domestic violence or any form of abuse.

[8] We thank Magaly Marrogán, Coordinator of the Service of Parenting Coordination of the Department of Justice of Navarra, for the useful information she gave us.

[9] *Documento Base Para el Desarrollo de la Coordinación de Parentalidad*. See cuemyc.org/wp-content/uploads/2020/03/DOCUMENTO-BASE-CP.pdf. See, too, the Good Practice Guidelines for the Parenting Coordinators (2020) from the College of Psychologists of Catalonia (psiaracopc.cat/wp-content/uploads/2021/02/2020_ACTUALIZACION_DIRECTRICES_DEL_COPC_PARA_LA_COORDINACION_DE_PARENTALIDAD_30.11.2020.pdf). As a recent useful bibliography, see Vilella (2021).

More specifically, in cases of gender violence, separating and divorcing couples have to go to the special court of Gender Violence against Women. There is no possibility of mediation because mediation is legally prohibited in cases of gender violence by Spanish Organic Law 1/2004 for Integrated Protection Measures against Gender Violence (art 44.5) and by the State Pact against Gender Violence of 2017 (Proposal 116).

A research study has been carried out in the Autonomous Region of Aragon on the difficulties of family mediation in cases of gender violence, domestic violence or child abuse from the perspective of the professionals concerned.[10] This research was done by a professional association of social workers from December 2018 to October 2019. The professionals interviewed in the research believe that family mediation should be excluded in cases when the court has ruled that gender violence has taken place. They are uncertain whether mediation can be in used in cases without a court ruling – possibly because the case has not yet reached the courts. This is currently a controversial issue in Spain.

In cases of serious child abuse, the professionals believe that family mediation is not appropriate because the child is in a vulnerable situation.

More specifically, advances have been made in Spain both with respect to protection for child victims in the context of gender and domestic violence. Specifically, Law 4/2015 includes some specific provisions affecting victims of gender violence. But above all, it was the passing of the Organic Law 8/2015, of 22 July, and the Law 26/2015, of 28 July, *modifying the system for the protection of infancy and adolescence*, which represented a substantial advance in the matter dealt with here.

The most significant modification made by the Organic Law 8/2015, of 22 July, is to consider children and minors under the care and custody of abused women to be victims of gender violence and not just mere witnesses,[11] as they were considered before. Therefore, the civil or criminal judge will be able to adopt judicial measures that involve prohibiting the aggressor from approaching and communicating with the child. In this sense, children come to be considered as *direct victims* of gender violence against them and not mere indirect victims or witnesses of the violence suffered by their mothers.

The child is considered to be a direct victim of gender violence from the moment that the child is present in the place where the aggression against the mother takes place, irrespective of whether the child only witnesses the aggression or whether the child intervenes (ie between the mother and the aggressor). Therefore, even though the aggressor acts against the mother and not the child, in such cases minors deserve special protection by the law.

For these reasons, the Organic Law 4/2004 (modified by the Organic Law 8/2015) for Integrated Protection Measures against Gender Violence now

[10] See Mesa Raya (2020).

[11] See Picontó-Novales (2018: 441–58).

not only has the direct protection of women who are victims as its objective, but instead extends its special protection to children under the guardianship, care or custody of the victims. This makes it possible to adopt protection measures for any child, regardless of whether that child is the aggressor's child.

The Organic Law 8/2015 also acknowledges the possibility of requesting precautionary measures to protect child victims of gender violence. It acknowledges the possibility of suspending parental responsibility or custody of children of a parent, custodian or guardian if they are accused in proceedings for domestic violence. Moreover, the fact that the measure refers to them being accused means that it can be adopted simply as a precautionary measure before there is a conviction for an act of gender violence, without prejudice to the penalties that could finally apply or the decisions that are finally taken in the civil proceedings that regulate parental responsibility or care and custody of the child.

However, these measures to protect child victims of gender violence have not had sufficient impact in practical terms, especially in judicial practice.[12]

In this sense, the State Pact against Gender Violence proposes that shared custody should not be granted in cases of gender violence or if a protection order is in place (proposal 144). In addition, visiting arrangements should be suspended in all cases where a minor has witnessed, suffered or had to live with acts of gender violence (proposal 145).

In its 2019 Report, the State Attorney General's Office[13] highlighted the lack of protection suffered by these children and the need to apply civil protection measures and to supervise them. In this sense, Reyes Cano and Martín Nájera[14] consider that the measures on the suspension of parental authority, shared custody or contacts with the children on the part of the aggressor have been limited because the law allows the judge to decide whether to apply them or not.

More recently, Organic Law 8/2021 of 4 June (also known as 'the Rhodes Law') has very recently been passed by the Spanish Parliament and published in the official gazette (BOE 5 July 2021). This law guarantees the fundamental rights of children and adolescents, whether physical, psychological or moral, against any form of violence. Part of this law was expected to come into effect at the end of 2021 and the remainder next year.

The Organic Law 8/2021 pays special attention to protecting the best interests of children in situations of family breakdown and in cases where children live in family environments marked by gender violence. More specifically, the judge can agree to the precautionary suspension of the exercise of parental responsibility and/or the exercise of guardianship, custody or the visitation and communication regime in order to remove children from danger or avoid harm to their family environment. It also establishes as mandatory the imposition

[12] See Gómez Fernández (2018).
[13] See Fiscalía General del Estado (2019).
[14] See Reyes Cano (2019: 19); Martín Nájera (2020).

of the penalty of deprivation of parental responsibility on those convicted of homicide or murder in the cases in which the perpetrator and the victim had children in common and also in cases where the victim was a son or daughter of the perpetrator.

IV. CHANGES IN THE SPANISH FAMILY JUSTICE SYSTEM RESULTING FROM THE COVID-19 CRISIS

As previously mentioned, the Covid-19 pandemic has been a factor in determining the promotion of ADR. The APLMEP is the best test of the new landscape. It has also been a determining factor in the generalisation of Online Dispute Resolution (ODR). We are confident that online resources will remain. Although we will not discuss the ODR ecosystem (especially online mediation) further here, but we should note that the experts are discussing the best way to use this, and how to provide adequate skills and training for online professionals.[15]

In addition, during the pandemic, public administrations and bar associations have used videos and advertisements in the media to gain publicity regarding the usefulness of ADR. In a remarkable case, Catalonia promoted a free mediation programme during the state of alarm, with the name 'Dialogue and Agreement to deal with COVID-19' (Mediation and Covid-19). It was adopted by the Resolution Jus/848/2020 1 April.[16] This Resolution established the continuation of the procedures developed by the Center for Mediation of Private Law of Catalonia and the initiation of the aforementioned programme of free mediation. When regulating some aspects of the programme, it was emphasised that consultations related to childhood, people with disabilities and other vulnerable groups would be prioritised.

Even though it had already been under discussion, the Covid-19 crisis may have provided a great opportunity for the development of ADR, both from the sociological–political and from the legal perspective (the increase of litigation) (Belloso Martín, 2020: 191–206). But, today, the first step is the real development of the aforementioned APLMEP, which will change the coordinates for conflict resolution. Until its approval, the rest is speculation.

That said, the government has adopted for the first time measures to manage the situation and to prevent the collapse of the courts in the Royal Decree-Law 16/2020, of April 28, on procedural and organisational measures to deal with COVID-19 in the field of the Administration of Justice.[17] Unfortunately, the text did not take ADR into account. As Belloso Martín points out, 'it would have

[15] See Terrats Ruiz and Armadans Tremolosa (2021: 115–28). See also Cerdeira Bravo de Mansilla (2021: 257).

[16] Diari Oficial de la Generalitat de Catalunya n 8114, 17 Abril 2020.

[17] Real Decreto-ley 16/2020, de 28 de abril, de medidas procesales y organizativas para hacer frente al COVID-19 en el ámbito de la Administración de Justicia (BOE n 119, 29 April 2020).

been convenient, at least, to implant one information session on mediation in civil and commercial procedures' (Belloso Martín, 2020: 200).

From the legal perspective in family courts, the RD-L 16/2020 introduced a summary trial for family conflicts (Arts 3–5). Here, we present the objectives of this specific procedure (Art 3) and some aspects of the procedure as such, oriented towards the speed that was advocated.[18]

> **Article 3. Scope of the special and summary procedure in family matters.**
>
> During the state of alarm and up to three months after its end, the following demands will be decided through the special and summary procedure regulated in articles 3 to 5 of this royal decree-law:
>
> a) Those that deal with claims relating to the restoration of balance in the visitation or joint custody regime when one of the parents has not been able to attend the established regime in its strict terms and, where appropriate, joint custody is in force, as a result of the Measures adopted by the Government and other health authorities in order to prevent the spread of COVID-19.
> b) Those whose purpose is to request the review of the definitive measures on marriage charges, economic alimony between spouses and maintenance recognized for the children, adopted on application the provisions of article 774 of Law 1/2000, of 7 January, of Civil Procedure, when the review is based on a substantial change in the economic circumstances of spouses and parents as a result of the health crisis produced by COVID-19.
> c) Those who seek the establishment or review of the obligation to provide maintenance, when the claims are based on the substantial change of the economic circumstances of the relative obliged to pay as a consequence of the health crisis produced by COVID-19.
>
> Therefore, we identify three specific matters: 1. Reestablishment of balance in the visitation rights or joint custody regime when one of the parents has not been able to comply with what is agreed in the parents' agreement or it has been established in the sentence; 2. Review of definitive measures on economic issues (family expenses, alimony and compensatory pensions); 3. Establishment or review of the maintenance obligation.

The notion of a *special and summary procedure* – the description employed in the Royal Decree-Law – is aimed at speeding up the process and making it more agile. The procedure begins by means of a demand, which describes the facts and grounds on which the claim is based, as well as the documentation to prove them. If the claim is related to the modification of measures for economic reasons, the demand must be accompanied by a certificate showing the monthly amount received as a benefit or subsidy (that justifies the claim). Once issued for processing, the parties, and the Public Prosecutor if necessary (the law does

[18] This is not the place to analyse in full the impact of Covid-19 on family law fields in our country (for instance, alimony, custody exercise or parental responsibilities). See as a useful bibliography, Departamento Jurídico de Sepín Familia y Sucesiones (2020); Lepín Molina and Ravetllat Ballesté (2021).

not explain anything more), will have a hearing within the 10 working days following the admission of the claim, in which the defendant will be interviewed orally. In addition, when the procedure is about custody, the children can be heard in a reserved manner if the court deems it appropriate (and in any case, if they are more than 12 years old).

The parties attend the hearing with the evidence they have and such evidence must be taken, as well as those that may be agreed ex officio, as an act of the hearing. If this was not possible, the evidence has to be provided within the time indicated by the Judge, which may not exceed 15 days. Once the hearing has been carried out, and the conclusions of the parties have been formulated orally, the Judge issues a resolution orally or written in the next three working days. In the event of being made orally, the resolution must be documented with a succinct justification. The parties can appeal against the resolution unless it was issued orally and all parties were present at the act and expressed their wish not to appeal.

We must emphasise the time limit linked to these matters: during the state of alarm and the following three months. The initiative was taken to avoid the feared collapse of the courts. We must also add that we lack further information about how this procedure has worked, but family lawyers were sceptical and legal commentators were also mistrustful of the effectiveness.

V. CONCLUSIONS

Finally, we offer some conclusions about the progress of ADR in Spain and likely developments in the future.

It is important to note that there are substantial differences in family mediation between the Autonomous Communities. Family mediation is much more developed in some communities, such as Catalonia, The Basque Country, Valencia, Murcia, Navarra and Madrid. In the case of Aragon, following a decision of regional policy makers (the Justice and Interior Department of the Aragon Government), family mediation is only possible within the context of the judicial process, although the law allows extra-judicial mediation. There are many voices (experts, social workers, psychologists and other agents in this field) who are critical of this policy decision and who wish to see a broadening of the preventive nature of mediation (Mesa Raya, 2020).

The Autonomous Communities with more advanced mediation processes include both intra-judicial and extra-judicial forms; moreover, they are extending mediation to other areas such as conflicts in communities, associations, property disputes and insurance.

There are also differences between the Autonomous Communities in the area of parental coordination. Some communities have welcomed the figure of the Parental Coordinator (Catalonia, Navarra, Valencia, Murcia), while others have rejected it (The Basque Country).

We are, now, at a relative impasse, despite the complexity of the situation in family conflicts and the level of overwork in the courts. We have to wait and see how the APLMEP, the draft bill for the transformation of justice, will evolve. It does seem uncontroversial that different ADRs will have a prominent role. Some experts and practitioners worry that mediation is not given the importance it deserves in the APLMEP. We would like to think that the existence of the law 5/2012, a specific regulation, will be a sufficient guarantee for the legislator.

In the field of family conflicts, we discovered other emerging forms of ADR, such as parenting coordination and collaborative law, which we must also take into consideration. In fact, collaborative law may have an important place in future because lawyers seem not to dislike it (Lauroba, 2020b: 43–60). But there are opposing sensitivities in dealing with forms of ADR, even mediation. Among the legal practitioners we discover enthusiastic mediation (and other ADR) groups along with distrustful sectors. A large number of lawyers fear that their clients would be less protected with ADR, because they, as experts in family law, are undervalued or even forgotten. That is why we appreciate the effort to implicate lawyers in the mediation procedures in the Catalonian law 9/2020, and this also seems to be a goal of the APLMEP. Moreover, in Spain, Judges also disagree on ADR. The European Association of Judges for Mediation (GEMME) supports numerous initiatives to promote mediation,[19] but we find a number of sceptical judges, too.

A very controversial issue in Spain is the advisability of mediation in some cases of gender violence.[20] From an international perspective, mediation is prohibited by the Convention of the Council of Europe on preventing and combating violence against women and domestic violence (Art 48), which was ratified by Spain in 2014. Also, mediation is absolutely prohibited by Spanish Law (2004) and in the State Pact against Gender Violence (2017) in these cases.

Despite this legal prohibition there is some criticism by some professionals, experts and researchers who consider that the prohibition should not necessarily be applied in certain cases of gender violence, where there may be some advantages for the victims, and which might be able to provide more effective prevention against this form of violence. But those who defend the possibility of mediation in such cases emphasise the necessity of taking several precautions. This continues to be the subject of debate.[21] For example, which cases should be subject to mediation? What professional qualifications would a mediator need to mediate in these cases?

It should be remembered that a very great amount of work and effort has been made in Spain to give visibility to the serious social problem of violence against women and to include it within the penal sphere. For this and other

[19] See mediacionesjusticia.com.

[20] See Picontó-Novales (2019: 251–62).

[21] This controversy also exists within feminist groups: see González Ferrer (2020: 225–55).

reasons, considerable care should be taken over the possible introduction of mediation in this area, which continues to be the subject of considerable debate.

REFERENCES

Belloso Martín, N (2020) 'La sociedad del post-covid 19: oportunidad para impulsar y consolidar la mediación' in G Cerdeira Bravo de Mansilla and C Pilia, *Mediación, conciliación y arbitraje tras la pandemia* (Santiago, Chile, Ediciones Olejnik).

Castillejo Manzanares, R (dir), Alonso Salgado, C and Rodríguez Alvarez, A (coords) (2013) *Comentario a la Ley 5/2012, de Mediación en asuntos civiles y mercantiles* (Valencia, Tirant lo Blanch).

Cerdeira Bravo de Mansilla, G (2021) *Aspectos jurídicos del coronavirus* 2nd edn (Madrid, Ed Reus).

Departamento Jurídico de Sepín Familia y Sucesiones (2020) *Efectos del COVID-19 en el Derecho de Familia y Sucesorio* (Madrid, Editorial Jurídica Sepín).

Duplà, Mª T (coord) (2012) *El régimen jurídico de la mediación familiar en España. Análisis de la normativa autonómica* (Ed Andavira, Santiago de Compostela).

Fiscalía General del Estado (2019) *Memoria 2019*: Capítulo 3.1.3 (Hijos de víctimas de violencia de género. Otras víctimas): www.fiscal.es/memorias/memoria2020/FISCALIA_SITE/index.html.

García Sánchez, I (2019) 'Comentarios al anteproyecto de ley de impulso a la mediación' in Barral Viñals, I (dir), Viola Demestre, I and Pérez Daudí, V (cords), *El sistema ADR/ODR en conflictos de consumo: aproximación crítica y prospección de futuro* (Ed Atelier, Barcelona).

García Villaluenga, L, Rogel Vide, C (dirs) and Fernández Canales, C (coord) (2012) *Mediación en asuntos civiles y mercantiles. Comentarios a la Ley 5/2012* (Ed Reus, Madrid).

Gómez Fernández, I (2018) 'Hijos e hijas víctimas de la violencia de género', *Aranzadi Doctrinal Magazine* 8.

González Ferrer, Y (2020) 'Mediación familiar con perspectiva de género. Una necesidad impostergable para la efectiva resolución armónica de conflictos' in García Mayo, M (dr), *La mediación en las diversas disciplinas jurídicas* (Ediciones Olejnik, 2020).

Lauroba, E (2018) 'Instrumentos para una gestión constructiva de los conflictos familiares: mediación, derecho colaborativo, arbitraje ¿y?', *InDret. Revista para el Análisis del Derecho* 4.

Lauroba, E (2020a) 'La Ley 9/2020, de 31 de julio, de modificación del Libro II del Código Civil de Cataluña y de la Ley 15/2009 de Mediación en el ámbito del Derecho Privado: Una reforma prudente con onda expansiva', *Revista CESCO de Derecho de Consumo*, revista.uclm.es/index.php/cesco/article/view/2566.

Lauroba, E (2020b) 'El derecho colaborativo como ADR y como herramienta de la abogacía del futuro' in G Cerdeira Bravo de Mansilla and C Pilia, *Mediación, conciliación y arbitraje tras la pandemia* (Ed Olejnik).

Lepín Molina, C and Ravetllat Ballesté, I (2021) *Covid-19 y Derecho de Familia* (Valencia, Ed Tirant lo Blanch).

Magro Servet, V (2020) 'La Ley de mediación obligatoria para resolver los conflictos civiles ante la crisis originada por el Coronavirus', *Diario La Ley*, no 9618, 22 April.

Martín Nájera, P (2020) 'La Protección de los menores víctimas de violencia de género', *Ley del Derecho de Familia* 27.

Mesa Raya, C (dir) (2020) 'Informe de Investigación, ¿Cómo implementar un sistema de mediación familiar en Aragón' in Documentos Técnicos Colectivos de Trabajo Social 2: www.researchgate.net/profile/Jorge_Gracia_Ibanez/publication/341992345_Como_implementar_un_sistema_de_mediacion_familiar_en_Aragon/links/5edd260092851c9c5e8baed1/Como-implementar-un-sistema-de-mediacion-familiar-en-Aragon.pdf.

Ortuño, P (2020) 'Comentario de urgencia a la Ley 9/2020, de 31 de julio, de modificación del Libro II del Código civil de Cataluña y de la Ley 15/2009 de Mediación en el ámbito del derecho privado', *Laley, Mediación y Arbitraje* no 3, julio-septiembre.

Picontó-Novales, T (2018) 'Contact Disputes and Allegations of Gender Violence in Spain', *Journal of Social Welfare and Family Law* 40(4).

Picontó-Novales, T (2019) 'Violencia de género y mediación' in JL Argudo (dir), MA Júlvez and FA González Campo (coords), *Mediación y tutela judicial efectiva. La justicia del siglo XXI* (Madrid, Ed Reus).

Reyes Cano, P (2019) *El olvido de los derechos de la infancia en la violencia de género* (Madrid, Ed Reus).

Saavedra, M (2019) 'Comentarios al anteproyecto de ley de impulso a la mediación' *Indret* 3.

Terrats Ruiz, G and Armadans Tremolosa, I (2021) 'Plataformas tecnológicas y Covid 19: utilización en el contexto de la mediación y la coordinatión de parentalidad', *Anuario de mediación y solución de conflictos* 8.

Vilella, Mª del P (2021) *Hacia un Nuevo modelo de Derecho de familia. Análisis de las figuras y herramientas emergentes* (Ed Dykinson).

Part C

Innovative Practice

8

Experimenting with a Non-Adversarial Procedure for Child-related Parental Disputes in the Netherlands

MASHA ANTOKOLSKAIA, MARIT BUDDENBAUM
AND LIEKE COENRAAD

I. INTRODUCTION

TO COMBAT HIGH-CONFLICT divorce by making the divorce procedure less adversarial and diminishing subsequent legal and personal conflicts between separated parents is currently a high legal and policy priority in the Netherlands. It has even been proclaimed as one of the Government's national policy goals in the 2017 Coalition Agreement that forms the basis of the current Dutch Coalition Government.[1]

High-conflict divorce was brought onto the Dutch political agenda in 2013. In that year, a dramatic family murder case hit the headlines of national newspapers.[2] A divorced father, who had been involved in a child-related struggle with his ex-wife for five years, killed himself and his two sons. He did so, after receiving a phone call from the police that the mother had filed a child abuse complaint against him, out of fear of losing the shared residence order regarding his boys. This case generated attention on all levels of society and led to a policy campaign against high-conflict divorce. In the following year, the Dutch Parliament discussed the lessons from this case together with a plan to improve the situation for children of (high-conflict) divorce.[3] At the same time, the Children's Ombudsman released an alarming report on the impact of high-conflict divorce cases on children and made recommendations for improving the situation (De Kinderombudsman, 2014). In 2015, the Government launched

[1] 2017–2021 Coalition Agreement *Confidence in the Future* (10 October 2017) 9.

[2] See eg 'Broertjes zouden onder toezicht komen' *NOS* (Hilversum, 18 May 2013); 'Politie bevestigt vondst lichamen Ruben en Julian' *Algemeen Dagblad* (Rotterdam, 19 May 2013); 'Vader bereidde moord op zijn zoons tot in detail voor' *Algemeen Dagblad* (Rotterdam, 6 June 2013).

[3] Kamerstukken II 2013/14, 33836 no 3.

the 'Divorce Challenge' call, inviting societal partners to come up with ideas that would reduce the number of high-conflict divorce cases by 50 per cent. The 'Divorce Challenge' led to 506 submissions from academics, professionals and grassroots organisations. Five of these proposals were selected by an expert panel to be developed and implemented (Schrama, 2018: 680). Although the Government reserved five million euro for the winning projects, none of these projects have been financed and/or put into practice (yet). In 2016, the Government created the 'Platform for Separating without Damage'[4] and entrusted to it the distribution of the reserved money and the implementation of the selected proposals. This Platform, created to bring together all the relevant initiatives and parties, did not however proceed with coordinating the implementation of the winning proposals. Instead, in 2018, it released its own Action Plan containing other proposals to improve the situation for children involved in high-conflict divorce (Van Beuningen and Rouvoet, 2018). In the meantime, the judiciary also reflected critically on the problem of high-conflict divorce cases and published its own Vision statement in 2016.[5] This Vision statement was based on the results of the evaluations of various pilots held in different courts. At the time of writing, there are at least three independent uncoordinated large-scale pilots, aimed at making the Dutch divorce procedure less adversarial. One – 'Joint Access to Court'[6] – was initiated by the judiciary and is loosely connected to the Platform. Another – 'The Family Representative'[7] – is a bottom-up initiative from a group of judges, mediators and lawyers and financed by the Dutch Council for Legal Aid. The third – 'The Legal Counter'[8] – started more or less under the auspices of the Platform, but little is known so far about its design.

This peculiar situation forms the background to this chapter. Many legal and non-legal questions need to be answered in order to understand how and why the Netherlands got to this point. In this contribution, we will try to tackle only three of them. First, we will try to briefly address the problems and uncertainties surrounding defining and estimating the prevalence of high-conflict divorce in the Netherlands. Second, we will review how Dutch divorce law and procedure could discourage or fuel high-conflict divorces. Finally, we will discuss at some length some of the current initiatives to make the Dutch divorce procedure less adversarial in order to improve the situation with high-conflict divorce.

[4] Platform Scheiden zonder Schade (2018) *Scheiden … en de kinderen dan? Agenda voor Actie.*

[5] Raad voor de Rechtspraak (2016) *Visiedocument Rechtspraak (echt)scheiding ouders met kinderen.*

[6] Raad voor de Rechtspraak (2021) 'Procedure gezamenlijke toegang ouders': www.rechtspraak.nl/organisatie-en-contact/Organisatie/Rechtbanken/Paginas/procedure-gezamenlijke-toegang-ouders.aspx, accessed 24 July 2021.

[7] 'De Gezinsadvocaat: Schakel tussen zorg en recht' (2020): www.gezinsadvocaat.nl, accessed 24 July 2021.

[8] Nederlandse Orde van Advocaten (2020) 'Pilot Samenwerken in de eerstelijn': www.advocatenorde.nl/pilot-samenwerken-in-de-eerstelijn, accessed 24 July 2021.

II. HIGH-CONFLICT DIVORCE: WHAT ARE WE TALKING ABOUT?

Despite all the attention, there is not yet any broadly accepted, workable definition of high-conflict divorce either in the Netherlands or on an international level. We have no ambition to present an overview of either Dutch[9] or international discussion on this point, but rather aim to signal the problem arising from the absence of consensus. The Dutch Children's Ombudsman spoke of high conflict if a divorce is accompanied by such tensions and conflicts between parents, that they lose sight of the interests of the other parent and/or the children (Inspectie Jeugdzorg and Inspectie voor Gezondheidszorg (2013): 35 fn 11; De Kinderombudsman, 2014: 16). Elsewhere, he suggested using Glasl's escalation ladder (De Kinderombudsman, 2012: 4–5 and 10) a well-known validated instrument for conflict diagnosis. Many definitions have been proposed and almost every report, study or article uses its own. In order to avoid a kind of Babylonian confusion, we think that instead of trying to develop an all-embracing definition, it would be more practicable to make a validated checklist of the characteristics of a high-conflict divorce and to label a problematic divorce as a high-conflict one if it displays a certain number of the listed characteristics.

The exact number of high-conflict divorces in the Netherlands is difficult to determine. This is partly because of the absence of a shared definition: it is simply not clear what should be counted. The other problem is that relevant specific statistical data is not being collected. Therefore, all current figures come from estimates based on the existing general data.[10] On the basis of the figures gathered by the Child Protection Service, the Children's Ombudsman estimates that 3,500 children are trapped in high-conflict divorces every year and that in the Netherlands a total of approximately 16,000 children are affected by high-conflict divorce (De Kinderombudsman, 2014: 16). Another more substantiated and detailed estimate arrives at a figure of approximately 6,000 children per year (Spruijt, 2013: 266; Geurts and ter Voert, 2014: 72–73). The Children's Ombudsman survey among lawyers found that about 20 per cent of all divorces can be classified as high conflict. This high figure is unlikely, as only about 19 per cent of all divorces are contested. Besides, in this estimate all divorces with and without children are taken into account. The Vision Statement of the judiciary estimated that 15–20 per cent of divorcing parents fail to make child residence and contact agreements and therefore have high-conflict potential (Raad voor de Rechtspraak, 2016: 3).

It is worth noticing that since high-conflict divorce has come under the spotlight, many scholars and professionals report that the number of high-conflict divorces is growing. However, there is no hard empirical evidence either supporting or dismissing these claims. In order to explore the real dynamics

[9] See eg Antokolskaia (2016) 31.
[10] See eg ter Voert (2020).

of high-conflict divorces, large-scale multidisciplinary research is needed. In the absence of any clarity as to the prevalence and the dynamics, it has been maintained that it was not so much the high prevalence, but rather the growing awareness of the harmful short- and long-term effects of high-conflict divorces on children, that has attracted attention to the problem.[11]

Thus, it can be concluded that the prevalence of high-conflict divorces in the Netherlands can be estimated only very roughly and comes down to somewhere between 10–15 per cent of all divorce and post-divorce child-related procedures. How does this relate to the situation in other countries? A 2019 multidisciplinary research into the problems with parental compliance with child residence and contact arrangements after divorce presents some comparative data from Australia, Denmark and Norway (Antokolskaia et al, 2019). All these systems find a small group of approximately 10 per cent of divorcing parents engaged in high-level divorce and post-divorce child-related conflicts. Parents from this group are typically not capable of sorting out their disputes themselves even when assistance is provided. Instead, they litigate. This group seems to be system-resistant, as all three examined countries report that their systems cannot solve the problems of these parents. Parents from this group are often characterised by the presence of multiple risk factors such as drugs and alcohol abuse, severe mental health problems, a low IQ, insufficient ability to provide care, and domestic violence (Antokolskaia et al, 2019: 296, 297 and 313). The empirical research and the study of existing data, conducted in the framework of the same 2019 research, reveal that in the Netherlands parents involved in high-conflict divorce display more or less the same characteristics. Therefore, there is no indication that the prevalence of high-conflict divorce in the Netherlands is much higher than in other Westernised countries. Moreover, these findings give rise to the question whether any changes in the family justice system can help this system-resistant group out of the high-conflict track. Perhaps we should look for the solution in non-legal quarters?

III. HOW ADVERSARIAL IS THE CURRENT DUTCH DIVORCE PROCEDURE?

In 2019, approximately 34,000 formal relationships (marriages and registered partnerships) were dissolved in the Netherlands. Additionally, 21,000 ancillary matters, concerning spousal maintenance, division of matrimonial property, child support, child residence and contact were brought to court (ter Voert, 2020).

Since 2013, the solution to the problem of high-conflict divorce has been sought in improvement of the divorce procedure. Multiple legal, ADR and behavioural interventions, aimed at making divorce procedure less likely to

[11] See eg Antokolskaia (2016) 33.

escalate, more efficient and more problem-solving, have been put forward and some have been tried out. Some proposals have made their way to the legislature; others have been dropped or are still in the pilot phase.

Starting from the major no-fault divorce reform in 1971, roughly three periods in the development of Dutch divorce law – each with its own policy priorities – can be distinguished. In the period from 1971 until around 2004 further liberalisation and eradication of the last remnants of fault were the main priorities. In the next period, lasting from around 2004 until 2013, the main policy concern was ensuring (equal) involvement of both parents in the lives of their children after divorce. In the current period, which started somewhere around 2013, the focus of attention has shifted to searching for solutions for high-conflict divorce problems.

As a result of these developments, the current Dutch substantive divorce law is relatively liberal and the current Dutch divorce procedure is easily accessible and relatively short and inexpensive. The only ground for divorce is the irretrievable breakdown of marriage. Despite some earlier proposals to implement an administrative divorce procedure, the divorce procedure is still a judicial one. In addition, registered partners with minor children have to dissolve their partnership through a judicial procedure (Coenraad, 2014: 371). Legal representation of spouses in a divorce procedure is mandatory and spouses lacking sufficient means are entitled to legal aid. There is no mandatory separation period or waiting period before spouse(s) can file for divorce.

There are substantial differences between the consensual divorce procedure upon a joint petition of the spouses and the contested divorce procedure upon a unilateral petition. The consensual joint divorce procedure is non-adversarial. Spouses can file a joint divorce petition only when they have no disputes, meaning that they agree on the divorce itself and – if they have minor children – are able to make a compulsory parenting plan (this requirement was implemented in 2009). About 66 per cent of all divorcing couples opt for a joint divorce procedure (ter Voert, 2020). In such a procedure, the spouses do not need to prove the irretrievable breakdown of the marriage as, under Dutch law, a joint petition constitutes an irrefutable presumption thereof. Spouses could also present to the court their agreement on other ancillary matters, such as the division of matrimonial property, allocation of the matrimonial home or spousal maintenance, in order to receive a kind of a consent order. However, this is not mandatory.

If spouses have no dispute, they can both be represented in court by the same lawyer. They can also choose to be represented by two lawyers, but this is not required.[12] The consensual divorce procedure resembles in many ways the special procedure in England and Wales. In principle, it does not involve a court hearing and the divorce order, including a consent order on the issues the parties agreed

[12] eg, if one or both spouses would feel better protected if a personal lawyer would review the arrangements and agreements on their behalf, it would be wise to each be represented by a separate lawyer.

on, and is granted within weeks after filing the petition. In theory, the judge has the task of examining the compliance of the arrangements in the parenting plan with the requirements of domestic and international law and the best interests of the child. However, in consensual cases, this is a rather marginal examination. In practice, the judge has neither enough time nor the necessary background information to be able to really assess the arrangements. Thus, in the great majority of cases, such judicial control comes down to mere rubberstamping.[13] Only if something in the arrangements really stands out or if an eventual child hearing[14] gives rise to questions can the judge order an oral hearing in order to get more information for performing a real assessment (Coenraad, 2010: 88–89).

The contested divorce procedure is potentially adversarial. Each spouse has to be represented by their own lawyer. In the Netherlands, approximately 34 per cent of all divorce procedures are unilateral. However, not every unilateral procedure is a contested one. In the majority of unilateral procedures – which amounts to circa 19 per cent of all divorce cases – a unilateral divorce petition is not contested (ter Voert, 2020). This means that only around 15 per cent of all divorce cases are contested (unilateral procedures). A contested procedure is a more or less classical legal 'tournament' in which two parties, each represented by their own lawyer, take stands on opposite sides. A spouse, filing a unilateral divorce petition, has to present proof of the breakdown; for example, aiming to convince the judge that continuation of marital cohabitation has become intolerable and there is no prospective of restoration of an adequate marital relationship.[15] However, irretrievable breakdown as such is seldomly contested and, even if it is contested, the court always finally grants divorce if the petitioning spouse keeps persisting. The real struggle in contested divorce cases is not about the dissolution of the marriage as such, but about the ancillary matters: child residence and contact arrangements, child support, spousal maintenance and the division of matrimonial property.

As already mentioned, the divorcing spouses start the contested divorce procedure by taking written positions against each other. This initial written phase of the divorce proceedings is truly adversarial and merely focuses on the dispute, therefore, it may polarise the parties and possibly turn their legal dispute into a battle that both parties want to *win*, rather than a problem they want to *solve*. These position statements are often substantiated with compromising evidence, for instance aimed at disqualifying the other party as a parent.

This danger of escalation of the conflict is already well known and much is done in order to mitigate it. Spouses are encouraged to resolve their disputes before filing a divorce petition. This may be done through mediation or an

[13] See eg Coenraad (2010) 81–94; Tomassen-van der Lans (2015).

[14] ie, in the Netherlands, children at the age of 12 years and older are invited for a private conversation with the judge in order to give their views on the divorce or separation of their parents. In Dutch, these conversations or consultations with children are called *kindgesprekken*.

[15] Kamerstukken II 1968/69, 10213 no 3, 14.

informal meeting between the two parties and their respective lawyers prior to the formal legal proceedings. If this attempt succeeds, they could resort to the joint procedure. For a fortunate few, who can afford it, there is also the possibility of collaborative divorce with a team of lawyers and other professionals (Chin-A-Fat, 2010). The lawyers are bound by the rules of the professional Code of Conduct of the BAR, stating that the lawyer should bear in mind that amicable settlement is to be preferred to an adversarial court procedure.[16]

There are also specialised family lawyers-mediators, specially trained in mediation techniques. However, every lawyer accredited by the BAR is entitled to represent parties in a divorce procedure. Some lawyers, not specialised in family law, still approach divorce cases as battles they want to win for their client (and not for the family as a whole) (Allewijn, 2020). Even when the unilateral petition has already been filed, if the court finds that the parties might benefit from mediation, they could, with their consent, be referred to mediation before the first hearing. During the oral hearing, the judge tries to de-escalate conflicts and could refer the parties to mediation or another intervention.[17] However, the damage done during the initial written adversarial stage can sometimes be irreparable. The conflict can escalate to such an extent that when the judge finally sees the parties, all attempts to de-escalate their conflict and induce them to work together as parents, would be in vain.

Amid the quest for making the contested divorce procedure less adversarial, there are also voices emphasising the positive aspects of the classical adversarial procedure (Forder, 2019). Even though these elements carry the risk of polarisation and escalation, the adversarial procedure with two lawyers offers safeguards and protection to parties who simply cannot see eye to eye. It is, after all, an age-old procedure that safeguards the principle *audi alteram partem* and the right to a fair trial (Coenraad and Ingelse, 2017: 19 and 40–41). It should not be underestimated that, even though the adversarial process can escalate a conflict between parties, it also offers a controlled environment to resolve a dispute within the limits of the law.

In the end, it should also be noted that parents who have had a consensual divorce are not protected against getting into high-conflict procedures after the divorce procedure is finished. Post-divorce parental conflicts and re-litigation often results from non-compliance with residence, contact, child support and other child-related arrangements. In a sample of 344 divorce cases from 2010, Tomassen-van der Lans has found that 8 per cent of the couples, who initially filed a joint divorce petition re-litigated after divorce (13 out of 171 couples) and 13 per cent of the couples, who initially divorced through a non-contested unilateral divorce procedure re-litigated afterwards (13 out of 102 couples)

[16] Nederlandse orde van advocaten, 'Gedragsregels advocatuur' (2018), https://regelgeving.advocatenorde.nl/content/gedragsregels-advocatuur, accessed 24 July 2021.

[17] See eg Coenraad and Ingelse, (2017) 45; Coenraad and ter Voert (2021) 139.

(Tomassen-van der Lans, 2015: 118, table 5.17). Therefore, the key to solving the problems of high-conflict divorce lies not only in a de-escalating *divorce procedure*, but also in finding solutions that prevent the escalation of parental conflicts and resulting re-litigation *after* the divorce.

IV. PREVIOUS ATTEMPTS: COMPULSORY PARENTING PLAN

Before 2009, the spouses in both the consensual and the contested procedure were completely free to choose between adjudicating ancillary matters during the divorce procedure, postponing adjudication until a later moment, or settling them out of court. After the introduction of the compulsory parenting plan in 2009, this freedom was partly restricted for separating spouses and registered partners with minor children. Henceforth, they have to present a parenting plan together with a joint divorce petition as well as with a unilateral divorce petition. A parenting plan has to contain arrangements on child support, child residence, contact and consultations between parents and information exchange.

Introducing the compulsory parenting plan was an attempt to resolve problems with post-divorce cooperation between parents in general and, more specifically, the problem of loss of contact between the child and the non-resident parent, most often the father. A study from 2002 showed that about 25 per cent of children did not see their father at all and another 25 per cent had poor contact arrangements (Spruijt et al, 2002). Growing dissatisfaction with this situation, along with pressure from fathers' rights groups persuaded politicians to search for remedies. The introduction of the compulsory parenting plan is a good example of politically driven legislation, introduced without any preceding research (Antokolskaia, 2017b: 252).

On 1 March 2009, the Dutch legislature introduced the compulsory parenting plan into Dutch law.[18] Since then, all separating parents in the Netherlands – whether they are married, in a civil partnership or informally living together – should make a parenting plan. The parenting plan is, in essence, an agreement between the parents on the consequences of their divorce or separation for their minor children. As such, it should contain agreements on child maintenance, contact arrangements, where the children are to reside and the exchange of information and arrangements for consultation on child-related matters. The objective of the parenting plan was to make parents, from the very beginning, think of the consequences of their separation for the children and to make legally binding, tangible arrangements.[19] On the ground that parents would be more likely to comply with self-made agreements than they would with court orders imposed by a judge, the legislator hoped that the parenting plan would reduce post-divorce conflicts and re-litigation.

[18] Article 815 and 828 of the Dutch Code of Civil Procedure.
[19] Kamerstukken II, 2004/05, 30145 no 3, 1–2.

Since its implementation in 2009, there has indeed been a significant increase in the number of child-related agreements in the Netherlands. However, various evaluations have indicated that these agreements did not lead to better compliance or fewer parental conflicts and re-litigation. In her doctoral thesis, Tomassen-van der Lans has observed that the implementation of the compulsory plan did not lead to any decrease of child-related re-litigation within two years after divorce (Tomassen-van der Lans, 2015). In both 2008 (prior to the implementation of the compulsory parenting plan) and 2010 (after the implementation of the compulsory parenting plan), re-litigation remained stable at 9 per cent (Tomassen-van der Lans, 2015: 115, table 5.13).

Later evaluations of the parenting plan indicated that one of its weak points was the focus on the end result: the parenting plan itself, rather than support for the parents throughout the divorce process (Antokolskaia et al, 2019: 46). The parenting plan can be made by the parents themselves or with the help of a mediator or a lawyer. However, an explicit link to mediation and other types of support is missing (Chin-A-Fat, 2006). As a result, parents have been left to their own devices in making the parenting plan. Parents also appeared not to fully understand the dynamic nature of the parenting plan and the need to constantly adjust it as the children grow older and other circumstances change. This has led to a great deal of litigation relating to accommodating later changes in the parenting plan.

Another problem is the *one size fits all* approach to the parenting plan: all parents, no matter the level of conflict, are obliged to make a parenting plan. It has been suggested already prior to the implementation of the compulsory parenting plan, that roughly three groups of (divorcing) parents can be distinguished:

(1) parents who are still willing and able to communicate well;
(2) parents who have problems in communicating with one another, but are not trapped in an irreconcilable conflict; and
(3) parents who are trapped in an irreconcilable conflict (Antokolskaia, 2005: 741 as mentioned in Antokolskaia et al, 2019: 19–20).

Each of these groups needs a tailor-made targeted approach. For instance, the parents from the first group do not really need to be persuaded, as most of them have been already making child-related arrangements prior to 2009. In contrast, the parents from the third group appeared to remain unable to agree on a parenting plan, despite the pressure imposed on them after the parenting plan became compulsory. The second group is the group for whom the incentive to make a parenting plan works most beneficially. However, this group would have benefited much more if the obligation to make a parenting plan had been accompanied by proper assistance and mediation.

The sanction for failing to present a parenting plan together with the divorce petition is inadmissibility of the divorce petition (Coenraad, 2014). However, courts impose this sanction very exceptionally and only in the rare cases where the petitioner's appeal on the exception clause has failed. The 'escape clause' allows the court to accept a divorce petition without a parenting plan if the petitioner provides evidence that in this particular case making a parenting plan cannot be reasonably expected (Coenraad, 2014). Initially, this clause was meant to be interpreted rather narrowly: for example, in cases of domestic violence or where it is impossible to trace the other parent (Tomassen-van der Lans, 2015). In practice, however, courts appeared to apply the escape clause rather leniently (Tomassen-van der Lans, 2015: 46 and 280).

Large-scale empirical research into the effects of the parenting plan on legal and non-legal parenting conflicts allowed De Bruijn to conclude that the implementation of the compulsory parenting plan was a noble but unsuccessful attempt to decrease the amount of post-separation conflicts. But it has been too ambitious to try to force parents to come to mutual agreements with regard to their children at the time that they are ending their relationship (de Bruijn, 2017: 62).

Another large-scale multidisciplinary study concluded in 2019, has summed up the findings of the previous evaluations of the parenting plan and added its own empirical research looking into the effects of the parenting plan (Antokolskaia et al, 2019). All studies show that, on the one hand, the parenting plan became an integral part of the Dutch divorce procedure: the vast majority of child-related arrangements of divorced parents in formal relationships are in the form of a parenting plan. But on the other hand, it appears that parenting plans have almost no effect on parents' behaviour after divorce and do not live up to the expectation that they would help to reduce post-divorce child-related conflicts between parents (Chin-A-Fat, 2014). Some authors have even suggested that the implementation of parenting plans has made the situation worse (Spruijt, 2013).

V. NEW FOCUS OF ATTENTION: NON-ADVERSARIAL DIVORCE PROCEDURE

Much was learned from the fiasco of the parenting plan: the new proposals emphasise supporting parents throughout the divorce process; conflict prevention and de-escalation during the pre-litigation stage; and non-adversarial resolution of parental disputes in court.

A. A New Job Description for the Family Judge: The Interventionalist Judge

The idea of the interventionalist judge (*regierechter* in Dutch) came from the judiciary itself. It emerged from local initiatives piloted in several district courts. In the 2016 Vision statement, the judiciary has endorsed this idea and gave the interventionalist judge a crucial role in the proposed non-adversarial procedure for contested divorce procedures (Raad voor de Rechtspraak, 2016: 15–17).

The interventionalist judge model has been successfully piloted, evaluated (Antokolskaia et al, 2017a), and already functions in the current procedural setting. The interventionalist judge takes on a more proactive role as 'case manager' of contested divorce cases. Therefore, the judge receives special training in conflict diagnosis and mediation techniques. It enables the judge not merely to examine the legal side of the case, but also to estimate the level of the conflict, apply mediation techniques during the oral hearing and explore the best approach to resolving the dispute. There are several possibilities at the judge's disposal: make an order straight away; try to move the parties towards an amicable settlement with the help of a mediator; or refer the case to specialised help (such as a course on improving communication skills). During the family proceeding, the judge speaks to both parents and the children – if the latter are old enough and willing to be heard. The best interest of the child is the interventionalist judge's primary concern.[20]

In line with the growing influence of mediation and the increased focus on the emotional aspects of a divorce or separation, acquiring mediation skills is an essential part of the training of current and prospective (family) judges. However, it should be made clear that, while applying mediation techniques during oral hearings, the judge does not perform the same role as a mediator. The judge merely uses mediation techniques for uncovering parties' underlying interests and assessing the conflict level (Coenraad and ter Voert, 2021: 134; Coenraad, 2019: 5; Raad voor de Rechtspraak, 2016: 16).

Another innovative aspect of the interventionalist judge is that the same judge would do all hearings related to the same divorce case – including any subsequent cases on ancillary matters. This continuous involvement allows the judge to get really familiar with the case and the parties, and spares the parties the necessity of telling the same story several times. There have been warnings that such close involvement could lead to a confirmation bias and hamper the judge's impartiality. However, the evaluation revealed that neither the participating judges nor the parties and their lawyers saw that continuing with the same judge as a problem. Some judges have thereby indicated that if they felt that their impartiality might be compromised, they would pre-emptively remove themselves from the case (Antokolskaia et al, 2017a: 80). On the whole, the empirical evaluation of the pilot of the 'interventionalist judge' has led to the positive conclusion that the interventionalist judge can offer parents and children a more targeted, tailor-made approach (Antokolskaia et al, 2017a: 40, 49 and 107–09).

B. New Pilots: Joint Procedure for Couples with a Dispute

Although the idea of a more proactive interventionalist judge is proving to be a success, its potential is diminished by the counterproductive aspects of the

[20] See eg Raad voor de Rechtspraak (2016) 16 and 17; LOVF (2018) 3; Coenraad (2019) 4 and 5.

adversarial procedure. Before the interventionalist judge enters the stage and can try to persuade parties towards an amicable and durable solution of their dispute, the couple has already gone through the potentially conflict-escalating and polarising written phase of the divorce procedure.

Therefore, two pilots have been started in order to tackle the adversarial aspects of the current divorce procedure: the pilot 'Family Representative' aims to improve the prelitigation stage and the pilot 'Joint Access to Court' aims to depolarise the written part – the most adversarial part of the divorce procedure.

i. Pilot 'Joint Access to Court'

The idea of joint access to court for spouses with a dispute was proposed in the Vision statement of the judiciary in 2016. This new type of joint procedure would allow separating couples with a dispute to submit a joint petition, using the non-adversarial joint procedure. This is quite a revolutionary idea since the joint procedure has up until now been strictly reserved for spouses without a dispute. In 2021, two district courts – of The Hague and of Den Bosch – started pilots involving this joint access procedure (Raad voor de Rechtspraak, 2021).

The main potential benefit of the joint access procedure is that it becomes possible to skip the phase of written petitions and counter-requests and in this way avoids the 'tournament model' that potentially leads to the polarisation of couples and the escalation of their conflict. At the same time, the oral hearing allows both parties to be heard by an interventionalist judge.

An important question regarding the new joint petition for couples with a dispute is whether they should be represented by one or two lawyers. The judiciary and the Platform 'Separation without Damage' both propose representation by one single 'family representative'. The family representative is a professional who acts as a representative not for one or both spouses, but rather for the whole family, including the children. The judiciary insists that the family representative must be a lawyer-mediator, whereas the Platform suggests that the representative does not necessarily need a legal background, and can also be a mediator, specialised in behavioural science. The family representative is supposed to serve as the entry to the joint divorce procedure for couples with a dispute. After an intake, the family representative starts mediation, aimed at resolving all disputes out of court and presenting a joint petition along with a complete parenting plan. In cases where this is successful, the divorce can be dealt with as a regular joint divorce procedure without a dispute. If consensus on all aspects of the parenting plan cannot be reached, the new joint procedure provides for a possibility to file a joint divorce petition without a complete parenting plan. In this petition, the family representative has to indicate on which issues the parties have reached agreement and on which they did not. After that, an interventionalist judge will hear the parties and decide either:

- to grant the divorce order along with orders on unresolved child-related issues and a consent order on issues the parties did agree on; or

- to designate the remaining unresolved issues too complicated to be handled in the current joint procedure and refer the couple to a contested procedure where both parties are represented by their own lawyer.

Before its legal implementation, various stakeholders should first agree on the profile of the family representative. Should it be a lawyer-mediator or is a legal background not necessary? In the current pilots, the family representative is a lawyer. Another point to note is the voluntary nature of this procedure during the pilots. The couple has to choose to participate in the pilots. It remains to be seen if the target audience – couples with a dispute that could still be resolved with the help of a family representative – would actually enter this procedure voluntarily. This sampling strategy carries the risk of self-selection bias which could make it difficult to extrapolate the results of the pilots to the whole population of divorcing parents with disputes.

ii. Pilot 'Family Representative'

Another pilot, the 'Family Representative', is taking place from 2021 until 2023 in the south of The Netherlands.[21] In this pilot, the idea of a family representative, representing the whole family, including the children, has a rather different interpretation. In this pilot, the family representative is a specialised family lawyer, who aims to guide parents and their children throughout the whole divorce process, by offering and coordinating tailor-made, efficient and de-escalating legal and non-legal help. In essence, the family representative oversees a family's divorce trajectory from the moment they come forward with their plan to separate until after the divorce procedure is finalised. Participation in the pilot is voluntary. After the intake, the parties are subjected to an initial conflict diagnosis. According to the existence of the disputes and the presence and the intensity of the conflicts, the couples are triaged into three categories: 'green' – little to no disputes and conflict; 'orange' – substantial conflict; and 'red' – high level of conflict.[22] This initial categorisation of a couple could be adjusted over the course of the procedure, following the dynamics of that couple's conflict.

The family representative acts as a case manager and, in the pre-litigation phase, does not act as a lawyer or mediator of the parties herself, but rather directs the family to interventions and professionals from various disciplines (ie financial, psychological and child-focused) tailored to the family's specific needs. If parties are able to make a complete parenting plan, the family representative presents a joint petition to court. The parties in 'red' cases can – if rendered necessary by the family representative – be represented in the pre-litigation phase

[21] 'De Gezinsadvocaat: Schakel tussen zorg en recht' (2020): www.gezinsadvocaat.nl, accessed 24 July 2021.

[22] The different phases of conflict indicated with colour codes are based on the escalation model of Glasl, which is oftentimes used in mediation and the training of mediators. See eg Brenninkmeijer et al (2017) 124–27.

by their own lawyers. However, these lawyers work under the supervision of the family representative with the aim of presenting to the court a petition which indicates the issues on which the parties agree, and presents – in neutral, non-polarising terms – the issues on which the parties did not reach an agreement. During the court hearing, the parties are also represented by these lawyers and the family representative, all bound not to escalate the conflict.

The expected benefits of this pilot are the tailor-made, highly professional, efficient early interventions during the pre-litigation stage and avoiding the escalating elements of the contested divorce procedure, while keeping the benefits of legal representation of both parties by their own lawyers during the litigation. The potential weak points are self-selection bias linked to voluntary participation in the pilot and the possible high costs of the specialised professional help.

VI. CONCLUSION

Prevention and de-escalation of high-conflict divorce have been high on the agenda of Dutch politicians, the judiciary and other professionals for many years. Lawyers, judges and other professionals have been developing more and more knowledge and tools in order to help separating couples (and their children) with the legal and emotional aspects of the divorce (procedure) and its consequences. Since 2013, various proposals for solutions to decrease the amount of high-conflict divorce and separation cases have been made, and various pilots and experiments have been carried out. In more recent years, the adversarial procedure, in which parties are each represented by their own lawyers and thus risk polarisation of their positions and losing sight of the interests of their child(ren), has been critically reflected upon, leading to proposals for a new non-adversarial procedure for parents *with a dispute*. These pilots only began in 2021 and, at the time of writing, even preliminary results are still awaited. So, it is much too early to speculate whether these proposed non-adversarial procedures will prove to be successful in the pilot settings and suitable for implementation into the family justice system later on.

There are worries that no matter what kind of divorce procedure or intervention, the 10 per cent system-resistant high-conflict group will keep fighting and litigating. This concern, however, does not justify abandoning efforts to diminish the adversarial aspects of the current Dutch divorce procedure, in which parties with even a minor dispute are forced to take stands on the opposite sides of the tournament field. The years of trial and error have taught us that every new proposed measure has to allow for tailor-made solutions targeting each specific group of parents with a conflict. In the next two years, we will have a lot of interesting material to analyse and we will know more on whether and to what extent different groups of divorcing parents could benefit from a less adversarial divorce procedure.

REFERENCES

'Broertjes zouden onder toezicht komen', *NOS* (Hilversum, 18 May 2013).

'Politie bevestigt vondst lichamen Ruben en Julian', *Algemeen Dagblad* (Rotterdam, 19 May 2013).

'Vader bereidde moord op zijn zoons tot in detail voor', *Algemeen Dagblad* (Rotterdam, 6 June 2013).

Allewijn, D (2020) 'Naar een vredestichtende advocatuur' in AJ Akkermans, G de Groot and AT Marseille (eds), *Het probleemoplossend vermogen van het rechtssysteem: Inleidingen op de lustrumconferentie van het Netherlands Institute for Law & Governance, Amsterdam, november 2019* (Den Haag, Boom juridisch).

Antokolskaia, MV (2005) 'De voorstellen tot hervorming van het echtscheidingsrecht: naar de vorm modern, naar de inhoud een stap terug' *WPNR*, 6636.

Antokolskaia, MV (2016) 'Vechtscheidingen: Meer om over te vechten?' *UCERF Ars Aequi*.

Antokolskaia, MV et al (2017a) *Evaluatie pilot preventie vechtscheidingen en pilot regierechter echtscheidingen* (Research Memoranda Raad voor de Rechtspraak).

Antokolskaia, MV (2017b) 'Het verplichte ouderschapsplan heeft gefaald, hoe nu verder ... ?' in R de Jong et al (eds), *In verbondenheid': Opstellen aangeboden aan Professor mr. Paul Vlaardingerbroek ter gelegenheid van zijn emeritaat* (Deventer, Wolters Kluwer).

Antokolskaia, MV et al (2019) *Naleving van contact-/omgangsafspraken na scheiding: een rechtsvergelijkend en sociaalwetenschappelijk perspectief* (WODC, Ministerie van Justitie en Veiligheid).

Brenninkmeijer, A et al (2017) *Handboek Mediation 6th edition* (Den Haag, SDU).

Chin-A-Fat, BES (2006) 'Het ouderschapsplan als wondermiddel? De rol van mediation in het nieuwe echtscheidingsrecht' in MV Antokolskaia (ed), *Herziening van het echtscheidingsrecht: administratieve echtscheiding, mediation, voortgezet ouderschap* (Amsterdam, Uitgeverij SWP).

Chin-A-Fat, BES (2010) '*Collaborative Divorce:* de overlegscheiding vindt haar weg in Nederlands' in MV Antokolskaia and LM Coenraad (eds), *Het nieuwe scheidingsrecht: ouderschapsplan, positie van het kind, regierechter en* collaborative divorce (Den Haag, Boom Juridische uitgevers).

Chin-A-Fat, BES (2014) 'Vijf jaar ouderschapsplan: de vechtscheiding voorbij?' *FJR*, 53.

Coenraad, LM (2010) 'Het toezichthoudend oog van de rechter ziet in werkelijkheid weinig. Toets door de rechter van ouderschapsplannen en' in MV Antokolskaia and LM Coenraad (eds), *Het nieuwe scheidingsrecht: ouderschapsplan, positie van het kind, regierechter en collaborative divorce* (Den Haag, Boom Juridische uitgevers).

Coenraad, LM (2014) 'Voices of minor children heard and unheard in judicial divorce proceedings in the Netherlands' (2014) *Journal of Social Welfare and Family Law* 36(4).

Coenraad, LM (2019) 'Regie en rechter in scheidingszaken' *FJR*, 3.

Coenraad, LM and Ingelse, P (2017) 'Afscheid van de klassieke procedure? Vernieuwen + behouden = versterken' in *Afscheid van de klassieke procedure? Handelingen Nederlandse Juristen-Vereniging 2017-I* (Deventer, Wolters Kluwer).

Coenraad, LM and ter Voert, M (2021) 'De positie van mediation en van rechtspraak in familiezaken' in M Dubelaar, L Glas, A Terlouw and M ter Voert (eds), *Conflictoplossing: het domein van rechters? Een vergelijkende studie naar rechterlijke en alternatieve conflictoplossing in verschillende rechtsgebieden* (Deventer, Wolters Kluwer).

de Bruijn, S (2017) *Reaching agreement after divorce and separation: Essays on the effectiveness of parenting plans and divorce mediation*, (Ede, GVO drukkers en vormgevers, doctoral thesis Utrecht University).

De Kinderombudsman (2012) *Ondertoezichtstelling bij omgangproblemen*: www.dekinderombudsman.nl/system/files/publications/2019-Publicatie%20aanmaken/2012.KOM5A%20OTS.pdf, accessed 24 July 2021.

De Kinderombudsman (2014) *Vechtende ouders, het kind in de knel: adviesrapport over het verbeteren van de positie van kinderen in vechtscheidingen*: www.dekinderombudsman.nl/publicaties/rapport-vechtende-ouders-het-kind-in-de-knel, accessed 24 July 2021.

Forder, C (2019) 'Liever advocaten: over de Divorce Challenge en de plannen voor vernieuwing van de echtscheidingsprocedure' *NJB*, 1559.

Geurts, T and ter Voert, M (2014) 'Evaluatie van het ouderschapsplan en misvattingen in de media', *FJR*, 3.

Inspectie Jeugdzorg and Inspectie voor Gezondheidszorg (2013) *Casusonderzoek Zeist: Onderzoek na het overlijden van twee kinderen*: advocatencomite.nl/GRONDSLAGEN/COGNITIEVEWENDING/blg-254047.pdf, accessed 24 July 2021.

LOVF (2018) *Professionele Standaarden Familie- en Jeugdrecht* (Raad voor de Rechtspraak).

Nederlandse Orde van Advocaten (2018) 'Gedragsregels advocatuur': regelgeving.advocatenorde.nl/content/gedragsregels-advocatuur, accessed 24 July 2021.

Nederlandse Orde van Advocaten (2020) 'Pilot Samenwerken in de eerstelijn': www.advocatenorde.nl/pilot-samenwerken-in-de-eerstelijn, accessed 24 July 2021.

Raad voor de Rechtspraak (2016) *Visiedocument Rechtspraak (echt)scheiding ouders met kinderen*: www.rechtspraak.nl/SiteCollectionDocuments/visiedocument-vechscheidingen.pdf, accessed 24 July 2021.

Raad voor de Rechtspraak (2021) 'Procedure gezamenlijke toegang ouders': www.rechtspraak.nl/organisatie-en-contact/Organisatie/Rechtbanken/Paginas/procedure-gezamenlijke-toegang-ouders.aspx, accessed 24 July 2021.

Schrama, W (2018) 'Waar twee vechten …', *Ars Aequi.*

Spruijt, E (2013) 'Kind in (v)echtscheiding, op weg naar verbeteringen' *FJR*, 10.

Spruijt, E et al (2002), *Het verdeelde kind. Literatuuronderzoek omgang na scheiding* (Utrecht, Capaciteitsgroep Kinder- en Jeugdstudies Universiteit Utrecht).

ter Voert, M (2020) 'Factsheet Scheidingen 2019' (WODC).

Tomassen-van der Lans, M (2015) *Het verplichte ouderschapsplan: regeling en werking* (Den Haag, Boom Juridische uitgevers, doctoral thesis VU Amsterdam).

van Beuningen, AHWM and Rouvoet, A (2018) 'Scheiden … en de kinderen dan?' *FJR*, 36.

9

Legal Needs across the Family Justice System: Who Needs What, Where and When?

The Contribution of CLOCK, a Community Outreach System in England and Wales

JANE KRISHNADAS

I. WHAT IS A FAMILY COURT FOR?

IN THIS CHAPTER I will respond to the overriding question 'What is a Family Court for?', by arguing that for a family court to have any purpose, it must first and foremost be accessible to all, so that a judge is able to make an informed decision based upon adequate evidence. The first section will explain the history of legal aid and review the government's objectives and rationale for reducing legal aid. Drawing upon wider research I will consider the prioritisation of public funding for legal representation in the public sphere of family law, where the local authority is a party to the proceedings, compared to the significant withdrawal of legal aid in private law proceedings, where the parties and children may be exposed to the same risk, but are expected to manage the proceedings alone.

The chapter will draw upon my 'Transformative Methodology' (Krishnadas, 2008), which gives central place to the experience of the litigant in person, in order to understand legal needs across the family court system. This chapter will focus upon how understanding 'who' does the court recognise as litigants in person in the court system?; 'what' is the capacity of the litigant in person to conduct proceedings?; and 'where' are litigants in person placed within public or private family law proceedings? – and how this impacts their access to a right to a fair hearing. CLOCK applies the transformative methodology to reflect the legal subject's agency, revalue their capacity and relocate their position across the public and private courts through a collaborative, holistic and community response.

A. Background to the Legal Aid Reforms in England and Wales

Following LASPO, Lady Hale in the Supreme Court presented a poignant and comprehensive reminder of the role of the courts as being inextricably linked with access to justice in the *Unison* case (*R (Unison) v Lord Chancellor* [2017] UKSC 51, at para [68]):

> At the heart of the concept of the rule of law is the idea that society is governed by law. Parliament exists primarily in order to make laws for society in this country. Democratic procedures exist primarily in order to ensure that the Parliament which makes those laws includes Members of Parliament who are chosen by the people of this country and are accountable to them. Courts exist in order to ensure that the laws made by Parliament, and the common law created by the courts themselves, are applied and enforced. That role includes ensuring that the executive branch of government carries out its functions in accordance with the law. In order for the courts to perform that role, people must in principle have unimpeded access to them. Without such access, laws are liable to become a dead letter, the work done by Parliament may be rendered nugatory, and the democratic election of Members of Parliament may become a meaningless charade. That is why the courts do not merely provide a public service like any other.

The principle of 'unimpeded access to the courts' has been diminished by the Legal Aid, Sentencing and Punishment of Offenders Act 2012 (LASPO). The Ministry of Justice set out four objectives and justifications for removing everything from the scope of legal aid unless specifically included; 'to discourage unnecessary and adversarial litigation at public expense, target legal aid to those who need it most, make significant savings in cost of the scheme and deliver better overall value for money for the tax payer' (*Post-Implementation Review Evidence Gathering Exercise Terms of Reference*, Ministry of Justice, 2018).

The House of Commons Justice Committee concluded 'while it had made significant savings in the cost of the scheme the Ministry had harmed access to justice for some litigants and had not achieved the other three out of four of its stated objectives for the reform' (*Impact of Changes to Civil Legal Aid under Part 1 of the Legal Aid, Sentencing and Punishment of Offenders Act 2012*, Eighth Report of Session 2014–2015).

Nearly a decade since the significant withdrawal of legal aid in private law proceedings, the steep rise in the number of litigants in person now seems to be an accepted consequence of the cuts. Litigants in person have been widely referenced in policy reports as a uniform category, and there has been little research with regard to the identity of the litigants in person and the complex nature of their cases, which are often presented as a private matter for the parties to be able to resolve by themselves, leading to a surge in litigants in person in private family law proceedings.

B. The Privatisation of Family Disputes and the Public Duty to Protect against Harm

The President of the Family Court, Sir Andrew McFarlane, proposed a Private Law Working Group (in 2018) to respond to the surge in applications for private law children arrangements. The Private Law Working Group conducted an extensive consultation and produced a report which directed strategies to 'look to the future and to continue to contemplate ways in which the Family Court, and more widely society in general, can best support children and families following parental separation'. Overall, the report highlighted the need for a 'wider social responsibility moving cases out of the court system' and an overall 'shift from private law to mediation' (March 2021).

Wong and Cain (2019), refer to Hunter et al (2017), Kaganas (2017) and Mant (2017) in their understanding of the privatisation of family as 'a neo-liberal ideology of "responsibilisation" where parties are encouraged to be responsible for resolving their "private disputes"'.

Though most academic and policy commentaries highlight that legal aid is still available for domestic abuse cases, my research listening to the experience of survivors of domestic abuse has demonstrated that the evidence criteria for the merit test and limitation of the means test has resulted in many domestic abuse survivors being excluded from access to legal aid, and hence acting as litigant in persons in private law proceedings. Similarly academic and policy reports have assumed that parties have access to legal aid when there is a risk to a child, without appreciating the gap between those who cannot access funding in domestic abuse cases due to the restrictive means and merit test.

Pragna Patel is the co-founder and Director of Southall Black Sisters (SBS), a not-for-profit, secular and inclusive organisation, established in 1979 to meet the needs of Black (Asian and African-Caribbean) women to challenge all forms gender-related violence against women. Patel highlighted the human rights approach of CLOCK:

> Due to the cut back in legal aid, SBS is witness to an unprecedented rise in the numbers of abused women having to represent themselves in legal matters and to the growth of discriminatory religious forums for dispute resolution in minority communities. Both these developments have a devastating impact on the most vulnerable in our society. Initiatives like CLOCK are vital because they can help to ensure that the most vulnerable can access justice and assert their human rights (2015, CLOCK National Launch: clock.uk.net/pages/testimonials).

II. HOW THE CLOCK FOR ACCESS TO JUSTICE BEGAN

Clock (the Community Legal Outreach Collaboration Keele) was started in 2012 by the University of Keele, as a direct response to listening to 'Voices of Experience': a self-help group of mothers who had lived in a refuge since escaping domestic abuse, and now sought to rehabilitate their lives (Krishnadas, 2018). The women had completed the 'Freedom Programme' to identify and understand patterns of abuse, and how 'children are affected by being exposed to this kind of abuse and very importantly how their lives are improved when the abuse is removed' (Craven, www.freedomprogramme.co.uk). Soon after completing the programme, the women received court papers demanding they attend the family court to respond to their ex-partner's application for access to the children, known as Child Arrangements (under the Children Act 1989). Together they shared their fear of having to prepare for and attend court proceedings without a lawyer.

The Legal Aid, Sentencing and Punishment of Offenders Act 2012 (LASPO) came into effect in 2013. LASPO withdrew publicly funded legal aid from all private family law proceedings, ie any dispute between individuals. Legal aid only remained available for cases where the state had an interest, ie public law cases, and in private law cases for domestic violence and child protection, yet critically this is conditional upon passing the merit and means test. The merit test requires the submission of specific evidence, which many of the women were unable to access due to the nature of the domestic abuse. Further many women from the self-help group explained that having returned to work on a low income and part-time basis, they did not pass the means test, to qualify for legal aid, and did not have sufficient funds to be able to afford a solicitor to represent them in court. The women were anxious as to how they would be able to prepare and present their evidence to the court. If they did not adequately present their evidence or comply with the court directions, children could be ordered to reside with the ex-partner, or the local authority could intervene to assess whether the mother was acting in the best interests of the child, with the possibility that the child could be taken into the care of the welfare authority.

Law students at Keele University were studying an active research-led module 'Law in Action' based on my underpinning 'Transformative Methodology', which gives a central place to those who are marginalised (Krishnadas, 2008). The students listened to the narratives from members of 'Voices of Experience' (Whatton, 2010) and prepared an account of the women's journey from leaving a violent relationship to entering the family justice system. This narrative was presented to representatives from a range of public, private and third sector bodies, including Staffordshire Police, the Regional Law Society, the Court Service, Stoke and Staffordshire North Citizens Advice Bureau, the local domestic violence support services (Arch and New Era), and the sexual violence support service (Savana).

After listening to the student presentations, the respective organisations established the CLOCK Steering Committee with a representative of 'Voices of Experience' and each of the multi-agency partners from legal practitioners, mediators, court staff, domestic violence and sexual violence housing and welfare services. The Steering Committee delivered an intense collaborative training programme on how law students could signpost for legal and charitable support, and where this was not available, they could assist litigants in person engage with court proceedings in a new and innovative role: the 'Community Legal Companion'.

The Community Legal Companion was based upon the principles established within the McKenzie Friend Practice Guidance (*Practice Note (McKenzie Friends: Civil and Family Courts)* [2010] 1 WLR 188), which had been developed following the 1970 Court of Appeal case which confirmed that litigants in person had a right to lay assistance from a friend, when they were representing themselves (*McKenzie v McKenzie* (1970) 3 WLR 472). The Practice Guidance sets out that litigants have the right of reasonable assistance from a lay person, sometimes called a McKenzie Friend, who may: (i) provide moral support for litigants; (ii) take notes; (iii) help with case papers; and (iii) quietly give advice on any aspect of the conduct of the case.

The Steering Committee was mindful of a range of concerns regarding the role of the McKenzie Friend due to the lack of any training or regulation, and the increase in the number of fee-paying McKenzie Friends, which has since been summarised in a research report by Smith, Hitching and Sefton (2017). The Community Legal Companion presented a distinct development of this role, by confirming that the student would be trained by the CLOCK Steering Committee to identify eligibility and signpost for legal aid, affordable fixed fee or charitable services; only where legal aid was not available would they assist directly within the capacity of the McKenzie Friend Guidance on a no-fee basis. The unique role of the Community Legal Companion was presented to the Designated Family Judge and District Judges at the Stoke on Trent Family Court, for which His Honour Judge Ross Duggan noted:

> These are very difficult times for those involved in litigation in our courts. Public funding for legal representation is not so widely available as it was in the past but the cost of engaging solicitors is prohibitive. In this context the local scheme called the 'Community Legal Outreach Collaboration, Keele' is a very welcome development. The judges of Stoke-on-Trent County Court have met representatives from CLOCK and we have been very impressed by the scheme. The presence of trained volunteers in our court on a daily basis will provide a valuable source of support for many Court Users facing difficult issues. We feel fortunate that this imaginative scheme is based locally. We look forward to supporting the development of the scheme. (clock.uk.net/pages/Testimonials)

The Community Legal Companions were trained to listen to the litigant in person in order to signpost for mediation, legal aid, an affordable fixed fee, or pro bono support, with the understanding that the legal subject's position might change through the legal process, according to whether and when they may access professional legal advice and support.

The Stoke on Trent Family Court established a CLOCK Desk at the entrance to the court where the Community Legal Companions provided direct support for litigants in person. This support ranged from assisting them to fill in court forms, arranging the paper work, accompanying them to formal proceedings and note taking.

A support worker from the domestic violence refuge stated:

> CLOCK have been efficient and reliable in organising legal companionship for my service user whose case is unique and complex, as she is a victim of domestic violence yet legally defined as a respondent. I know how grateful my service user is for having such support, which has been both generous and vital given her situation. CLOCK is a necessary service for vulnerable individuals who either cannot afford legal advice or aren't seen as eligible for support due to their unique circumstances. (clock.uk.net/pages/Testimonials)

In 2015, following the sustained contribution of CLOCK to the Stoke on Trent Family Court, and sharing of good practice amidst the court service, the judiciary and academia, CLOCK has been cascaded to 10 University Law Schools with their respective community partners to deliver the CLOCK Community Legal Companion training and service in the Stoke, Brighton, Canterbury, Oxford, Leicester, Wolverhampton, Liverpool and York court centres, providing a local, collaborative and holistic response to community legal needs. In 2019, the Family Operations and Liaison Officer for the Judicial Office confirmed that the President of the Family Court Sir Andrew McFarlane

> is of the view that Clock offers valuable support to litigants in the absence of legally aided representation. He whole heartedly endorses the work of Community Legal Companions. I hope that this will enable you to cascade Clock across the UK court service. Thank you for your ongoing work assisting and supporting litigants in these difficult times. (email, 12 December 2018)

To date, CLOCK has been embedded in the training and operational practice of 70 public sector, legal practitioner and charitable services. Maclean and Eekelaar describe CLOCK as a 'virtuous circle of activity which benefits clients, students, and the university, lawyers and the courts' (2019: 166). Yet the rise in the signposting of cases from public services has created a wider concern regarding access to justice for litigants in person in the private family courts.

III. CLOCK: A HUMAN RIGHTS-BASED APPROACH

The question of 'What is the Family Justice System For' is fundamentally a human rights question, as under the European Convention on Human Rights (ECHR) everyone has the right to a fair hearing (Art 6) and the right to family life (Art 8).

Steel and Morris v the United Kingdom (Application No 68416/01, Fourth Section, 15 February 2005) ruled that the lack of legal aid violated Art 6 ECHR, ie the right to fair proceedings: 'each side must be afforded a reasonable opportunity to present his or her case under conditions that do not place him or her at a substantial disadvantage vis a vis the adversary'.

Article 8 ECHR protects the right to respect for family life, home and correspondence. There may be no interference with the protection of this right by a local authority, unless lawful, hence it is a qualified right which is balanced against the rights of the child under the welfare principle to protection against the risk of significant harm.

The Director of Legal Aid Casework has the authority to grant legal aid under s 10 of LASPO in cases otherwise excluded from the scope of legal aid where, in its absence, there would be the risk of a breach of the applicant's ECHR rights within the meaning of the Human Rights Act 1998. The Government estimates that only 5 per cent of otherwise excluded cases will receive this 'exceptional case' funding.

According to *Steel and Morris*, the right to fair proceedings is dependent upon an assessment of (i) the applicant's capacity; (ii) the complexity of the relevant law and procedure; and (iii) what is at stake for the applicant.

One leading legal aid practitioner said:

> We support CLOCK as it is an invaluable service within the area which has greatly assisted a significant number of people. In working with CLOCK we have been able to identify people who were unaware that they were eligible for legal aid and in some cases even identify and successfully apply for Exceptional Case Funding. For those unable to access legal aid, CLOCK has helped support litigants in person within the Court process and also signposted to various agencies to support those people. (clock.uk.net/pages/Testimonials)

Yet exceptional case funding is still restricted to the means test, hence those who lack the capacity to manage proceedings, with complex issues and significant issues at stake, are left to try and manage their case alone.

IV. CLOCK AS A TRANSFORMATIVE METHODOLOGY

CLOCK was designed according to a 'Transformative Methodology' based upon my underpinning research in the post-earthquake rehabilitation in Latur, India, which listened to the voices of experience of women from domestic abuse self-help groups who had shared their views and concerns on how to claim their rights (Krishnadas, 2008).

Though the experiences of these women were distinct in their geographical, political, and cultural perspectives, there is commonality in how listening to the voices of experience of survivors of domestic abuse informed the importance of understanding the direct experience of complex and intersecting needs in times of crisis, as they navigated rights claims within the family, community, state and international legal systems.

The transformative methodology draws upon feminist critical perspectives on how and whether law may be empowering or oppressive for women (Krishnadas, 2019). Sharon from 'Voices of Experience' illustrated the historic concerns of feminist legal discourse (Smart, 1989; Kapur, 1996) in her poignant question; whether it was better to stay on the island of abuse or jump into the shark-infested waters of the legal system? Similarly, the women in the post-disaster site in India reflected upon the dilemma of engaging with the personal laws according to their religion, or to risk being ousted from their community if they entered the family court. In each of the scenarios the women progressed the critical dilemma between the legal strategies through engaging and transforming rights strategies. The women negotiated their identities as women, wives and mothers according to familial and community identities, their complex needs regarding rights to marital home and maintenance of the children and, critically, how their experience was marginalised in the private sphere of the personal laws compared to when they engaged with public proceedings.

The transformative methodology places the experience of those most marginalised to reconstruct traditional rights theory based on post-colonial feminist discourse to question the four dimensions of rights claims, as applied through CLOCK.

Who is claiming rights? How identity may be understood to reflect agency; ie the applicant's capacity to represent themselves, with consideration to the wider context of their identity informed by an understanding of how their gender, sexuality, race, class, ability, nationality, religion, language, age, literacy level and mental health may all impact upon how the person is able to access and engage with the court process.

What is being claimed? How capacity may be revalued according to the applicant's complex needs, the intersectionality of the issues and what is at stake for the applicant?

Where are rights being claimed? How are legal issues allocated in private and public family law proceedings, and how are cases which cross over the public and private courts addressed?

… and critically in the application of CLOCK:

When are rights claimed, understanding how legal needs may be transitional at different points in time?

The transformative methodology highlights that each of these factors are interdependent, intersectional and transitional, demanding a collaborative and holistic system for signposting litigants in person for access to justice.

V. CLOCK: DATA TO INFORM THE FAMILY COURT PRACTICE

Since LASPO there has been an even greater scarcity of resources for providing early legal advice and legal representation. The CLOCK evidence demonstrates that the vulnerability of clients, and complexity of the cases is still increasing, with many applicants being refused legal aid on narrow technicalities.

Between 2012 and 2021 CLOCK assisted more than 5,000 litigants in person, and in 2019 CLOCK assisted nearly 50 per cent of the approximately 100 child arrangements applications submitted in the local Stoke on Trent family court.

The CLOCK data questions and challenges the Ministry of Justice's assumption that litigants in person have access to fair proceedings, and highlights the barriers faced in light of the wider literature on access to the family justice system (Choudhry and Herring, 2017).

If we review applications on the secure clock.uk.net portal, we see that during the Covid-19 crisis, in the period 18 March 2020 to 18 March 2021, there were 212 applications for CLOCK assistance. Of these, 170 were child arrangement matters, 35 per cent had been signposted to CLOCK by the local authority children's services, and 18 per cent by doctors' surgeries, domestic abuse support services, and the Children and Family Court Advisory and Support Service (CAFCASS). The local authority referrals to CLOCK included risks of non-return of the child, domestic abuse substance abuse, mental health issues and parents who had had no contact with their child for over a year. This demonstrates the level of complexity of the cases and what was at stake for the litigants in person, having to face court alone.

A. Who is Making these Claims?

The statement by the President of the Family Division, Sir Andrew McFarlane, Law Working Group, that 'too many parents are becoming reliant on the courts' (March, 2021), led to the Nuffield Family Justice Observatory study, (the 'Nuffield study') to trace 'Who is coming to Court in England? Cusworth et al (2021). Drawing upon feminist critiques of the concept of the legal subject as an autonomous entity in family law (Diduck, 2016), there is a deep concern regarding the assumption that they should be able to able to sort out their own private relationships, without an adequate understanding of the gendered and inter-dependent nature of family relations.

One service user of CLOCK noted:

> I was recently helped by Clock and would just like to email to say how grateful I was to the service!! I have been through the worst 12–18 months of my life and at first I had no help what so ever!! I could not afford a solicitor and there were massive safeguarding issues regarding my ex-partner who was fighting in court with full legal representation, for unsupervised contact! CLOCK was really helpful, told me how great I had done so far and helped to make me feel calm and got me in touch with a solicitor who tried her best to get me legal aid. The solicitor tried her hardest to get me the help of legal aid even offering group therapies to help myself come to terms with things but unfortunately legal aid was denied. Clock never gave up and still persisted in getting me the help I needed and along came the Community Legal Companion. Without an organisation like Clock and a willing student taking her

own time to help I would have drowned in all the jargon of massive legal words and the overwhelming time I spent in a court room! (clock.uk.net/pages/Testimonials)

The Nuffield study aimed to 'build a profile of families in private law proceedings and their pathways and outcomes to enable us to better understand the characteristics, needs and vulnerabilities of the families involved in private law proceedings'. The study presents important findings regarding the upward trend in private law applications, the link between deprivation and private law applications and, as reflected in the 'Voices of Experience' narratives, 'the majority of private law cases are mainly brought by fathers, usually the non-resident parent'. The report notes the need for '[a] more in-depth look at the pre-court needs and vulnerabilities of adults and children including the prevalence of mental health difficulties, domestic abuse and other child protection issues' and concludes 'a key priority will be exploring the overlap between public and private law cases'.

The CLOCK data presents an initial insight into the presentations of domestic abuse, mental health difficulties and vulnerabilities, as the majority of applicants expressed anxieties regarding the court process. Of the 170 applications for CLOCK assistance, 57 referred to experiences of domestic abuse and raised concerns for their children's well-being and impact upon their mental health restricting their ability to represent themselves in the court proceedings.

Wong and Cain note that 'many couples are no longer eligible for legal aid except through the domestic/sexual abuse gateway' (2019: 3). Yet the majority of CLOCK applicants who have a background of domestic abuse have not been eligible for legal aid due to the strict means and merit test, and so are faced with having to conduct the proceedings as litigant in persons despite facing emotional and mental health barriers.

In recent interviews of CLOCK service users by the Separating Families' Justice Working Party (Justice) (forthcoming), one litigant in person facing fact finding hearings involving domestic and or sexual violence, expressed that she would not have proceeded with the hearing if she had not had the assistance of the Community Legal Companion, who had signposted her to Savana for support of an independent sexual violence adviser. The litigant in person reflected that if she had not gone through with the fact finding hearing, she had been told that this could have led to the children being removed from her care.

CLOCK has been critically important in signposting for legal aid and multi-agency support. CLOCK has helped to identify potential pro bono support and signposted to the charitable services for mental health, domestic and sexual abuse support. Where legal aid is not available, CLOCK has assisted within the remit of the lay volunteer McKenzie Friend role to enhance the agency of the litigant in person to face proceedings, and monitor and raise policy concerns regarding the risk of unfair hearings.

B. What is Being Claimed? What is at Stake?

The Nuffield study highlighted concerns regarding the emergence of 'a justice gap, where certain sections of the population can no longer afford to bring private law applications following the removal of legal aid from private law cases in 2013, other than for some survivors of domestic abuse'. Although there was an exemption for domestic abuse cases granted when LASPO withdrew legal aid, the means test has also restricted accessibility of legal aid regardless of the extent of the merits of the case, which remain dependent upon strict evidential criteria. The following summary reviews a sample of the complexity of cases which have been signposted to CLOCK, in relation to domestic violence, mental health and parental separation.

Of the 170 applications for CLOCK assistance, 76 had been referred by the Local Authority Children's Services, Children and Family Advice and Assistance Service (CAFCASS), Schools, Health Services, domestic abuse and sexual abuse services, indicating the rising complexity of the cases. The role of the Community Legal Companion is to signpost for legal aid or pro bono support, and support the applicant in gathering evidence for the LASPO means and merit test. As Choudhry and Herring explain, '[w]hile LASPO largely facilitates the protection of the human rights of domestic abuse victims seeking orders for occupation and non-molestation orders under the Family Law Act 1996 (they) argue it does not protect victims who are seeking financial orders or child arrangement orders' (2017: 153). Choudhry and Herring set out the human rights provisions in relation to Art 6 ECHR depending upon the circumstances of the case with regard to the importance of what is at stake for the applicant and the applicant's capacity to represent him or herself effectively (*Steel and Morris v the United Kingdom* (Application No 68416/01, Fourth Section, 15 February 2005), the complexity of the relevant law or procedure (*Airey v Ireland* (1979) 2 EHRR 305, para 24), and where the '[e]xpert evidence is involved of a complex nature' (*Mantovanelli v France* (1997) 24 EHRR 370).

CLOCK cases have demonstrated the limitations where the litigant in person cannot provide evidence for eligibility for access through the Domestic Violence Gateway. In the Community Legal Companion training, representatives from the domestic abuse service 'New Era' and Staffordshire Police have provided a series of reasons why the domestic abuse criteria are not found to have been met, due to the non-reporting of incidents to the police due to fear of reprisals, the invalidation of the experience as not wanting to 'take up police time', and the difficulties in evidencing patterns of domestic abuse and control and coercion. Furthermore, CLOCK cases have evidenced the financial barriers for accessing medical reports, medical evidence of drug and alcohol testing, and the barriers to accessing mental health reports. CLOCK have noted a further concern regarding the limited understanding of the LASPO evidential criteria for the merit test, from doctors, social workers and independent domestic violence advisers, and independent sexual violence services. One of the leading CLOCK partners in Stoke, a local Legal Aid Solicitor, Anna Brunt of Lewis Rodgers, has created LASPO templates for the use of the local authority, and special domestic and sexual violence support services, to facilitate the submission of evidence for the merit test. However there is is a difficulty for the local authority to confirm that a party is a victim or perpetrator if there is an ongoing assessment of the facts of the case. Further, the litigant in person remains subject to a means test and there is a lack of resources to signpost for professional and charitable services.

As set out in the 2020 Family Justice Council Debate 'What are Family Courts for?' I noted how:

> Our Designated Family Judge was very keen that CLOCK community legal companions were not just welcoming people to the court with carrier bags full of papers etc, but that our aim was to try and signpost them out to services for holistic, early intervention and rehabilitation support through a collaboration of rape crisis, domestic violence services, housing, Cafcass and the Citizens Advice Bureau.

As highlighted within the debate, and as this chapter seeks to evidence, when drawing upon data during the Covid-19 lockdown, the difficulty we are facing is that those cases are being signposted by the under-resourced law firms and charities back to CLOCK for direct assistance in court. There seem to be cross over cases between the public and private law domains, and many of the cases that are signposted to us come from our local authority Children's Services, doctors and schools. So, it may be argued that because of the funding cuts to the professional public and private services, there is nowhere for the cases to go, in which case it would be better if those services were better resourced to support families out of court. But it could also be argued, as I would suggest, that the fact that the local authority, rape crisis and domestic abuse services, are all signposting back to CLOCK, indicates the serious allegations of risk of harm to children and the importance of court intervention as part of a holistic collaborative project.

C. Where is a Case Allocated within the Justice System?

The CLOCK statistics highlight how the question 'what is at stake for the applicant' is related to where the case is located; whether in public or private legal proceedings. The President of the Family Court initiated a parallel Public Law Reform Programme alongside the Private Law Reform Programme. The Public Law Working Group aims to consider measures which may be taken to 'divert those public law applications made by local authorities to the Family Court' which could be 'stepped down', with a focus on: (a) the internal processes undertaken by local authorities to determine whether and when to issue an application to the court for public law orders; (b) the extent to which there is compliance with the pre-proceedings protocol; (c) the identification of 'blue water cases' to be contrasted with the 'grey cases', as considered by the Chief Social Worker, including the increase in the number of children returning home to their parent(s) under care or supervision orders in some local authority areas. Yet CLOCK data highlights how the areas of private family law and public care cases have both been detrimentally affected, with CLOCK going as far as to suggest that the lack of legal aid in some cases constitutes 'a significant breach of public duty in relation to failing to safeguard the child against the risk of harm' (Livingstone, 2018).

During the Covid-19 pandemic, the CLOCK partners developed emergency signposting procedures to respond to the rise in demand for CLOCK assistance and the wider impact on services. CLOCK data highlights the significant rise in the number and complexity of private law proceedings particularly during the Covid pandemic. The CAFCASS regional manager noted an increase of 33,000 cases in private law since two years earlier, and the Strategic Manager of Children Services in Stoke noted the highest rise of domestic violence cases in December 2020, with a combination of mental health and substance abuse high risk factors. Anna Brunt, the Director of Lewis Rodgers, a legal aid practice, noted an increase of 25 per cent in domestic abuse cases when they were already working at full capacity. The Stoke-on-Trent family court manager noted the backlog of private cases due to the Covid restrictions and the increasing complexity of cases – some of which were asking to be listed for a court hearing of 4 to 5 days due to the seriousness of the allegations.

As set out in the CLOCK data, the cases signposted by the local authority and schools indicate cases where there have been welfare concerns and the local authority had initially been involved but the case had been moved to private law proceedings. CLOCK has been able to identify a significant number of cases referred by the local authority to CLOCK. The distinction between whether a case is allocated to private or public law proceedings rests upon whether the local authority consider it has met the 'threshold' of there being a risk of harm to the child, in order to legitimise local authority intervention (s 31 of the Children Act 1989). However if a case is considered below this 'threshold', the parties will no longer be eligible for legal aid, even where the local authority may be involved in the case, ie on discharge of a care order, or where the case crosses over into public law proceedings.

CLOCK's concerns have been submitted to the Local Family Justice Board stating:

> We are concerned by the increased number of cross over cases signposted by the Local Authority Children Services, GP and Schools which involve domestic abuse and the impact on mental health and risk of harm to children. As they do not meet the threshold for public law proceedings they are diverted to private law, though there may still be elements of public law through local authority involvement. Where the litigant in person is not able to access legal aid due to the difficulty in producing and collating evidence for merit, or due to not meeting the means test on the basis of a limited income and due to the DV impact on mental health finds the litigant in person will

> find it difficult to collate and present evidence in complex proceedings, which limits the Judge's role to make fully informed decisions where there are significant issues at stake. (Local Family Justice Board, *Escalation Report*, December 2021)

The Nuffield study has highlighted that a key priority for the family court is to explore the overlap between private and public proceedings (Cusworth et al, 2021). Jay et al (2019) (UCL Legal Epidemiology Group) noted that though 'a distinction is drawn between public and private children law in England, there is evidence that many cases are "hybrid" and children involved in private law cases may go on to be subject to public law applications'. The authors also noted that 'Research that focuses solely on private or public law may miss the true extent to which children appear in family law proceedings in England over their childhood'.

Jay et al's report corroborates the crossover of cases, with the finding that 3.4 per cent of children subject to private law in their large cohort study became involved in public law proceedings within 4.25 years of their original hearing.

In other university CLOCK projects similar concerns have been raised, for example by the York University CLOCK Domestic Abuse Working Group led by Carmel Offord of IDAS (the Independent Domestic Abuse Service). Representatives from CAFCASS and the local authority have noted the different criteria for identifying risk which critically determines the allocation of the case to the public or private legal system, or cases which have crossed over, and whether a party is eligible for legal representation.

CLOCK has submitted evidence to the National Family Justice Board raising concerns regarding the delay in court proceedings and the difficulties for judges in gathering clear and reliable evidence due to the limited capacity of the litigant in person and the complexity of the proceedings.

The barriers faced in the early stages of proceedings have a significant effect on:

(i) delays in court proceedings likely to cause harm to children in proceedings;
(ii) difficulties in gathering reliable evidence for fair decision making where there are significant issues at stake for the parents;
(iii) the impact on social workers having to give evidence and be cross examined by the litigant in person;
(iv) an incomplete picture of the impact of the domestic violence on the litigant in person regarding mental health and control and coercion and the impact on their ability to confidently present their own case;
(v) the CAFCASS or local authority reports may be relied on to make an initial order without providing the litigant in person the opportunity to present their evidence.

CLOCK has expressed concern over the significant judgments which are being delivered to litigants in person at the magistrates' court level without the opportunity of legal representation to present their evidence in a coherent and legally informed manner. In a recent case the legal adviser advised that the magistrates should order 'no contact at all', for a mother who had experienced a mental health crisis, highlighting the criteria of what is at stake for the litigant in person, and the distinction between the right to representation under Art 8 ECHR in public law proceedings, compared to the withdrawal of such entitlement in private law proceedings.

CLOCK has called for the issue to be addressed at national level as the public and private reforms encourage the 'safe diversion' of cases to private law proceedings. Yet once in private law it is assumed the matters are resolvable between parties, without appreciating the capacity of the litigant in person. The applicant's identity, and the issues at stake raise concerns regarding potential breaches of the right to fair proceedings, the right to family life, and the welfare rights of the child, depending upon whether the judge allocates the case to public or private law proceedings.

The CLOCK partners have shared their concerns and proposed that a cross-agency solution is needed for a better understanding of how the impact of domestic abuse on mental health can impact the ability of litigants in person to present the evidence for their case, and how this limits the judge's capacity to assess risk in private law proceedings.

VI. CONCLUSION: CLOCK – A COLLABORATIVE AND INTERSECTIONAL APPROACH TO IDENTIFYING RISK

His Honour Judge Perry, Designated Family Judge, affirmed that '[t]he Community Legal Companion role carried out by CLOCK at Stoke on Trent Combined Court has proved invaluable in assisting litigants in person, *whose voice might otherwise have not been heard in obtaining access to justice*' (HHJ Perry, 2019, clock.uk.net/pages/Testimonials) (emphasis added).

Following on from listening to 'Voices of Experience', CLOCK has explored how the agency, capacity and location of the litigant in person are intersectional and interdependent factors which need to be addressed in a coherent and holistic manner, to understand whether a person has the agency to represent themselves, the capacity in relation to what is at stake, according to whether the case is located in the public or private sphere.

In Sir Andrew McFarlane's address to the Jersey International Family Law conference in 2021 he set out:

> two broad categories of private law case that come before the Family Court. Those which raise safeguarding issues, and where protection is sought by way of court order for a parent and/or children, and those which do not … Cases of domestic abuse, or where other safeguarding issues arise, are in a different category and are already afforded a very high priority in the work of the Family Court generally. It is, awfully, the case that allegations of domestic abuse feature in more than half of all the cases that come before the court. Addressing and appropriately dealing with domestic abuse is, therefore, and must certainly remain, at the very heart of the court's work.

The categorisation of private law cases according to the identification of risk, regarding domestic abuse and safeguarding issues, creates a welcome layer between the allocation of cases as public or private law matters. Yet the critical issue is how, who and on what basis/evidence will these categories will be decided? Social worker managers have highlighted that though the risk may not meet the threshold to be a public law matter, the risk factors may still be high, particularly where the children may have witnessed domestic abuse and may be subject to ongoing control and coercion through child arrangement matters. Sir Andrew McFarlane noted the recent developments of the Domestic Abuse Act 2021 which has further taken steps to recognise children as victims of domestic abuse. The President noted that the Court of Appeal in *Re H-N* [2021] EWCA Civ 448 has sent a clear message that judges should be alert to 'an over-arching pattern of coercive and controlling behaviour', and judges will be trained 'how to conduct fact-finding hearings in a way that focuses on coercive and controlling behaviour, avoids slavish adherence to a Scott schedule of allegations, yet keeps the timing of any such hearing within reasonable and proportionate bounds' and, critically, to understand and 'enhance each judge's understanding of the traumatic nature of domestic abuse upon victims, and the impact that such trauma may have on their ability to participate in proceedings' (McFarlane, 2021).

Although McFarlane noted that 'domestic violence is in a different category', it is essential that this category is provided with the same resources of public funding as those within public care proceedings to support litigants to be able to present their case. CLOCK has recommended that in order for the litigants to be able to present the evidence in fact finding hearings, public funding should be available where orders are made for medical reports, mental health assessments, drug and alcohol testing, and supervised contact. CLOCK has also argued that there should also be legal representation in fact finding hearings to enable the court to gather the required evidence to prioritise the welfare of the parties and the child. Overall CLOCK advocates that public funding should be available for all cases in private and public care proceedings which involve allegations of domestic abuse, and or social work assessments for supervised contact, special guardianship orders, interim care orders, supervision orders and family assistance orders.

CLOCK submitted the evidence to the Ministry of Justice LASPO Review, after which Lucy Frazer QC, MP, Parliamentary Under Secretary of State for Justice accepted that:

> '[t]he CLOCK evidence submission has raised particular issues with the financial eligibility test in family which demands; i) a comprehensive review of the legal aid means testing thresholds, ii) proposals for extending eligibility for non-means tested legal aid for parents, or those with parental responsibility, who wish to oppose applications for placement orders or adoption orders in public family law proceedings and iii) to expand the scope of legal aid to cover special guardianship orders, hence extending public funding for private family law.

The recommendations noted:

> Beyond legal aid, we have announced a number of policies that build on the evidence received from CLOCK, and other organisations; …
>
> For instance, the excellent work that CLOCK does in supporting people to resolve their legal problems underlines the value of effective signposting, coordination and advertising of the support already available. As such, we are undertaking a pilot to explore how we can better coordinate and signpost legal support, as well as launching an awareness campaign for legal support and legal aid.

Hence, the overriding question 'What is the Family Court For?' demands an engaged and collaborative triage and signposting of cases according to the risk factors within the case, according to the needs of the litigant in person, the complexity of the case and what is at stake for the litigant in person. Based upon listening to Voices of Experience, this chapter proposes a collaborative, intersectional and holistic system to signpost applicants to multi-agencies to support their complex needs, and to identify and assess risk for parents and children against the risk of harm. The answer to the question returns to the overriding public duty of the state to make public funding available to ensure litigants have the resources to effectively present their case to enable the family court to make fair and informed decisions to safeguard parents and children from the risk of harm.

REFERENCES

Reports/Resources

CLOCK, 'Testimonials': clock.uk.net/pages/Testimonials.

Craven, P, 'The Freedom Programme': freedomprogramme.co.uk/lwd.php.

House of Commons Justice Committee (2015) *Impact of Changes to Civil Legal Aid under Part 1 of the Legal Aid Sentencing Punishment of Offenders Act 2012*, Eighth Report of Session 2014–2015.

Justice Working Party (forthcoming) 'Improving Access to Justice for Separating Families', Justice Working Party.

Krishnadas, J (2021) 'Falling through the Public and Private Divide in Family Law', Social and Legal Studies Association Conference, April 2021: www.youtube.com/watch?v=OYtyNNqwzbk.

Livingstone, E (2018) 'Devastating' Sector responds to LASPO Review, The Justice Gap: www.thejusticegap.com/devastating-legal-aid-sector-responds-to-laspo-review, October 2018.

Local Family Justice Board, *Escalation Report*, December 2021.

McFarlane, Sir A (2021) 'Supporting Families in Conflict: There is a Better Way', Address by Sir Andrew McFarlane to the Jersey International Family Law Conference 2021.

Ministry of Justice (2018) *Post-Implementation Review Evidence Gathering Exercise. Terms of Reference* ('Ministry of Justice LASPO Review').

Private Law Working Group (March 2020): www.judiciary.uk/announcements/message-from-the-president-of-the-family-division-private-law-working-group-report.
Public Law Working Group (March 2021): www.judiciary.uk/wp-content/uploads/2021/03/March-2021-report-final_clickable.pdf.

Articles

Choudhry, S and Herring, J (2017) 'A Human Right to Legal Aid? The Implications of Changes to the Legal Aid Scheme for Victims of Domestic Abuse', *Journal of Social Welfare and Family Law* 39(2), 152–67.
Cusworth, L, et al (2021). *Uncovering Private Family Law: Who's Coming to Court in England?* Summary (London, Nuffield Family Justice Observatory).
Diduck, A (2016) 'Autonomy and Family Justice', *Child and Family Law Quarterly* 133.
Hunter, R, et al (2017) 'Access to What? LASPO and Mediation' in A Flynn and J Hodgson (eds), *Access to Justice and Legal Aid: Comparative Perspective on Unmet Legal Need* (Oxford, Hart Publishing) 239–54.
Jay, M, Pearson, R, Wijlaars, L, Olhede, S and Gilbert, R (2019) 'Using Administrative Data to Quantify Overlaps between Public and Private Children Law in England' (UCL Legal Epidemiology Group).
Kaganas, F (2017) 'Justifying the LASPO Act; Authenticity, Necessity, Suitability, Responsibility, and Autonomy', *Journal of Social Welfare and Family Law* 39(2), 168–88–88.
Kapur, R and Cossman, B, *Subversive Sites* (Sage, New Delhi).
Krishnadas, J (2008) 'Rights as the Intersections: Rebuilding Cultural, Material and Spatial Spheres – A Transformative Methodology' in R Dasgupta (ed), *Cultural Practices, Political Possibilities* (Cambridge Scholars).
Krishnadas, J (2018) 'CLOCK: "The Community Legal Companion" as an Agent of Change: A Transformative Methodology' in L Thomas et al (eds), *Reimagining Legal Education* (Oxford, Hart Publishing).
Krishnadas, J (2019) 'From East to West, Can Feminist Legal Strategies be Transformative? Post-Disaster to Everyday Times of Crisis', *Jindal Global Law Review* 10, 247–68.
Maclean, M and Eekelaar, J (2019), *After the Act, Access to Family Justice after LASPO* (Oxford, Hart Publishing).
Mant, J (2017) 'Neoliberalism, Family Law and the Cost of Access to Justice', *Journal of Social Welfare and Family Law* 39(2), 246–58.
Smart, C (1989) *Feminism and the Power of Law* (London, Routledge).
Smith, L, Hitchings, E and Sefton, M (2017), 'Fee-charging McKenzie Friends in Private Family Law Cases: Key Findings from the Research Report', *Family Law* 971.
Whatton, M (2010) *Beaten Down, Rising Up, Standing Tall* (Voices of Experience).
Wong, S and Cain, R (2019) 'The Impact of Cuts in Legal Aid Funding of Private Family Law Cases', *Journal of Social Welfare and Family Law* 41(1).

Part D

Major Policy Change

10

Developing Holistic and Inclusive Family Justice in Argentina

JULIETA MAROTTA*

I. INTRODUCTION

THIS STUDY LOOKS at how family law has embraced working with other disciplines to enable victims of domestic violence achieve access to justice in Buenos Aires, Argentina. Roderick A Macdonald analysed the understanding of the concept of access to civil justice and identified five waves (Macdonald, 2010: 492–521). The fifth and most recent wave recognised a holistic and inclusive understanding of access to justice (Macdonald, 2010: 507–08). It is important to consider how laws are drafted and administrated, as well as how other disciplines (together with the law) can assist in achieving conflict resolution. Therefore, the term 'access to justice' broadens its boundaries to include enabling conflict resolution and societal order. Access to justice recognises the importance of the law, and the courts and judges value international law and constitutional principles, multidisciplinary assistance and the active participation of parties. This study focuses on understanding how multidisciplinary assistance is perceived within the fifth wave, and uses Buenos Aires, Argentina, as a case study to understand this relationship.

In Buenos Aires, the fifth wave of access to justice began to emerge with the developments of laws and the way access to justice is understood. In this context, multidisciplinary assistance developed within the law and its administration as an essential tool for approaching domestic violence cases in a holistic manner (Masciotra, 2020: section X).

Domestic laws in Buenos Aires recognise that domestic violence cases demand a particular response in order to ensure that victims obtain proper access to justice (Bruce et al, 2007: 12, 14–16, 19, 35; Commission on Legal

* The author is grateful to Soledad Barbona for her contribution to the understanding of the design and functioning of the Family Court in the Province of Buenos Aires. Moreover, the author is grateful to all the interviewees for their contribution to this research.

Empowerment of the Poor, 2008: 43; Van De Meene and Van Rooij, 2008: 6–8; Gramatikov and Porter, 2010: 26–27). As mentioned by a prosecutor expert on domestic violence in an interview, 'the problem of domestic violence is very dynamic because it is an issue that is becoming increasingly relevant in different societies, in the media, and we are constantly experiencing a change in jurisprudence.' Moreover, victims need 'access to a well-functioning' judicial system (Commission on Legal Empowerment of the Poor, 2008: foreword) where providers are trained to understand domestic violence cases and grant victims a chance to enforce their rights (Bruce et al, 2007: 13). Victims need to be provided with viable ways to overcome obstacles that may inhibit or deter their access to justice; for example, physical distance, opening hours, costs, delays, complexities in the judicial system and legal procedure, and sociocultural obstacles (Macdonald, 2010: 510–15). Furthermore, they need to be given viable opportunities and chances to fully pursue their legal rights; for example, the flexibility to work with parties in the search for remedies (Van De Meene and Van Rooij, 2008: 10–11, 15–16).

Different justice systems implement different legal and structural responses to domestic violence. Some systems of justice, such as those in Ontario (Canada) and New York (US), have incorporated an integrated approach to domestic violence cases, through the Integrated Domestic Violence Courts, to centralise legal claims and the delivery of assistance (National Institute of Justice; Ontario Court of Justice). Other justice systems, such as that of Buenos Aires, Argentina, maintain the system's division between the criminal and civil aspects of cases but incorporate elements designed to expand the legal assistance offered, aiming for a more holistic approach to the problem. In both types, the resolution of conflicts is not limited to a court decision based on legal reasoning and experts from different disciplines are consulted to assist in the formation of the decision.

The current policy approach to access to justice in Buenos Aires, Argentina, considers the need for a holistic understanding of the problem of domestic violence, which calls for multidisciplinary interventions. Therefore, a number of policy initiatives have been implemented to incorporate the holistic approach. This study analyses those policy interventions to understand how family law has welcomed cooperation with other disciplines in order to provide victims of domestic violence with access to justice. The study also relies on empirical evidence to understand the impact of such policy initiatives by justice providers on victims of domestic violence.

II. METHODOLOGY

This study uses qualitative methods to answer the research question and follows a case study approach in Buenos Aires, Argentina. This jurisdiction was selected due to the number of policies implemented in recent decades to improve the rights of access to justice for victims.

A legal analysis was undertaken to understand how the law incorporated the holistic approach to domestic violence and multidisciplinary assistance. Moreover, the justice system was described in order to show how organisations were designed to respond to the holistic approach to domestic violence and multidisciplinary assistance. Lastly, an empirical analysis was conducted to address how justice providers and victims reacted to multidisciplinary assistance.

The legal analysis looks at laws enacted in the City of Buenos Aires (hereinafter, City) and applicable to the Public Prosecutor's Office and laws enacted in the Province of Buenos Aires (hereinafter, Province) and applicable to the Family Courts. This approach allowed us to look at the incorporation of multidisciplinary assistance as applicable to the Public Prosecutor's Office and the Family Courts. The laws analysed are: (i) Civil and Commercial Code of 2015, article 706 (hereinafter, the Code) (Congreso de la Nación Argentina, 2014); (ii) Federal Law 24417 of 1994: Law against Domestic Violence (hereinafter, Law 24417); (iii) Federal Law 26485 of 2009: Law on the Right of Women to Live Free of Violence (hereinafter, Law 26485); (iv) Provincial Law 12569 of 2001: Law on Family Violence (hereinafter, Law 12569); (v) Internal Regulation 16 adopted by the Public Prosecutor's Office of 2010 to assess, assist, and intervene in domestic violence complaints (hereinafter, Internal Regulation).

The description of the justice system looks at the Public Prosecutor's Office for the City (hereinafter, PPO) and its multidisciplinary office known as the Victims and Witness Assistance Office. This is a multidisciplinary office tasked with providing immediate intervention in domestic violence cases involving the PPO (Internal Regulation). It also looks at the Family Courts of the Province (hereinafter, Family Courts), which are composed of a judge, a family counsellor and a multidisciplinary support team composed of one psychiatrist, one sociologist and three social workers (*Cuerpo Técnico Auxiliar*) (Law 11453, 1993 which creates Family Courts).

The empirical section includes the results of in-depth interviews with justice providers and victims.[1] Some of the interview questions were open-ended, while others were semi-structured. In both instances, leading questions were not used.

The justice providers consist of specialised prosecutors tasked with handling high-risk domestic violence cases at the PPO, which includes criminal judges with jurisdiction in the City and family judges and secretaries with jurisdiction in the Province. The sample is composed of: (i) in-depth interviews undertaken between 2012 and 2014 with the four specialised prosecutors at the PPO: 'JP[identification number]'. Interviews with specialised prosecutors were

[1] With the exception of the interviews undertaken with family judges and secretaries, the data used for this study was collected for the doctoral thesis of the author. For a comprehensive description of the data and the method used to collect it, see Julieta Marotta, 2017, Access to Justice and Legal Empowerment of Victims of Domestic Violence through Legal Organizations in the City: A Qualitative Empirical Legal Study, PhD dissertation Maastricht University/United Nations University, chapter 2 section 2.2 (www.merit.unu.edu/about-us/profile/?staff_id=1594&stage=2#pub).

enriched by input from interviews with the multidisciplinary group that works at the Victims and Witness Assistance Office: 'SP[identification number]'; (ii) two interviews with male criminal judges conducted in 2014: 'CrimJ[identification number]'; (iii) one interview conducted with a family judge and two interviews with secretaries to the family judge in 2019: 'FamJ[identification number]'. One of the two secretaries was interviewed five times between 2019 and 2021 with follow up questions as this study progressed.

The selection of the sample of criminal judges was chosen using a convenience sample constructed from recommendations by a gate keeper, who was a lawyer working at the PPO in the design of the Victims and Witness Assistance Office. As a result, the sample is not representative of the entire population of judges, but it does aid in understanding the perceptions of judges.

The selection of the sample of family judges was based on the commitment of judges and secretaries to incorporate a holistic approach to domestic violence. Hence, the results of this section reflect best practices.

In-depth interviews were conducted with 54 victims who obtained access to the PPO between 2012 and 2014. Interviews with victims were identified as 'V[1 or 2 making reference to the first or second interview] [identification number]'. Thirty-one out of the 54 victims who agreed to the first interview at the PPO also took part in a second interview. The majority of these second interviews were conducted over the telephone, to avoid asking victims to travel to the PPO. Observations and fieldwork notes were also used to track contextual information, perceptions and the main lessons learned. Field notes were also used to prepare for future interviews, as well as to analyse and triangulate data.

III. LEGAL FRAMEWORK AND JUSTICE SYSTEM

This section analyses how the legal framework and justice systems of the City and Province incorporated multidisciplinary assistance to rule on domestic violence cases. The multidisciplinary teams at the PPO were incorporated by the Internal Regulation that created the Victims and Witness Assistance Office, whereas they were incorporated by provincial law in the Family Courts. In both cases, these incorporations were motivated by Law 24417, Law 26485 and international standards that recognise that in domestic violence cases the full repair of the damage exceeds the legal sphere. As a result, legal remedies (such as child support, divorce, probation or incarceration) are being broadened to include welfare, economic and psychological health-related remedies (UNGA, 2005: art 10).

The main changes in the legal framework started in 1994 with Law 24417. The drafting of Law 24417 was motivated by article 14bis of the Argentine Constitution, which addresses, among other things, the duty of the state to provide holistic protection to the family (Fernández Touriño, 2003; Medina, Yuba and González Magaña, 2013: 362). Law 24417 requires judges to evaluate the risks using a diagnosis of inter-family relations drafted by a multidisciplinary group composed by experts in family violence (Law 24417, art 6; Law 26485 art 29; Medina, Yuba and González Magaña, 2013: 262–63, 335).

Law 24417 introduced the formation of the multidisciplinary team, but it does not address the specific disciplinary composition, nor does it oblige judges to make use of them (24417, art 3, 6–7; Medina, Yuba and González Magaña, 2013: 332, 335–36). Law 12569 for the Province, on the other hand, commands judges to rely on an interdisciplinary report to determine the damage suffered by victims and allows them to request reports from experts of other civil societies (Law 12569, art 8, 29; Medina, Yuba and González Magaña, 2013: 334). Moreover, the Executive Order of Law 24417 instructs the creation of information and advice centres located in hospitals, as well as the creation of judicial assistance centres and the National Council of Women to ensure a holistic approach to domestic violence (Executive Order 235/1996). The diagnosis made by the multidisciplinary team is intended to assist judges rather than overrule the rights recognised in substantive law nor the legal procedure (Medina, Yuba and González Magaña, 2013: 263). Judges can contest these reports (Law 24417, art 3; Medina, Yuba and González Magaña, 2013: 332).

In 2009, Law 26485 introduced more tools for women to enforce their right to a life free of discrimination and violence. The law calls for a transparent and expeditious proceeding by creating specialised and multidisciplinary state organisations. It guarantees a holistic approach to the assistance of victims, defined as services in charge of 'preventing, detecting, recording and approaching the different types and ways of violence against women, according to the different communities' (Executive Order 1011/2010, art 10). Further, the law specifies the need for a multidisciplinary team of professionals, as well as incorporating the need to provide training to providers (Law 26485, art 10).

Law 26485 assigned to the National Council of Women the creation of organisations that can provide multidisciplinary and free assistance to victims of gender violence (Law 26485, art 9). In addition to this, the executive is called on to promote and strengthen the creation of state and non-state organisations to implement a holistic approach to gender violence (Law 26485, art 11).

In 2015, a new Code took effect in Argentina.[2] The Code recognises the particularities of family procedures and the need to regulate resulting specificities (De la Rúa, 2012; Medina, 2012: 440–49). The Code therefore includes the principle of equality by recognising human diversity (Lorenzetti, 2012; Lorenzetti, Highton de Nolasco and Kemelmajer de Carlucci, 2012: 4), and incorporates general principles for family procedures. Article 706 states that the process in family matters should respect the principles of effective judicial

[2] This paragraph is borrowed partly, and sometimes verbatim, from the work of Marotta and Parise, 'On Codes, Marriage, and Access to Justice: Recent Developments in the Law of Argentina'; Congreso de la Nación Argentina, *Código Civil y Comercial Argentino.*

protection and require family judges to be specialised and engage with a multidisciplinary team for consultation (Castillo and Carol Lugones, 2008; De la Rúa, 2012: 2; Medina, 2012: 446–47).

These changes in the law have had consequences for the design of the justice system. For example, the PPO and the Family Courts were adjusted to respond to the holistic approach to domestic violence and the multidisciplinary assistance. The PPO created the Victims and Witness Assistance Office (hereinafter, Office). The Office allows victims the possibility to meet with a lawyer, a psychologist and a social worker. This multidisciplinary team meets with the victim to discuss the conflict and drafts a report that is referred to the public prosecutor.

The Family Courts also rely on this team of experts who evaluate the characteristics of the cases, assess the damage and risk and send a report to the judge. These reports assist judges in granting holistic and timely measures to prevent the problem from escalating and in achieving a long-term solution (Medina, Yuba and González Magaña, 2013: 342–62).

Multidisciplinary reports help the courts to provide preventive and comprehensive assessments (JP1a). Therefore, prosecutors can dedicate more time to conducting in-depth investigations, finding ways to gather evidence in order to bring cases to trial, receiving training on the dynamics and characteristics of domestic violence and utilising all available tools to resolve this multidimensional type of conflict. Furthermore, family judges can make expedited decisions that can protect the victim from an increase in the likelihood of being harmed. However, the PPO does not have the capacity for granting long-term assistance and can instead refer victims to other organisations that do. The Family Courts have a number of legal options at their disposal to follow-up on cases (for example, setting up hearings to understand how a therapy is going, arranging for the installation of a panic button) and a long term solution is more feasible when parties are engaged in the treatments (FamJ001; FamJ002; FamJ003). Hence, the multidisciplinary teams assist justice providers in making short term decisions to reduce the risk of harm, and in Family Courts, they might assist in following up with the parties on the impact of long-term strategies on family dynamics (FamJ002).

IV. HOW JUSTICE PROVIDERS WELCOME MULTIDISCIPLINARY ASSISTANCE

> Interviewer: What type of 'justice' could you grant without the interdisciplinary groups?
>
> Interviewee: One that is incomplete. It would be a formality. […] We would not be able to understand beyond what [victims] verbally tell us in the interview, beyond the discourse. Because I am a lawyer. I can participate in training, I can undertake research, I can get involved in the case to want to know more, but I do not count on the tools […] to have a deeper understanding of the why of the family dynamics. (FamJ1)

This section analyses how justice providers make use of multidisciplinary assistance to rule on domestic violence cases. In domestic violence cases, justice providers are expected to provide an expeditious answer in order to protect victims. The type of measures justice providers can enforce should also be in accordance with the type of violence feared and the family dynamics, contemplating the risk that any action might awaken (Law 26485, arts 26–27; Medina, Yuba and González Magaña, 2013: 343–62). Justice providers collaborate with multidisciplinary offices and other teams to determine effective measures, which frequently entail a change in the behaviour of the parties (Medina, Yuba and González Magaña, 2013: 361).

Most justice providers understood that the assistance of other disciplines was essential in order to solve problems in a holistic manner (Marotta, 2017: chap 4; JP1; FamJ1; FamJ2) because the teams were able to provide a technical analysis of the family dynamics (as mentioned by FamJ1: they allow Family Courts to 'grant measures which are more respectful of the reality that parties encounter'). The members of the multidisciplinary teams can work jointly or individually, depending on the needs of the case and the instructions of the judge (FamJ3).

When making decisions, prosecutors take into consideration, to some extent, the reports made by the multidisciplinary team of the Victims and Witness Assistance Office. Family judges manifested a closer relationship with the teams and more frequent communication. Among the disciplines mentioned, psychologists and psychiatrists are the ones most frequently referred to as being essential for victims to be able to sustain the process and work on a long-term solution (JP1; FamJ1; FamJ2). A family judge, on the other hand, was against pressuring parties to see a psychological therapist and instead left that decision to their discretion (FamJ3; Medina, 2008). This interviewee further argued that some socio-economic sectors could not afford therapy and hence, compliance with the measurement was unrealistic.

In domestic violence cases, criminal judges can impose penalties, whereas family judges can impose preventive measures (Bentivegna, 2015). On the one hand, the enforcement of penalties was mentioned as a challenge due to the lack of evidence (JP8a; JP7a; JP11a; JP12a, CrimJ11) and the consequences that such a penalty could have on the family (CrimJ11). In the words of CrimJ11: 'The son [of the abuser] of seventeen years old, or a little less, came and said, "My dad is in jail and during the last twenty days no money came into this house."' On the other hand, the enforcement of preventive measures and following up on their efficiency was also mentioned as a potential challenge due to the capacity of courts to follow up with the volume of cases (FamJ1, FamJ3), and the dynamics of domestic violence, in which it can take years before the victim is empowered to leave the environment (FamJ1).

Interviewees at the Family Court agreed that the multidisciplinary teams were essential to understanding the family dynamics and determining the best approach to helping parties in resolving the conflict (FamJ1, FamJ2, FamJ3). It also helped them to grant decisions faster and more accurately, because experts were able to understand and visualise patterns or pathologies faster and more accurately than they could (FamJ1, FamJ2). However, in some family courts, multidisciplinary teams are not always consulted (FamJ3) due to the high volume of cases. Hence, they usually intervene only in cases where the risk is greater (FamJ3). For example, if a victim calls about a harassment case in which the aggressor no longer lives with her and the verbal aggression was an isolated act, the judge may decline to call in the multidisciplinary team and instead grant preventive measures such as an anti-panic-button and a restraining order. If, on the other hand a victim lives with the aggressor and approaches the police after experiencing physical violence, the judge will grant immediate preventive measurements and request the intervention of the multidisciplinary team to understand the impact of these measures on the family dynamics.

Family judges are deep thinking playmakers. They need to know how to balance the legal options, as well as with the multidisciplinary teams, the array of referrals available, the other organisations (for example, the executive body), and the needs of the families. In their words: 'We have good laws, but those laws needs to be made effective' (FamJ2; González Freire, 2018). Family judges get to know parties through the complaints submitted at the Police Station for Women and the Family, through the interdisciplinary reports and/or through the hearings stated in article 11, Law 12569. Most of the time, by the time the hearing begins, judges have already considered the complaint and report mentioned above (FamJ1). Hearings are usually held when the case is of medium or high risk and the parties are usually represented by a lawyer (FamJ3). A judge explained that when the lawyers arrive, they need to change their mind set and reinforce the purpose of the hearing, which is one where there are no winners or losers, but rather one where a compromise for a better future is discussed (FamJ2). During the hearing, family judges explain to parties separately the extent of the preventive measures and both family and criminal judges agreed that it had a 'powerful' effect for the parties to see them during that event (FamJ1; CrimJ11).

The multidisciplinary teams are brought into the case to provide a diagnosis of the family situation for the judge who will complement the legal options (FamJ1). The teams help judges to become more acquainted with the parties and with the conflict at hand (FamJ2). Moreover, when an enforced preventive measure is not working, the family judge can withdraw the preventive measure and request the parties to meet again with the multidisciplinary team (FamJ3, FamJ1). Based on the results, the family judge might try different preventive measures (FamJ1); request the participation of other family members in the process (FamJ1); or give intervention to another governmental or non-governmental organisation with expertise in a specific problem, for example, group therapies to empower victims (FamJ1, FamJ2). Here, a smooth and formalised collaboration between state and non-state organisations is mentioned as being necessary to obtain a holistic result (SP2; SP3; SP4; SP5; SP7; SP8; SP14; SP16; SP18; SP19; SP20; SP22; SP24; SP25). According to one interviewee: 'We need other state organisations (SP13) because the complexity of the problem of domestic violence requires not only ... a multidisciplinary approach, but also ... an inter-state organisational approach' (SP21). A smooth collaboration between organisations allows victims to approach the organisation to which they have been referred to with realistic expectations (SP23). The need for articulation to enable a proper collaboration was mentioned as a problem by the PPO (SP9; SP17; SP15), but not by the Family Courts. However, family judges did mention a lack of resources to assist the population in a holistic way (FamJ3).

Interviewees explained that they needed to be creative (FamJ1) and innovative (FamJ2) because their role was not limited to granting a preventive measurement but also to working with the options available and more (FamJ2). FamJ2 counted 25 years of service and explained the number of innovations she undertook. For example, she successfully petitioned the Provincial Supreme Court for the use of ankle bracelets to track the aggressor and founded three organisations. One organisation assists aggressors to learn how to control their emotions, another assists survivors of violence, and the third is a shelter which provides victims with a space to live in and with labour skills. All of these examples highlight the need for a multidisciplinary approach to domestic violence, as well as the importance of the role of the judge in knowing the resources at their disposal, the needs of the population they serve and the willingness to go the 'extra mile'. As mentioned by FamJ2,

> Family courts are the 'thermometer of a society.' Because here I can see who eats and who does not eat, who works and who does not work, if they have addictions or not ...
>
> What is the role of a family judge? It is not being closed to people, it is accompanying them. [...] understanding that you will help all family members. [...] not a conflict where one wins and other loses. No. Here, you accompany them on their life path. You will not spend your entire life with them, but you will give them the tools so that later in time they can perform differently.

V. HOW VICTIMS CONSIDER MULTIDISCIPLINARY ASSISTANCE

This section analyses how victims perceive the multidisciplinary assistance they received as a tool to solve their problems. Interviews helped to understand the values and obstacles experienced by victims when receiving multidisciplinary assistance. Interviewees mentioned three offices that had provided them with multidisciplinary assistance. These offices are: the Domestic Violence Office,[3]

[3] The Domestic Violence Office is an organisation to assist victims established in 2006. The office is open every day of the year during the entire day. Its aim is to ensure access to justice for victims of domestic violence and to support judges to enact decisions with celerity. Therefore, the office offers an entrance to the justice system with a holistic approach to violence, and the comprehensive reports that they draft allow family judges and prosecutors to provide immediate preventive measures. These reports are written by a multidisciplinary team composed of a lawyer, a psychologist and a social worker.

Victims and Witness Assistance Office[4] and the Comprehensive Centres for Women.[5] This section helps to understand the relationship with victims and the multidisciplinary assistance provided by these offices.

The incorporation of multidisciplinary assistance in domestic violence cases is considered a necessary element to allow for the exercise of rights (Burton, 2008: 11). In the view of the victims, the solution to their problems demanded a multidisciplinary approach. When asked about what type of solutions were sought to solve their problems, the majority selected multidisciplinary solutions.[6] However, victims also find the holistic approach to be demanding due to the number of options available from which they must choose, and the number of requests they are required to comply with (ibid: 21–50; V2_19; V1_27; V1_30; V1_46; V1_24; V1_45; Epstein, 1999). Moreover, in justice systems such as the one in the City of Buenos Aires and the Province of Buenos Aires, victims find that having a civil and a criminal case in parallel triggers a variety of paths with numerous tasks and a number of organisations that get involved. These complexities created confusion for some victims and only a few victims understood the reasons for it. However, some victims felt empowered when knowing about the number of options because they saw a possible way out of their difficult domestic situations (V1_27; V1_30; V1_52).

The listening techniques used by multidisciplinary teams helped some victims to realise the importance of their problems (V18; V1_11; V1_12; V1_13; V1_17; V2_19; V1_23; V1_24; V1_25; V1_26; V1_27; V1_30; V1_31; V1_33; V1_37; V1_44; V1_52; V1_46; V1_53; V1_45; Molina, 2009; Zúñiga Basset, 2019). As one victim explained when asked about what she learned from her experience with the Domestic Violence Office: 'I stopped being the silly and naive woman everyone believed I was. [I learned] to make others respect me as a woman and not to allow offences, and in the worst case, I think I will dare to fight back' (V2_27). Another victim stated that the type of assistance given by the Domestic Violence Office enabled her to voice what she wanted from the complaint (V1_52). Moreover, some victims viewed these offices as 'clubs' that provided support and assistance, as well as places where they made many friends who had experienced the same situation (V1_17). Therefore, multidisciplinary offices may be useful in enhancing a sense of belonging to a group.

Victims relied on advice, referrals or their own intuition when choosing resources. The police station, lawyers, the Domestic Violence Office,

[4] The Victims and Witness Assistance Office assists prosecutors with comprehensive reports and assists victims in legal procedures. They are part of the PPO. Interviews and support are being provided by lawyers, psychologists and social workers.

[5] The Comprehensive Centres for Women were created in the city of Buenos Aires, Argentina to assist and provide guidance to women victims of domestic and sexual violence. The offices are decentralised in the city and offer legal advice and psychological (individual and in groups) and social assistance.

[6] 54.17 per cent opted for multiple options while 45.83 per cent chose only one.

psychologists and friends were the resources most frequently mentioned as being used by victims.[7] Referrals to psychologists were mentioned by some victims as important emotional support on how to handle problems, to improve their quality of life, and to understand their behaviour (V1_16; V1_17; V2_17; V1_41; V2_19; V2_28; V1_4; V1_37; V1_40; V1_13). Some victims did not feel convinced of the benefits of approaching psychologists, while others mentioned going or considering going to psychologists because it was a step they needed to follow (V1_9) or because they were pushed to go (V2_1; V2_12). Other victims were accessing psychological therapy before the submission of complaints and considered the therapy useful in coping with legal procedures (V1_19; V1_28; V1_43; V1_44).

It is perceived from the interviews that the skills of the trained professionals, rather than the technicalities are what help in conflict resolutions. For example, active listening by service providers at the Domestic Violence Office was interpreted as a sign of help, trust and confidence. This resulted in a sense of support and tranquillity (V1_1), a space for reflection (V1_27; V2_27) and provision of a unit that guides them step by step (V2_26), as well as performing telephone follow-ups (V2_27). Victims valued having their voices heard, as well as the opportunity to speak in a calm environment which made them feel tranquil and offered a space for self-reflection. However, because they could not understand their purpose, the repetition of questions and duplication of tasks was not positively perceived.

Some victims perceived the multidisciplinary assistance offered as personalised, where victims were not treated as case numbers but as individuals who were listened to by vocation-trained assistants (V1_34; V1_41) and where tools to deal with the problems were provided (V2_37). Other victims felt that the multidisciplinary approach to conflicts was ineffective because it was a repetition of information that had already been given and received (V1_1) and was not directly related to solving problems (V1_5, V1_32). Some victims viewed follow-up calls as a sign of support to continue with their cases, while others saw them as invasive.

VI. CONCLUDING REMARKS

This study confirms that we are experiencing a fifth wave of the concept of access to justice in which an expansion of the term 'access to justice' is observed. Boundaries are broadened in order to protect the goal of access to justice, which is the empowerment of parties to resolve conflicts. The appropriate legal framework equips justice providers with the tools they need to assist victims. Within

[7] The PPO is not mentioned as frequently as the former, and this can be explained by the fact that interviews took place at the premises of the PPO.

these tools, multidisciplinary teams are perceived by justice providers as key players in the resolution of conflict. There is no magic recipe for resolving family conflicts, but multidisciplinary teams can assist in finding tailor-made solutions.

Justice providers act as deep-thinking playmakers and they need to be knowledgeable, innovative and flexible in order to work with all the legal and non-legal tools they have at hand in order to assist a population in need. Justice providers found it essential to work within the boundaries of the law and understood the need to consult with and refer to other disciplines in order to overcome their limitations and ensure a holistic approach to domestic violence. However, justice providers acknowledged that their task was difficult since the population they serve has a number of socio-economic issues that also need to be addressed if the problem is to be approached holistically. The art of listening was mentioned as valuable by all groups of interviewees, and it is an essential soft skill for meeting the needs of different groups and providing them with the opportunity to access justice. Moreover, the population needs to be capable of understanding the system and the process in order to be able to participate. In the words of an interviewee:

> We live in a society, in general, where we do not listen to each other, where the word of one always goes over the word of the other. And the one who lacks the most is the least listened to. So, well, I sit down, I listen to them, let them talk and then I tell them, 'Look at what you said here, see if we can change to this way or the other.' (FamJ2)

REFERENCES

Bentivegna, S (2015) 'Medidas cautelares en los procesos por violencia familiar', *El Derecho – Diario*, Tomo 262: ED-DCCLXXV-278.

Bruce, JW et al (2007) 'Legal empowerment of the poor: from concepts to assessment' (US Agency for International Development).

Burton, M (2008) *Domestic Abuse. Literature Review* (University of Leicester, UK: Legal Services Commission).

Castillo, MC and Carol Lugones, M (2008) 'Violencia familiar y la interdisciplina. El abuso sexual intrafamiliar', *Derecho de Familia: Revista Interdisciplinaria de Doctrina y Jurisprudencia.*

Commission on Legal Empowerment of the Poor (2008) *Making the law work for everyone. Vol I*, Report of the Commission on Legal Empowerment of the Poor. New York: Commission on Legal Empowerment of the Poor and United Nations Development Programme, 110.

Congreso de la Nación Argentina (2014) *Código civil y comercial de la nación*: www.infojus.gob.ar/nuevo-codigo-civil-y-comercial-de-la-nacion.

De la Rúa, AF (2012) 'El procedimiento de familia en el Proyecto', La Ley.

Epstein, D (1999) 'Effective intervention in domestic violence cases: Rethinking the roles of prosecutors, judges, and the court system', *Yale Journal of Law and Feminism* 11, 3.

Fernández Touriño, SE (2003) 'Breves consideraciones acerca de la ley de protección contra la violencia familiar', *El Derecho – Diario*, Tomo 204: ED-DCCLXV-12.

González Freire, JF (2018) 'La soberanía procesal de los jueces', *El Derecho – Diario*: ED-DCCLXXVII-117.

Gramatikov, M and Porter, RB (2010) 'Yes, I can: subjective legal empowerment', *Tilburg University*, 46.

Lorenzetti, RL (2012) 'Aspectos valorativos y principios preliminares del anteproyecto de código civil y comercial de la nación', La Ley.

Lorenzetti, RL, Highton de Nolasco, E and Kemelmajer de Carlucci, A (2012) 'Fundamentos del Anteproyecto de Código Civil y Comercial de la Nación'.

Macdonald, RA (2010) 'Access to civil justice' in *The Oxford Handbook of Empirical Legal Research* (Oxford University Press) 492–521.

Marotta, J (2017) *Access to Justice and Legal Empowerment of Victims of Domestic Violence through Legal Organisations in the City of Buenos Aires: A Qualitative Empirical Legal Study* (Maastricht University / United Nations University): www.merit.unu.edu/training/theses/marotta_julieta.pdf.

Masciotra, M (2020) 'Principios generales en los procesos de familia', *El Derecho – Diario*, 289.

Medina, G (2008) *Comentario al fallo de la CCiv y Comercial Neuquén Sala II – 2008-05-08 DURACION DE LAS MEDIDAS EN VIOLENCIA FAMILIAR.*

Medina, G (2012) 'El proceso de familia' in *Comentarios al Proyecto de Código Civil y Comercial de la Nación*, 440–49.

Medina, G, Yuba, G and González Magaña, I (2013) *Violencia de género y violencia doméstica* (Buenos Aires, Argentina, Rubinzal – Culzoni Editores).

Molina, AC (2009) 'El niño en los procesos judiciales. Su derecho a ser escuchado y a ser parte. Distintas alternativas legales', *El Derecho – Diario*, Tomo 232: DCCLXX-714.

National Institute of Justice (no date) *New York Integrated Domestic Violence Court*: www.crimesolutions.gov/ProgramDetails.aspx?ID=435, accessed 4 May 2016.

Ontario Court of Justice, maintained by the J L (no date) 'Integrated Domestic Violence Court': www.ontariocourts.ca/ocj/integrated-domestic-violence-court, accessed 15 April 2016.

UNGA (2005) *Basic principles and guidelines on the right to a remedy and reparation for victims of gross violations of international human rights law and serious violations of international humanitarian law.*

Van De Meene, I and Van Rooij, B (2008) *Access to Justice and Legal Empowerment. Making the Poor Central in Legal Development Co-Operation* (Leiden University Press): books.google.nl/books?id=U_U84FKFBBQC.

Zúñiga Basset, M (2019) 'Acceso a la justicia de las personas con capacidad restringida', *El Derecho – Diario*, Tomo 282: ED-DCCLXXVII-760.

11

Raising Questions on the Family Justice System in Turkey: An Ambivalent Fragmentation

VERDA IRTIS

I. INTRODUCTION

THIS CHAPTER WILL describe increasing fragmentation in the family justice system in Turkey, showing both how family justice is already fragmented in Turkey and pointing out how this fragmentation is continuing through the inclusion of new elements.

I will draw on different exploratory/small-scale researches carried out mainly between 2018 and 2021. In other words, I will reconsider how family justice maintains its fragmented state as demonstrated in my text entitled 'Competing Logics, Norms and World Visions: The Family Justice System in Turkey' (2019) by taking into account policy changes, some of which are related to the consequences of the Covid-19 pandemic.

What does this increasing fragmentation show us? What can we see behind the 'transformations' that continue where 'everything is changing so fast; transformations are in transformation' (Irtis, 2019: 69)?

As sociologists of law, we know the importance of putting law and justice in context:

> In this respect, the very expression 'law and society' is sociologically puzzling for it assumes that law is not part of society. Sociologists of law therefore side with legal theorist Lon Fuller (1968) in saying that it would be more appropriate to speak of law-in-society, and to approach law accordingly as a social issue that begs for sociological elucidation, just as do other social institutions and social practices. (Deflem, 2008: 7)

This means that to understand the family justice system, the 'wider structural and cultural contexts' (Deflem, 2008: 208) should not be ignored.

In this case, considering the last two decades in the country, it will not be wrong to say that family justice is being challenged in various ways both in the field of justice itself and outside. The latter is expressed above all through issues concerning women, children, civil society and those in the field of religion.

Although secular in its constitution,[1] the Turkish Republic has gone through periods of strong ideological and political tension originating in the Ottoman Empire (Berkes, 2016) during its modernisation process.

As is known, the last few years have witnessed a non-negligible polarisation of society as a consequence of political pressures, but also probably as a consequence of what has not been expressed so far by some parts of the country's population for different socio-historical reasons. In saying this, without ignoring the weight of an authoritarian drift such that the country has never experienced in this way before, it also seems important to reconsider the role of the society in the arrival, installation and maintenance of such a situation. To put it another way, it would not be irrelevant to reflect on the formation of a certain type of common personality[2] via the institutions that are responsible for transmitting what is to be prescribed in bodies and souls in order to regulate and to contain society.

Thus, in the case of Turkey, it will not be inappropriate to say that modern law and justice are already a product of the antagonistic forces that are part of the country's tense history that is still ongoing. In other words, as the recent dynamics of the country have shown us, the dilemma between modernity and tradition, reason and belief, secular and sacred, not only persists, but continues to create new conflicts.

Turkish society bears, if one may say so, characteristics of pre-modern, modern and post-modern structures. The complexity of social life can be thought of as if 'society' and 'community' – two notions[3] referring to different forms of interaction – co-exist.

As for the law, which is 'a textual mass in perpetual motion' (Legendre quoted by Gordon-Krief and Hurbert Flichy, 2015: 145), in such a context, it seems to 'move' at a pace that is not easy to keep up with.[4] At the junction of global dynamics and local politico-ideological ones where the law seems to be increasingly instrumentalised, this 'movement' also influences as we can imagine, and as we shall see, the family justice system.

The different aspects of this fragmented justice will be reviewed in four parts: Family Courts, Family and Religious Guidance Centers/Offices, Mediation and Digital Space.

[1] Second article of the Constitution.

[2] As we know, the initial studies were in the domain of cultural anthropology, which also included psychology and psychoanalysis within it. The 'basic personality structure' of Abram Kardiner (1939) (1969 for the French translation) (with Ralph Linton) and Erich Fromm's 'cultural type' (1956: 78–83) in a Freudo-Marxist perspective can be cited as being among the most important.

[3] This is a well-known distinction.

[4] In connection with this, I would like to express that there might be points that I have missed despite many attempts to verify everything.

II. FAMILY COURTS

Firstly, in Turkey, the Family Court is rather a recent phenomenon. The first court was founded in 2003. Before this there was the Civil Court of First Instance (having jurisdiction over various matters, including family matters). These courts created by Law No 4787 are responsible for dealing with Family Law cases, part of the Civil Code of 2001.[5] Composed by a judge and supposed to have a pedagogue, a psychologist and a social worker as experts, they are planned to be created in each province and also in districts with more than 100,000 inhabitants (Irtis, 2019: 60).

These courts deal with cases related to marriage, divorce, adoption, establishment of paternity, custody of children, property regimes, and recognition and enforcement of foreign court decisions. The judge must come from the ordinary courts and is expected to be qualified for the position, preferably married, with a child, and over 30 years of age, as well as having a post-graduate degree in the field of family law. Similar characteristics are desired for the experts (Irtis, 2019: 60).

The measures taken for the adults and minors are protective, social and educational ones:[6]

> Concerning the procedural provisions, according to the characteristics of the cases, before proceeding with a case, courts should encourage a 'friendly settlement' (sulh bulmak) in order to protect respect, tolerance and mutual love within the family by identifying the problems faced by the spouses and children. In the case of necessity, the court seeks the experts' opinion. If 'peace' cannot be achieved, the judicial process continues. (Irtis, 2019: 61)

When we look at the facts and practices, despite the years that have followed since 2003, in terms of the number of courts set up or in terms of the number of qualified persons, the objectives set by the Law seem not to have been achieved. Trials are still held in the Civil Court of First Instance.[7] The lack of experts not

[5] Law No 4721 Civil Code (Especially the second book Family Law), Law No 4722 on the Application of the Civil Code and Law No 6284 on Protection of the Family and the Prevention of Violence against Women (2012).

[6] 'For "adults", they are supposed to encourage spouses to respect the obligations of the marital union, and if it is necessary to reconcile, to take the measures necessary for the protection of the economic assets of the family or the fulfilment of financial obligations arising from the marital union, to use public or private health or social service agencies, nursing homes or other places, or an educational institution or appropriate vocational courses. For "minors", they take the necessary measures for the supervision, maintenance and alimony obligation, place a minor whose physical and mental development is endangered or who are spiritually abandoned in the family in a public or private health institution or in a specialised training institution, take measures concerning the management and protection of children's property placed with local authorities, state based economic enterprises and banks, etc. All these measures are supposed to be followed up by one or more of the experts.' (Irtis, 2019: 61)

[7] For example, 49,388 divorce cases for the year 2020 (as the most recent available data), (*Adli İstatistikler 2020*: 179). For the same year, 197,173 cases were within the Family Courts (*Adli İstatistikler 2020*: 188).

only increases the burden on those appointed, but also jeopardises the monitoring of decisions and measures.

With respect to the current political situation, several observations lead me to suppose that there is a tendency among judges to prefer civil courts.[8]

Although I am not dealing here with the interactions within the courts, on the basis of a preliminary study it seems possible, with reference to Merton's typology (1997), to group the practices of judges as 'ritualists', 'innovators' (those who put in relation/in network the other actors) and 'conformists'.

III. FAMILY AND RELIGIOUS GUIDANCE CENTERS/OFFICES

Also, since 2002 under the direction of the Presidency of Religious Affairs, Family and Religious Guidance Offices have been institutionalised.[9] It is interesting to observe that the first offices were opened in 2003, the date for the first Family Court (Irtis, 2019: 64).

Initially, these offices were called 'Aile [Family] İrşat [showing the correct way, warning[10]] ve [and] Rehberlik [Guidance] Bürolarι [Offices]. Since 2015, they have been named 'Aile ve Dini [Religious] Rehberlik Bürolarι'. In 2019, again their name as well as the Directive were modified.

> The new Directive, which regulates the working procedures and principles of the Family and Religious Guidance Offices or Centers opened within the provincial and district muftis, and the duties and authorities of the personnel working there was prepared on the basis of the Law No. 633 and the Directorate of Religious Affairs Duties and Working Regulations.
>
> In the light of the Qur'an and Sunnah, the number of Family and Religious Guidance Offices, which started to be opened in 2003 to provide sound religious information about the family and to help for solving the problems that threaten the family and the individual within the family, reached 385, including 81 provincial [total number of cities] and 304 [over 973] district muftis. In addition to providing religious guidance and spiritual support services by answering questions from our citizens face-to-face, via e-mail and telephone, the bureaus carry out projects for the protection and strengthening of the family, along with different social-cultural religious activities.
>
> With the Directive, legal grounds were established for the transformation of offices, which meet the requirements as multi-service spaces, into Centers. Thus, the Family and Religious Guidance Office, which includes the interview room, education hall,

[8] Which should be verified. As I noted previously (Irtis, 2019: 70) the Coup d'Etat of July 2016 resulted in several dismissals among judges and prosecutors as well as lawyers who have had severe problems (including incarceration and suicide). Since then we also know that the conditions and procedures of education, training, selection and attribution have been changed, which would require a closer look.

[9] Whose roots should be looked at.

[10] This word comes from the Arabic: www.tdk.gov.tr, accessed 1 August 2021.

> children's play area, library/reading hall and masjid in one place, will begin to serve under the name of the Center.
>
> (…).[11]

The document below gives a broader idea of the content, vision and objectives of these Centers/Offices:

> Family and Religious Guidance Centers/Offices[12]
>
> The family is the most valuable institution that establishes the peace and trust of the society. The fact that the family rises on solid foundations nourished by love and compassion and has a balanced and healthy relationship network means the security of not only the individual but also a generation. It is a fact that the family, which is the building block of society, has to deal with serious problems in today's world where change is experienced at a stifling speed. Not only parents, but also children, young people and even grandparents are worn out by being alone with family problems in the course of life. Founded from this point of view, the Family and Religious Guidance Offices provide services in order to establish and protect a family structure that adheres to our national and moral values, to support family unity, to contribute to the solution of problems and to develop a social sensitivity.[13]

This is how they define themselves as well as how they describe their raison d'être:

> Definition
>
> Family and Religious Guidance Office, we are the religious guidance unit serving within our muftis with a team of religious officials.
>
> Our duties
>
> We provide religious guidance service with an encompassing and embracing approach to all our citizens who come to our offices for questions and problems or who apply by phone or e-mail. We enlighten our people with authentic information about the well-known mistakes that threaten the family. By organizing activities such as conferences, panels, seminars, projects, etc. in cooperation with other institutions and instances, we raise awareness about the family. We spread knowledge about the establishment and strengthening of a healthy family through long-term trainings such as family school and marriage school.
>
> Our mission
>
> In the light of the Qur'an and the Sunnah, we provide the society with correct religious information about the family based on moral knowledge, and contribute to the solution of the problems that threaten the family and the individual within the family from a religious point of view.

[11] dinhizmetleri.diyanet.gov.tr/Detay/200/aile-ve-din%C3%AE-rehberlik-b%C3%BCro-veya-merkezleri-%C3%A7al%C4%B1%C5%9Fma-y%C3%B6nergesi-yay%C4%B1nland%C4%B1, accessed 1 August 2021.

[12] In the preceding declaration, it was said that these Offices would be called 'Centers'. Nevertheless, as we observe, 'Centers/Offices' has been kept.

[13] dinhizmetleri.diyanet.gov.tr/Documents/aile%20g%C3%B6rev.pdf, accessed 1 August 2021.

Our vision

We aim to create a peaceful and healthy society with conscious individuals who have the right religious and moral knowledge, who are responsible for being a family.

Our principles

- To base our activities on sound knowledge based on the fundamental sources of the religion of Islam and reinforced by the cultural values of our ancient civilisation.
- To be fair and consistent in providing religious guidance and spiritual support to women, families, children, youth and the elderly.
- To create social awareness of the value and importance of the family by conducting joint studies with relevant public and non-governmental institutions and organisations.
- To take into account the sensitivities of the applicants in order to create an effective service texture.

Our goals

- To plan and continue our work with the awareness of establishing, protecting and strengthening a family devoted to national and moral values,
- To contribute to the solution by developing a sensitivity towards women, family, old, young and child problems with the unifying role of the family concept,
- To carry out activities to prevent negative attitudes and behaviors such as domestic violence, honor killings and gender discrimination that girls are exposed to'.[14]

It seems that

> of the 66,625 applications filed with the Family and Religious Guidance Centers/Offices in the last 7 years, 25,820 were about the questions related to the marriage, wedding and divorce, 20,800 to the family, 6,289 to the health, 4,747 to the children, 2,548 to the women, 3,444 to the young people and 2,977 of them to the social situation. In addition, 4,794 applications were made for issues such as domestic violence, including violence against women, cheating, child neglect and abuse, forced marriage at a young age and honour crimes.[15]

Video presentations, workshops, etc, as far as we can observe these activities, seem to be multiplying:

> Basic Family Awareness Trainings Were Conducted
>
> Martı [Vice-president of Presidency of Religious Affairs] noted that within the framework of the 'Family Protection and Social Awareness in the Prevention of Domestic Violence' project, panels, café lectures and Friday sermons were held in the pilot provinces of Eastern and Central Anatolia regions. Explaining that one of the titles of the 'First Step to Marriage' seminar, which was initiated within the framework of the 'Peaceful Family, Strong Society, Safe Future' project, was determined as the module

[14] Ibid.

[15] www.aa.com.tr/tr/turkiye/diyanetin-aile-ve-dini-rehberlik-burolarina-66-bin-basvuru-yapildi/1746487#, accessed 17 July 2021.

> 'Let Our Home Be a Home of Mercy', Martı informed that these seminars are intended for couples who apply for marriage at the mufti offices and municipalities. Martı said that within the project 'Basic Education for Family Awareness', religious leaders, instructors of Quranic courses and about 600 000 trainees were trained.[16]

It has been reported that 14,083 applications were made to these Centers/Offices in 2018 (the most recent available data) (*Din Hizmetleri Raporu 2018*: 122); 52 per cent of the applications were made face-to-face, 47 per cent by phone and 1 per cent by e-mail. While 61 per cent of the applicants to the Centers/Offices stated that they were married, 11 per cent were single, 4 per cent were widowed and 24 per cent did not provide information about their marital status. Of the applicants, 87 per cent were female and 13 per cent were male (*Din Hizmetleri Raporu*, 2018: 126). While 35 per cent of the clients did not provide information about their educational status, the highest number of applicants were high school, primary school and university graduates, respectively. It is observed that the applicants are predominantly in the 25–40 and 41–60 age groups, and the highest number of applicants are housewives, with a ratio of 36 per cent (*Din Hizmetleri Raporu 2018*: 127).

As it is declared,

> In 2018, 107 projects were implemented by Family and Religious Guidance Offices to provide solutions to local and regional problems throughout the country. Some of these projects are: Arrive at Serenity, Give Serenity; I Learn My Values by Playing; Our Mosque Blossoms for Everyone to Read; I am a Youth Empowered with Kindness and Empathy, I am a Smiling Future; The First Step from Me to 'Us': Family; Come to Us for An Evening Tea, Family Counselling Trainer Training. (Religious Services Report, 2018: 132)

In addition,

> a total of 2,178 personnel, 1,457 women and 721 men, work in these offices (…) [and] when we look at the distribution of office personnel by title, we record 772 preachers, 48 religious services and education experts, 925 Quranic course instructors, 314 imams and muezzins. The number of office staff (such as branch manager, auditor, data preparation and control operator) is 54. Office services are generally provided by preachers and Quranic course instructors. (Irtis, 2019: 65)[17]

Many of the facts mentioned both here and earlier (Irtis, 2019: 65–66)[18] remind us of the need to reflect on the meaning of including religion in the handling of family matters.[19]

[16] www.aa.com.tr/tr/turkiye/diyanetin-aile-ve-dini-rehberlik-burolarina-66-bin-basvuru-yapildi/1746487#, accessed 17 July 2021.

[17] It is important to note that as far as I could see these data remain still the most recent available. At the same time, since we can observe a growth in the number of the Centers/Offices, it can be supposed that the number of the personnel has also increased.

[18] For example, 'the attribution in December 2017 to the imams after muftis the capacity to perform the marriage ceremony, which was formerly done only by marriage officials in the municipalities' (Irtis, 2019: 66).

[19] It is a work in progress.

IV. MEDIATION

On the other hand, since being introduced in 2012, mediation (Law No 6325) can be considered for employment and commercial transactions to be in a phase of expansion, but it seems still at an emerging stage for family affairs.[20] As mentioned previously, in 2018, a new article was added to the Law, putting mediation 'as a condition of the case' (Irtis, 2019: 62), which explains this expansion. It also became mandatory in 28 July 2020 for matters related to some parties in consumer law especially due to the consequences of the Covid-19 pandemic. There are no official statistics available for the moment, but it seems that there is an increase in court cases concerning tenants who can no longer pay their rent in the current circumstances of increased inequality.

Under the Ministry of Justice, General Directorate of Legal Affairs, video presentations (on what is mediation, why, and who is the mediator, including the Presidency of the mediation service), communication of meetings, activities, indication of offices, publications etc show the continuing efforts to spread this negotiation technique.

When we look at this from the family justice side, we observe opposition to mediation as a compulsory stage before any trial in the domain of family justice as illustrated by the example of the Istanbul Bar Women's Rights Center:

> No Mediation in Family Law
>
> Recently, the issue of mandatory mediation in family law disputes has been on the agenda. A system of mandatory mediation was introduced, first in labour law disputes and then in commercial cases. Now mandatory mediation is attempted in family law cases. Alternative methods of dispute resolution are being attempted to replace the court/judiciary system, which is the duty of the state.
>
> [...] There is psychological, verbal, economic, sexual, social and physical abuse in almost all family law cases, especially divorce cases. As such, it is not possible to distinguish whether there is violence or not without a trial. For this reason, MEDIATION IS NEVER POSSIBLE in family law disputes.
>
> In some circles it is specified that compulsory mediation will only be exercised for the liquidation of the property regime. Property settlement is also a family law dispute. The conclusion of the divorce case, unfortunately, does not end the violence. With hundreds of women being killed and subjected to violence at an increasing rate each year, bringing women to the mediation table puts women's safety at risk. Given that 440 women were killed simply for being women and 317 women were exposed to sexual violence in 2018, the question of HOW WOMEN WILL BE PROTECTED is extremely important. As the mediator cannot be expected to ensure the safety of the woman, there is no doubt that her/his own safety is also at risk.
>
> [...]

[20] For more information on the content of Law No 6325, on legal aid, on the profile of mediators, on the structure of the organisation as well as on assumptions that I had formulated following 'mediation has something unclassifiable' (Bastard, 2005: 66) see Irtis (2019: 62–64).

> Again, in Article 137 of the HMK [Code of Civil Procedure] we see that; "After the mutual submission of motions, a preliminary examination shall be conducted. During the preliminary examination the court examines the conditions of the case and the first objections, fully decides the issues in dispute, takes the necessary measures for the preparation of the parties to present their evidence and the collection of evidence, encourages the friendly settlement for the cases on which the parties can freely dispose, and records these issues in the minutes. In accordance with the provisions of the law, THE JUDGE ALSO HAS THE POWERS TO INSCRIBE THE PARTIES TO THE AGREEMENT".
>
> With the current legal arrangement, as long as the parties are willing to reach a settlement, before filing a lawsuit, there is the possibility of issuing documents in the form of a peace verdict in accordance with Article 35/A of the Attorneyship Law, but including family law cases in the scope of mediation, especially by making it compulsory, will jeopardise women's safety and will not allow women to exercise their rights and will hamper its realisation.
>
> MEDIATION IN FAMILY LAW MEANS THAT DOMESTIC VIOLENCE IS INVISIBLE.
>
> MEDIATION IN FAMILY LAW IS A BARRIER TO WOMEN'S ACCESS TO JUSTICE.[21]

However, in the 'Human Rights Action Plan', under the signature of President Recep Tayyip Erdoğan, in 'Increasing Efficiency and Dissemination of Alternative Dispute Resolution Methods' it is foreseen that the scope of mediation in civil disputes will broaden. Other aims are specialisation for mediators in different fields; to increase the efficiency of the system via the amendment of the Law on Mediation in Litigation; to revise the Law on Mediation in Disputes; to determine the legal status of mediation centres and to create standards to establish and control these centres, to create judicial family mediation (in Turkish: *Mahkeme temelli aile arabuluculuğu müessesesi*) by also taking into account international conventions to avoid, especially, abuse of women and children in the divorce process (Human Rights Action Plan 2021: 56).[22]

It is interesting to note that this Action Plan corresponds to the moment when it was decided to withdraw from the Istanbul Convention.[23]

[21] www.istanbulbarosu.org.tr/HaberDetay.aspx?ID=14275&Desc=Aile-Hukukunda-Arabuluculuk-Olmaz-#:~:text=Aile%20hukuku%20kaynakl%C4%B1%20davalarda%20bilhassa,uyu%C5%9Fmazl%C4%B1klar%C4%B1nda%20ARABULUCULUK%20asla%20M%C3%9CMK%C3%9CN%20DE%C4%9E%C4%B0LD%C4%B0R, accessed 8 August 2021; www.istanbulbarosu.org.tr/HaberDetay.aspx?ID=14275&Desc=Aile-Hukukunda-Arabuluculuk-Olmaz-, accessed 18 July 2021.

[22] rayp.adalet.gov.tr/resimler/1/dosya/insan-haklari-ep02-03-202115-14.pdf, accessed 28 July 2021.

[23] Since 1 July 2021, Turkey is no longer part of this Convention. At the same time, a new law on violence against women has been created 'in order to combat violence against women more effectively and to act as a deterrent, the grounds for increased penalties for the offences of "intentional homicide", "intentional injury", "torture" and "deprivation of liberty" will also include the divorced spouse'. See basin.adalet.gov.tr/yargi-reformunun-4paketi-resmi-gazetede-yayimlanarak-yururluge-girdi, accessed 27 July 2021.

V. DIGITAL SPACE

As for the digitising environment, for more than ten years it has existed in all public services and also in justice (in a large sense). E-Bars, I-Bar (lawyers), websites, social media, audio conferencing, emails, intranets as well as video conferencing seem to be increasingly used (Irtis, 2019: 66).

E-Mahkeme (E-Court), a private firm, which has been the only online dispute resolution (ODR) example in Turkey since 2018,[24] still appears to be the only firm providing services for the new E-Lawsuits (that we will address below), but no longer in the domain of mediation. During an interview that I conducted in January 2020 with the head of this E-Court, who is a lawyer, my interviewee especially emphasised the cost and the importance of following the European example.[25] In his opinion, 'the state should make it mandatory/compulsory'. According to him, if mediation becomes as common as in the commercial and employment laws, the demand will increase and online options will gain greater importance. As he states, 'At the same time, the final place for decision remains Courts. But mediation can prepare the divorce by considering it with its economic, psychological and social dimensions'. As for domestic violence, which is a preoccupying subject in the country, he thinks that mediation can diversify the norms and would be better than classical justice.

A preliminary research through mass media (news, different platforms – law firms, mediation centers) for the purpose of observing the effects of the context of the Covid-19 pandemic in handling of family affairs revealed that as in many countries, courts had stopped work from March to June 2020.[26] It was striking to see how mediation was seen 'as the only solution' in the speeches of some lawyers.

Nevertheless, as far as I can observe, declarations/testimonies such as '[m] ediation is the legal vaccine of the pandemic […]' and '[w]hile the medicine is searching for the solution to the virus, law has found it in mediation'[27] which were frequent during the period of March to June 2020 are no longer so common.

[24] Now (as at July 2021), their new website is called 'E-Arabulucu' (E-Mediation). As we see in this new link the date of the foundation is expressed as 2017 ('by taking into account the preparation stages' as its Director stated to us).

[25] For a detailed presentation of this private investment, cf Irtis (2019: 67–69).

[26] As for the last containment between 29 April and 17 May 2021 it is said: 'The Council of Judges and Prosecutors General Assembly recommended postponing hearings, except for urgent matters, throughout the containment period. According to the recommendation decisions, negotiations and explorations will also be postponed, there will be no complete cessation of judicial services during the containment, and complaints and reports concerning crimes and criminals may be received.': www.trthaber.com/haber/gundem/hskdan-tam-kapanma-tedbirleri-durusmalar-ertelenebilir-576145.html, accessed 17 July 2021.

[27] www.haberler.com/pandeminin-hukuki-asisi-arabuluculuk-13295731-haberi, accessed 5 August 2021.

The Regulation (on the Conduct of Hearings by Audio and Video Transmission in Civil Courts) concerning E-Lawsuits in the Civil Courts came into force on 30 June 2021. As it is *officially* declared:

> E-HEARING IS IMPLEMENTED IN 738 COURTS AROUND TURKEY
>
> E-lawsuit, which has been implemented in courts as part of the Ministry of Justice's judicial reform strategy [it is related to the 'Fourth Package of Judicial Reform', 14 July 2021], is being employed in 738 courts around the country.
>
> The e-lawsuit, which was implemented as part of the digital transformation objectives in the judicial system, offers convenience in trials with time and labour savings. With the application, the intensity that can occur in courts, especially during the Covid-19 outbreak, is avoided. The e-lawsuit, whose software was developed by the Ministry of Justice's engineers with national and state resources and started to be employed on 15 September 2020, allows lawyers to attend civil court hearings via a video conferencing system. The e-lawsuit application, which is one of the digital transformation objectives of the judicial reform, is of great importance to facilitate access to justice services, while saving work and time for lawyers.
>
> […]
>
> 17 THOUSAND 665 E-LAWSUITS HAVE BEEN HELD
>
> The e-lawsuit can be applied in 96 consumer rights, 193 execution rights, 33 cadastres, 102 civil rights, 73 peace rights, 77 family rights, 116 enterprises, 42 first instance businesses, 6 intellectual and industrial rights courts throughout the country. With the online trial system, a total of 17,665 hearings have been held so far.

IT IS PLANNED TO BE ESTABLISHED IN 2000 COURTS BY THE END OF 2021

> The application, which is to be rolled out nationwide by the Ministry of Justice, is expected to be installed in 1,800 courtrooms and over 2,000 courts by the end of 2021.[28]

Taking these developments into account, a closer look at the consequences of this digitalisation for family justice is likely to be a necessity for the near future.

At the end, despite these interminable changes and modifications, the Family Courts still 'remain the hub in the sense that they are the place of "conclusion" for conflicts' (Irtis, 2019: 70) even if they are not far away from the politico-ideological pressures.[29]

VI. CONCLUDING REMARKS

Carrying out these observations as a kind of follow-up study to reflect upon the ways in which family matters are handled, I realise that looking at the

[28] basin.adalet.gov.tr/turkiye-genelindeki-738-mahkemede-e-durusma-uygulaniyor, accessed 28 July 2021.

[29] As we hear quite often even in divorce trials, the ideology of the judge may influence the decision reached.

(re)organisation dimensions (in this case from a far,[30] at least for the time being) allows one to grasp, I think, the shaping 'force' of current policies for the context under study. And, from there, it would perhaps also become plausible to reconsider 'The Force of Law'[31] to reflect on its limits.

In other words, what Ackermann, Bastard and Ietswaart express about the importance of 'considering the judiciary as a set of organisational units, the courts' (1989: 4) for the purpose of analysing the diffusion of innovation in the judiciary, fundamental to understanding change, points to how important it is not to treat 'law and the rules of judiciary' (Bastard and Mouhanna, 2007: 14) as the sole benchmarks, and to think about justice 'in an organisational perspective' (Ackermann and Bastard, 1988: 19).

In the case of Turkey, these recent developments and this increasing fragmentation lead us to summarise the present situation as being like a successive process of organising, disorganising and reorganising.

If we accept that the institution is embodied in the organisation – here, the organisation 'comes to be seen as a concrete modality' – in order to give it meaning (Hans, 2019: 370), we can assume that in these successive organisations, disorganisations and reorganisations resulting in a deficiency of a 'concrete modality' can explain both the difficulty of instituting and 'stabilising social relationships through the establishment of values, laws and regulations' (Hans, 2019: 369).

In other words, taking an interest in organisation can be a way to get closer to 'the unconscious and socio-political dimensions' (Hans, 2019: 371) of institutions. Then, it seems important to look at the social order when considering 'What is family justice for?'

Finally, how should we interpret these 'contradictory' policies and pressures toward norms? How can we begin to grasp, understand and situate everything that is happening? How does this 'double crisis' (politics and health) influence the ways in which family matters are handled? What are the links between this increased fragmentation and this 'polarisation'? Do these almost continuous changes (in the names, in the procedures, in the laws, extending the government's powers of the state of emergency related to the Coup d'Etat attempt of 15 July 2016,[32] etc) indicate an 'abnormal'/incoherent state and/or a state of a structured instability?[33] What 'use' do we make of law and justice? What is the place of the family, of women, of children 'in the background'? What are and

[30] It means that beside the Ministry of Justice, I was also led to look at the ways the Ministry of Family and Social Services and Presidency of Religious Affairs were organised and are being reorganised to get closer to the family justice system. In the broadest sense, 'in addressing the question "What is law?" one responds to the question of how society is organized' (Milovanovic, 2003: 1).

[31] This is with reference to: Bourdieu (1986).

[32] www.dw.com/tr/h%C3%BCk%C3%BCmetin-ohal-yetkileri-uzad%C4%B1/a-58305421, accessed 5 August 2021.

[33] Following (for example) the ideas of Montesquieu (1748) (1941 for the new edition), Durkheim (1894).

what will be the effects at the organisational and professional level that also influence family justice? Is there a danger that the laws, which are already not always accessible for the citizens, and accompanied by such permanent changes, become a source of even more distrust? These are only some of the question marks whose answers await the future.

REFERENCES

Ackermann, W and Bastard, B (1988) 'Efficacité et gestion dans l'institution judiciaire' *Revue interdisciplinaire d'études juridiques* 1, 20.

Ackermann, W, Bastard, B and Ietswaart, H (1989) 'La diffusion de l'innovation dans l'institution judiciaire' *Annales des Mines*, décembre.

Adalet Bakanlığı (2020) *Adli İstatistikler 2020* (Ankara, Adli Sicil ve İstatistik Genel Müdürlüğü).

Bastard, B (2005) 'Mais à qui profite la médiation familiale?' *Dialogue* 4, 170.

Bastard, B and Mouhanna, C (2007) *Une justice dans l'urgence. Le traitement en temps réel des affaires pénales* (Paris, Presses Universitaires de France).

Berkes, N (2016) Türkiye'de Çağdaşlaşma (İstanbul, YKY).

Bourdieu, P (1986), 'La force du droit. Eléments pour une sociologie du champ juridique', *Actes de la recherche en sciences sociales* 64(1), 3–19

Deflem, M (2008) *Sociology of Law. Visions of a Scholarly Tradition* (Cambridge, Cambridge University Press).

Diyanet İşleri Başkanlığı (2018) *Din Hizmetleri Raporu 2018*: dinhizmetleri.diyanet.gov.tr/Icon/SagSlider/2018%20Din%20Hizmetleri%20Raporuu.pdf, accessed 12 August 2021.

Durkheim, E (1894) 'Le crime, phénomène normal': classiques.uqac.ca/classiques/Durkheim_emile/crime_phenomene_normal/crime_phenomene_normal.pdf, accessed 12 August 2021.

Fromm, E (1956) *The Sane Society* (London, Routledge & Kegan Paul Ltd).

Gordon-Krief, D and Flichy, H (2015) *Et si le droit n'existait pas? Nous avocats, acteurs du contrat social* (Paris, Editions Débats Publics).

Hans, D (2019) 'Institution' in A Vandevelde-Rougale and P Fugier (eds), with the collaboration of V de Gaulejac, *Dictionnaire de la sociologie clinique* (Toulous, Erès), 368–70.

Irtis, V (2019) 'Competing Logics, Norms and World Visions: The Family Justice System in Turkey' in M Maclean and B Dijksterhuis (eds), *Digital Family Justice. From Alternative Dispute Resolution to Online Dispute Resolution?* (Oxford, Oñati International Series in Law and Society, Hart Publishing) 59–71.

Kardiner, A (1969) *L'individu dans sa société. Essai d'anthropologie psychanalytique* (Paris, Editions Gallimard).

Merton, RK (1997) *Eléments de théorie et de méthode sociologique* (Paris, Armand Colin).

Milovanovic, D (2003) *An Introduction to the Sociology of Law* (New York, Criminal Justice Press).

Montesquieu (1941) *De l'esprit des lois* (Paris, Garnier).

12

How Does a Legal System Deal with Malfunctions by Its Judicial Officers?

BELINDA FEHLBERG AND RICHARD INGLEBY

I. INTRODUCTION

AUSTRALIA'S FAMILY JUSTICE system has experienced significant change since the enactment of the Family Law Act 1975 (Cth) (FLA). While the longstanding pattern continues that only a small minority of separating couples rely on family law courts for contested final hearings to resolve their parenting and financial disputes (Australian Institute of Family Studies, 2019; Qu et al, 2014), responding to family violence and child abuse (along with other risk factors including mental illness and substance abuse) now comprises the 'core business' of courts (Kaspiew et al, 2015) that were not established with that work in mind. This is in the context of increased workloads arising from a widening of jurisdiction and a decline in resourcing over many years (Australian Law Reform Commission (ALRC), 2019: [2.13], [4.35]). Added to this, and at least partly due to underfunding of means tested legal assistance through legal aid (Joint Select Committee, 2020: [5.62]–[5.81]), unrepresented litigants are now common (ALRC, 2019: [3.69]).

The demands on judges are therefore high (ALRC, 2021: 26), but so are the consequences for vulnerable families if judges fall short of the required standards of conduct. While it has been said that '[t]he most important measure of the performance of the court system is the extent to which the public have confidence in its independence, integrity and impartiality' (Gleeson, 1999), the reality is that most families before the Australian family law courts are not in a strong position to complain if the conduct of the judge deciding their case falls short of those standards.

In this context, how does the Australian legal system – and specifically the Australian family justice system – deal with malfunctions by its judicial officers? Here, we use the term 'malfunction' to refer to an error which goes to the very nature of the judicial process. Mistakes in factual findings or disagreements as to questions of law are an inevitable consequence of human beings being the operators in any court system. In contrast, a malfunction for the purposes of our discussion is when the system itself goes wrong.

Three issues which have arisen in the Australia family law context, and which are the focus of this chapter, are:

(i) inappropriate personal relationships and interactions between judges and practitioners;
(ii) inappropriate exchanges between judges and practitioners/litigants in the courtroom; and
(iii) delays in delivery of judgment.

As we shall demonstrate, in relation to each of these three issues, there are important unanswered questions as to the required standards of behaviour; the consequences of departure from the required standards; and how consumers of the system (whether litigants or practitioners) are supposed to complain about such departures from required standards without compromising themselves.

II. ADDRESSING JUDICIAL MALFUNCTION: THE FEDERAL CONTEXT

Traditionally, Australia has subscribed to the view that '[j]udges are accountable through the public nature of their work, the requirement that they give reasons for their decisions and the scrutiny of their decisions on appeal' (Federal Circuit and Family Court of Australia, 2021), and 'there has been no formal, transparent process for lodging or investigating complaints against federal judicial officers for poor performance, nor a code of conduct against which judicial behaviour may be measured, nor have there been sanctions available short of removal from office by a vote of both houses of parliament' (ALRC, 1999: [2.147]). A parliamentary vote is required pursuant to section 72(ii) of the Commonwealth of Australia Constitution Act, which provides that judges of courts created by the Federal Parliament:

> shall not be removed except by the Governor-General in Council, on an address from both Houses of the Parliament in the same session, praying for such removal on the ground of proved misbehaviour or incapacity.

Since the late 1980s, increasing efforts to ensure transparency and accountability in the public sector have meant that 'courts have come under pressure to operate with a greater degree of efficiency, transparency and accountability' (ALRC, 1999: [2.250]). This has resulted in the establishment of independent bodies to investigate complaints about judicial conduct or capacity by some Australian states in relation to their judicial officers (for example the Judicial Commission of New South Wales (from 1986) and the Judicial Commission of Victoria (from 2017)), resembling approaches in other countries (for example, England and Wales, the United States and Canada).

In contrast, this has not occurred in relation to Australian federal courts, including the Family Court of Australia and the Federal Circuit Court of Australia (before 1 September 2021, the Family Court of Australia and Federal Court of Australia). Instead, in 2012 the Federal Parliament enacted the Courts Legislation Amendment (Judicial Complaints) Act 2012 (Cth) and the Judicial Misbehaviour and Incapacity (Parliamentary Commissions) Act 2012 (Cth) which, respectively, established a framework to enable the Chief Justices of federal courts (other than the High Court of Australia) to manage complaints that are referred to them, and a mechanism (parliamentary commissions) to be put in place following a resolution by each House of the Parliament to investigate specified allegations of misbehaviour or incapacity in relation to federal judges when required, to assist the Parliament when considering removal of a judge from office.

Subsequently, the family law courts established a system of internal review, providing 'a process by which complaints by a member of the public about judicial conduct can be brought to the attention of the Chief Justice and where appropriate the judge concerned' (Federal Circuit and Family Court of Australia, 2021). That process has the significant disadvantage of requiring the initiative of the complainant, and immediately identifying the complainant in a situation which is necessarily characterised by a power imbalance. It also provides the Chief Justice of the Family Court with considerable discretion as to how to deal with complaints. While there are also informal mechanisms available through the Bar (again, discussed later in this chapter) these mechanisms suffer from the same defects as the family courts' complaints process. Furthermore, the concept of 'judicial independence' means that there are limits as to what remedies are available. Although the Chief Justice may, at the end of the official complaints process, refer a complaint directly to the federal Attorney-General, to be considered by Parliament, history suggests that the likelihood of Parliament acting is remote: in the 120 years since Federation, no federal judge has been removed from office in Australia (Kirby, 2001). That position might have been tested following a recent internal inquiry by a 'Conduct Committee', commissioned by the Federal Circuit Court into the behaviour of a judge (Maley, 2021a). While the Committee found that the judge had engaged in inappropriate, sexualised behaviour towards two young women – a junior court employee and a law student – and recommended that the complaints be referred to the federal Attorney-General for her consideration, that step was no longer necessary once the judge (who had previously been disciplined for breaches of protocol, including failing to disqualify himself from hearing a case involving his former girlfriend) resigned (Maley, 2021b).

The current system of internal review does not apply to matters that are capable of being raised in an appeal (Federal Circuit and Family Court of Australia, 2021). Judicial conduct that amounts to actual or apprehended bias or denial of a fair hearing falls into this category. Where concern regarding bias arises, an application may be made during proceedings to the judge to recuse themselves (as occurred in *Charisteas*, considered later), but 'the judge who is the focus of the disqualification application for bias decides the application' (ALRC, 2021: 18). After judgment is delivered, the possibility of an appeal based on judicial conduct that amounts to actual or apprehended bias (or denial of a fair hearing) is technically available to litigants. However, the law on bias is 'difficult for lay people to understand' and 'its application is discretionary and unpredictable' (ALRC, 2021: 8). There are also 'systemic and ongoing issues impacting on judicial impartiality and perceptions of judicial bias that the bias rule is neither designed nor appropriate to manage', including '[b]ias resulting from heuristics, attitudes, and stereotypes' (ALRC, 2021: 11–12). Added to this, the appeals process is extremely expensive, and there are significant delays at two stages: before appeals are heard and when judgments are delivered. There is then the further expense of a rehearing. In most cases, an appeal is a luxury which the offended party cannot afford.

While it has been said that 'bona fide serious complaints against federal judicial officers are very rare' (ALRC, 1999: [2.248]), absence of data does not allow us to establish prevalence. As the ALRC has recently observed:

> Commonwealth courts do not collect data on reallocations, recusal, and disqualification, undermining transparency around how issues of judicial bias are dealt with and the ability to implement improvements to systems
>
> Some litigants and lawyers report experiencing bias in the Commonwealth courts, but available data is not sufficient to understand fully the extent of these experiences and the underlying reasons for them (ALRC, 2021: 10)

And of course, even if prevalence is low, impacts on those affected may be significant.

Against this backdrop, we now consider specific contexts where concerns regarding judicial malfunction have recently emerged, along with the action taken to seek redress and the family law system's response.

III. INAPPROPRIATE INTIMATE RELATIONSHIPS WITH COUNSEL

Australian family law practitioners comprise a relatively small and increasingly specialised group of something over 5,200 (Family Law Section, 2021) in a population of just under 26 million. The fact that specialist family law practitioners are one (albeit not the only) source of judicial appointments to Australian family law courts compounds a more general issue that judges in general are likely to be appointed from the ranks of legal practitioners (Attorney-General's Department, Court appointments, 2021): 'The very system of judicial appointment from the senior ranks of the profession means that such prior associations are inevitable' (*Aussie Airlines Pty Ltd v Australian Airlines Pty Ltd and Another* (*Aussie Airlines*) (1996) 135 ALR 753 per Merkel J at 760). Judges are often appointed to a court registry in the city or region in which they practised. By the time they are appointed to the bench, they are thus likely to enjoy close connections and networks with their colleagues, developed over years of attending university together or working in the same city or region, which may make the independence required of them in their judicial capacity challenging.

As the following discussion illustrates, when inappropriate relationships with counsel are apparent, the most obvious avenue for redress is the appeals process. As noted earlier, delay and cost will put this option beyond the reach of most. Even in a case where one might expect the answer to be 'open and shut', an appellant faces the risk of a departure from accepted standards being excused as 'a different interpretation of the application of a principle' as in *Charisteas* [2020] FamCAFC 162, considered later in this section. Indeed, the 'discretionary and unpredictable' application of the law on actual and apprehended bias, mentioned earlier, is particularly well-illustrated by the family law cases.

Back in 1995, for example, a firm line was taken by the Full Court in *Kennedy & Cahill* [1995] FamCA 157. In that case, the hearing took place on 29 September 1994 and the trial judge made orders on 8 November 1994. A solicitor who was in the full-time employment of the solicitors for the wife and who 'at times, had the sole carriage of the wife's case and at other times an advisory role' swore an affidavit on 24 January 1995 which included a statement that:

> My relationship with [the trial judge] began on 2 August, 1994. It is a serious and close personal relationship. I intend that the relationship continue.

The Full Court held that 'the appellant in our view is entitled to entertain a reasonable apprehension that her Honour might not bring an impartial and unprejudiced mind to the resolution of his dispute with the respondent'. The Full Court also made the following strong statement of principle:

> Public confidence in the judicial process depends upon judges determining their cases free from any suggestion of bias and influence of any kind. In our opinion, both the trial Judge and [the solicitor] had separate duties of disclosure. In the case of [the solicitor], he was bound to disclose his relationship with the trial Judge to the solicitor for the appellant, whilst her Honour was bound to disclose her relationship to the parties themselves or to have disqualified herself from hearing the matter. The relationship between her Honour and [the solicitor] which has continued uninterrupted since 2nd August, 1994 in our opinion has raised a question as to the integrity of the judicial process.
>
> … The Full Court of the Family Court has the clear obligation and responsibility to supervise the manner in which the trial judges of the Court exercise their judicial functions so as to ensure not only that the law is correctly applied but also that they are seen to act with the utmost propriety in the conduct of trials. This is not a question of justice being done but of justice being seen to be done.

Despite the clarity of the Full Court's statements in *Kennedy & Cahill*, a more recent Full Court (albeit with a strong and principled dissent by the Chief Justice) displayed a far more permissive attitude. *Charisteas v Charisteas and Others* (2020) 60 Fam LR 483 involved a case with 'an unfortunately long and tortured history' (*Charisteas v Charisteas* [2021] HCA 29, [1]). After proceedings which commenced in 2006 and a final hearing producing a decision which was then set aside on appeal, followed by a further lengthy interlocutory judgment, the third trial took place in August 2016 with final submissions due to be presented on 13 September 2016. On 9 September 2016, two of the respondents applied for the trial judge to disqualify himself by reason of his conduct during the hearing. The judge dismissed that application, and the Full Court dismissed an appeal against his refusal to disqualify himself (*XYZ Pty Ltd and Anor v Charisteas & Ors; ABC Pty Ltc & Charisteas and Ors* [2017] FamCAFC 112). The trial judge handed down his decision in February 2018. That decision was in the wife's favour and the husband appealed against those orders.

In May 2018, the husband found out that the judge and counsel for the wife had had contact on many occasions in person and by phone and by text message, between March 2016 (when the trial was listed for hearing) and February 2018 (when the decision was handed down). The husband's practitioners wrote to the wife's counsel (the judge having retired) asking for her written assurance that 'during the time the former Judge was seised of the [Charisteas] matter, [she] had no contact with him outside of court'. If that assurance could not be provided, she was asked to 'outline the circumstances of [her] dealings with him' (*Charisteas v Charisteas* [2021] HCA 29, [7]). The wife's counsel's response to this letter set out that she had met the trial judge for a drink or coffee on about four occasions between 22 March 2016 and 12 February 2018, had spoken with him by telephone on five occasions between January 2017 and August 2017, and that they had exchanged 'numerous' text messages from 20 June 2016 to 15 September 2017 and 'occasional' text messages from 15 September 2017 to 12 February 2018, with no text communication from 2 August 2016 to 19 August 2016 (when evidence was being led). The wife's counsel concluded that the communications 'did not concern the substance of the Charisteas case'. (*Charisteas v Charisteas* [2021] HCA 29, [8]).

The husband filed an amended notice of appeal, adding the ground that the 2018 'orders should be set aside and a retrial ordered because of a reasonable apprehension of bias on behalf of the primary judge' (*Charisteas* [2020] FamCAFC 162 per Alstergren CJ at [3]).

While the Full Court agreed that the relevant general statement of principle for reasonable apprehension of bias was:

> whether a fair-minded lay observer might reasonably apprehend that the judge might not bring an impartial mind to the resolution of the question which the judge is required to decide. (*Charisteas* [2020] FamCAFC 162 per Alstergren CJ at [39])

there was significant division regarding the application of that principle to the case. Chief Justice Alstergren dissented and would have allowed the appeal due to apprehended bias and remitted the matter for rehearing. The majority (Strickland and Ryan JJ) rejected the allegations of apprehended bias and dismissed the appeal. In doing so, the majority distinguished between communications during the trial and communications at other times, limiting the period during which it was necessary to avoid communications to the former. The majority reasoned that because the judge and the wife's barrister had not communicated over the period of the trial itself (thus indicating their appreciation of some of their obligations), the hypothetical observer would understand that the trial judge mistakenly understood that the obligation not to communicate continued and so would not see anything sinister in the judge's lack of disclosure. The majority further reasoned that the hypothetical observer would be 'able to tolerate' some degree of undisclosed private communication between a judge and the legal representative of only one party and would accept that the judge and counsel adhered to the professional restraint and did not discuss the case (as referred to in *Charisteas v Charisteas* [2021] HCA 29, [16]–[17], [20]).

In a unanimous decision, the High Court (Kiefel CJ, Gageler, Keane, Gordon and Gleeson JJ) allowed the husband's appeal, holding that apprehended bias was established and remitting the matter for rehearing. The Court concluded that a fair-minded lay observer, understanding 'that ordinary and most basic of judicial practice' (that there should be no communication when a case is underway between the judge and a parties or their legal advisers or witnesses without the knowledge and consent of the other party) would apprehend that the trial judge might not decide the case with an impartial mind, due to his communications with the wife's counsel (*Charisteas v Charisteas* [2021] HCA 29, [15]). In so holding, the High Court referred to the Full Court's reasoning as 'erroneous' as it failed to appreciate that even the *appearance* of departure from perceptions of independence and impartiality is prohibited, and conceived the hypothetical observer as a lawyer rather than as a member of the public (*Charisteas v Charisteas* [2021] HCA 29, [18], [21]).

The decision of the High Court represents a scathing attack on the trial judge and the wife's counsel; and a dismissive attitude to the sophistry in the Full Court's attempts to minimise the seriousness of the departure from acceptable standards.

Before the High Court's recent correction of the Full Court's decision in *Charisteas*, the case prompted the Federal government to ask the Australian Law Reform Commission to conduct a review of the laws relating to impartiality and bias applicable to the federal judiciary (Australian Law Reform Commission, 2020), with a final report due in December 2021. It is therefore possible that in the longer-term, the Full Court's unfortunate decision may (in combination with the High Court's decision) jettison any lingering tolerance for inappropriate intimate relationships between judges and counsel.

IV. INAPPROPRIATE EXCHANGES WITH PRACTITIONERS AND LITIGANTS

Judicial malfunction in the form of inappropriate exchanges with practitioners and litigants is a further issue of concern.

The main way in which such exchanges are likely to be the addressed is, once again, through the appeal processes. Indeed, the two majority judges in *Charisteas* – Ryan and Stickland JJ – were each members of two unanimous 2020 Full Courts which set aside decisions of trial judges on the basis that the their conduct towards a party's counsel during the hearing prevented a party from having a fair hearing.

In *Finch & Finch* [2020] FamCAFC 60 (Ryan, Aldridge and Tree JJ) the main concern was 'excessive judicial intervention', and in particular whether 'such interventions indicate that a fair trial has been denied to a litigant because the judge has closed his or her mind to further persuasion, moved into counsel's shoes and "into the perils of self-persuasion"' (*Finch & Finch* at [31]). The Full Court unanimously concluded that in the proceedings the judge's interventions were:

> … wholly unwarranted, unduly personalised, demonstrated an unfortunate entry by the primary judge into the arena, and did not adequately undo the consequences of the very forceful initial expression of a 'preliminary view' by the primary judge.
>
> It is no exaggeration to say that, during his cross-examination of the husband, virtually every time counsel for the wife commenced questioning on an issue, the primary judge's response was to either berate him by questioning the length of time it might take, the competence of the structure of his questions, or their relevance, or sought to impugn his integrity.
>
> During the wife's evidence, it was largely the same, albeit the primary judge's interventions often took an even more personalised form, and were exclusively directed to the wife herself. (*Finch & Finch* at [59]–[61])

The consequence was that:

> counsel for the wife was unable to properly conduct cross-examination of the husband in the face of the barrage of unwarranted interventions; we are less confident, but nonetheless persuaded, that the wife was precluded from properly giving her evidence under cross-examination by virtue of them also. There is a real danger that the trial was therefore unfair, and hence miscarried. (*Finch & Finch* at [67])

The relevant factual matrix was even more extreme in *Adacot & Sowle* [2020] FamCAFC 215 (Strickland, Ainslie-Wallace & Watts JJ), in which the father contended 'that the primary judge's conduct towards the father's legal representatives in the trial, was such that it not only gave rise to an apprehension of bias but also robbed the proceedings of any semblance of fairness and, as a result the proceedings miscarried' (*Adacot & Sowle* at [1]).

The Full Court observed that there were unwarranted criticisms of the father's Queen's Counsel's conduct at the end of the first day (*Adacot & Sowle* at [18]). On the second day the judge said to him: 'Do not be obtuse or rude. Try and improve from yesterday. Your performance was disgraceful' (*Adacot & Sowle* at [44]). On the third day that the trial judge's conduct deteriorated further. Even when the father's Queen's Counsel announced his appearance in the same manner as he had done on the previous two days, simply giving his name rather than his designation as Queen's Counsel, this was decried as 'a further amplification of your behaviour' (*Adacot & Sowle* at [60]). There was a comment slightly later that 'Your behaviour and demeanour has been demonstrable as a tautology in this trial' (*Adacot & Sowle* at [64]). In response to an innocent and irrelevant error by the father's Queen's Counsel (by giving the date when a subpoena issued rather than the date when documents were lodged with the court) the judge proceeded to require 'evidentiary reference' for every statement made and made repeated comments about the 'truthfulness' of what was being said. When the father's Queen's Counsel withdrew from the proceeding as a response to the personal nature of his interaction with the judge (*Adacot & Sowle* at [115]) and the instructing solicitor took over the conduct of the case, there was no improvement in the judge's behaviour with comments such as: 'It's not me that has got the cognition problem' (*Adacot & Sowle* at [84]).

The wife's lawyers attempted to defend the decision on appeal by the argument that the judge's comments were only directed to the lawyers and were 'separate from the facts and merits of the case' (*Adacot & Sowle* at [5]). The Full Court rejected this argument as follows:

> the primary judge, by his conduct, squarely raised an apprehension of bias and failed to afford the father a fair trial ... the primary judge's interventions, his cruel, insulting, humiliating and rude interactions with the father's Queen's Counsel and his solicitor, amounted to an abuse of the power of his position and, in our view must be redressed by allowing the appeal lest the integrity of the judicial system be undermined. (*Adacot & Sowle* at [116], [117])

In so holding, the Full Court concluded that '[t]he aspersions ... on the honesty of the father's Queens Counsel were without justification and should not have been made' (*Adacot & Sowle* at [35]); and that '[t]here was no basis for the primary judge to impugn the professionalism of the father's Queens Counsel in the manner he did or at all' (*Adacot & Sowle* at [67]).

It is difficult to argue with the conclusions in these two appeal decisions, but two important questions remain. The first is as to the consistency between the position of the appeal judges who were part of these two unanimous decisions but were also part of the majority of the Full Court who dismissed the appeal in *Charisteas*. The second is as to the extent of bullying or otherwise inappropriate judicial behaviour which is not corrected through the appeal process.

As regards the second concern, the two examples above are not unique. Of the respondents to the Victorian Bar's 2018 Quality of Working Life survey (in which 40 per cent of 2160 members participated), 59 per cent indicated that they had experienced judicial bullying (The Victorian Bar, 2018). Indeed, the experience of the Second-named author of this chapter includes being told by a trial judge: 'You're not totally Australian, your accent'. His attempted deflection of this comment to the effect that the only real Australians were those with Aboriginal heritage was met with the euphemistic: 'I meant in the sense that you didn't have your childhood here. Am I right about that?' The (statistically correct) response that 25 per cent of Victorians were not born here was met with the judge's statistically incorrect statement: 'I think we're getting somewhere in the region of 40 to 50 per cent of most Australians are born overseas'. The judge here probably had in mind the statistic that about 49 per cent of Australians were either born overseas *or* have a parent who was born overseas (ABS, 2016), but the racist assumptions underlying the error are unfortunately resonant for anyone with memories of Pauline Hanson's 1996 maiden Parliamentary speech with the statement that 'we are in danger of being swamped by Asians' (Hanson, 1996: 3859) and her 2016 return to Parliament with: 'Now we are in danger of being swamped by Muslims' (Hanson, 2016: 938).

In a more extreme case that also did not reach the law reports, the Full Court had to deal with the situation where a trial judge called for the Federal Police and asked them to sit in the courtroom because counsel for the husband insisted on making an objection to the wife's cross-examination. The Full Court held that there was an 'irresistible conclusion … that there was an absence of a fair trial' (*Marra & Marra* [1996] FamCA 137, per Barblett DCJ, Fogarty and Lindenmayer JJ). Given the importance of the decision and the novelty of the situation, it is at least curious why neither of the specialist family law reporting services have ever included this decision.

Inappropriate treatment of litigants by judges is also evident. This includes the recent experience of an unrepresented husband serving about a week in prison because of an order jailing him for contempt. The order was set aside by the Full Court (*Stradford & Stradford* [2019] FamCAFC 25) with the wife not only supporting the appeal, but also having asked the judge on two occasions not to send the husband to jail. In other words, the judge was effectively acting of his own motion. Further, the Full Court made clear that there was a premeditated aspect on the part of the trial judge, in that the threat of jail was openly raised at an earlier hearing when the judge told the husband that if he did not make full financial disclosure, 'bring your toothbrush' (*Stradford & Stradford* [2019] FamCAFC 25, at [20]). The Full Court was unanimously and unequivocally scathing of the judge for treating the issue of disclosure as a criminal issue of contempt of court, while also refusing to accord the husband the protections of being a defendant in criminal process or consider, as the legislation requires, whether other sanctions were more appropriate (*Stradford & Stradford* [2019] FamCAFC 25, at [68]–[70]).

How, then, does the 'system' make provision for the malfunction of inappropriate exchanges with counsel and litigants, including bullying? In addition to his successful appeal, the husband in *Stradford & Stradford* currently has a claim in the Federal Court for damages against the judge (The Age, 2021). This, however, will require the husband to establish that the doctrine of judicial immunity, which operates to the effect that judges cannot be civilly liable for their decisions, was lost. This has only rarely been held to occur. In addition, in response to concerns raised by the Law Council of Australia, Chief Judge Alstergren announced that the judge in *Stradford* would receive 'mentoring'

(ABC News, 2021). Complaints not capable of being raised in an appeal might be made through the Family Court's formal complaints procedure or the Bar, the difficulties surrounding which are considered in the next section.

V. DELAYS IN DELIVERY OF JUDGMENT

Another malfunction in the system is delay in the delivery of judgment.

Despite the publication of key data in relation to court performance in annual reports of the family law courts, lack of clarity surrounds the incidence and extent of delay. For example, in 2018, PWC reported that 68 per cent of Family Court judgments and 74 per cent of Federal Circuit Court judgments were delivered within three months (PWC, 2018: 66). This figure had improved to 83 per cent in the Family Court's Annual Report for the year 2019–2020 (Family Court of Australia, 2020, Part 3, Report on Court Performance). However, the corollary of the figures for judgments which are delivered within three months is that, respectively, 26 per cent and now 17 per cent of judgments were not delivered within three months of the conclusion of the hearing. Further, there was no discussion of how far beyond three months the delays extended. There is a significant difference between a slippage of four months and the delays of more than a year which feature in the reported decisions.

In *Wallis v Manning* [2017] FamCAFC 14, for example, there was a three-year delay in the delivery of judgment by the Federal Circuit Court judge after the conclusion of the trial of property issues before the judge (at [1]). In cases which relate to the best interests of children, the delay can end up determining the result if the relevant factual matrix changes sufficiently. In *Cavour* [2019] FamCA 478 the wife at trial sought a change of residence so that two teenage daughters, of whom she had been the primary carer pre-separation, could live with her in circumstances where they were currently living with the father and had had no contact with her for over 16 months. The daughters were entrenched in their opposition to the mother, and one of the issues which the trial judge had to consider was whether making orders against the wishes of the children would put them in danger if they chose to abscond from the mother's care. The hearing took place in the last week of August 2018. The judgment (which included an order 'That the mother spend time and communicate with the children in accordance with the children's wishes') was delivered in mid-July 2019, by which time the children were nearly a year older and any windows of opportunity to repair the relationship with their mother would be necessarily even more difficult.

More recently, in *Manifold & Alderton* ([2021] FamCAFC 61), the Full Court allowed the father's appeal against parenting and property orders delivered more than seven years after the initial trial had concluded and where the reasons for decision gave no explanation or justification of the delay. By the time the trial judge delivered her judgment the children, both of whom had special needs 'had grown from infancy to near adolescence and the parties' property bore little correlation to that which they owned when proceedings were first started in November 2012' (*Manifold & Alderton* [2021] FamCAFC 61, per Austin J at [87]). The Full Court agreed that the delay was 'integral to the appeal' and had 'impaired the primary judge's capacity to distil the issues, properly assess the evidence, and make necessary findings' (*Manifold & Alderton* [2021] FamCAFC 61, per Austin J at [88]). A further 'mischief' was that the court file had been lost before judgment was made, leading to the inference 'that her Honour, when determining the disputes, was deprived of and therefore did not take into account material evidence' (*Manifold & Alderton* [2021] FamCAFC 61, per Austin J at [89]).

So how does the 'system' make provision for the malfunction of delay? In relation to appeal, the Family Court has followed the more general approach of the High Court in *NAIS v Minister for Immigration and Multicultural and Indigenous Affairs* [2005] HCA 77 (similar to other jurisdictions, see: *Expectations Pty Ltd v PRD Realty Pty Ltd* [2004] FCAFC 189; *Clavel v Savage* [2015] NSWCA 61; *MM Constructions (Aust) Pty Ltd v Port Stephens Council* [2012] NSWCA 417) that it is ultimately the error rather than the delay which forms the basis for the appellate court to intervene. This is reflected in the Full Court's statement in *Rollings & Rollings* [2009] FamCAFC 47 at para [67] that:

> The authorities thus establish that if there is a delay between the conclusion of the hearing and judgment, presumably with contemporaneity of reasons, the delay is not in itself a ground of appeal and it is not, as argued in McCrossen, a denial of a fair trial and/or a miscarriage of justice. However the delay does mean that on appeal there has to be greater scrutiny of the findings made by the trial judge.

It follows that the delay itself is not a ground of appeal.

Although it can make an appeal court more likely to intervene, the general approach of the Full Court has been resistant to such arguments. The approach in *Feranti & Connor (Contravention Appeal)* [2009] FamCAFC 178 at [164] – that is 'well established by authority that delay in delivery of reasons, whilst unsatisfactory, particularly if unexplained, does not necessarily constitute appealable error. Rather, the reasons require much greater scrutiny than would otherwise be the case' – has been applied consistently in a way that makes clear that delay is not of itself a reason to challenge a decision (eg *Herridge v Handerson* (2011) 46 Fam LR 367 at [18]–[23], *Wynona v Friend* [2011] FamCAFC 6, [106] ff, *Doherty* [2014] FamCAFC 20 at [52]–[58] *Vismay & Shaw* [2014] FamCAFC 124 at [17], *Jarrett* [2015] FamCAFC 126 at [85]–[89], *Gillard* [2015] FamCAFC 169 at [65], *Velderman* [2020] FamCAFC 243 at [26], *Manifold & Alderton* [2021] FamCAFC 61 at [36]). It is interesting to speculate whether there would be an impact on judicial performance if it was.

Given that delay is of itself not a ground for appeal, what other avenues for redress are available? In relation to malfunctions including delay and bullying, and that cannot be dealt with by an appeal or other application to the court, family law courts have, as mentioned earlier, developed an 'official' judicial complaints procedure. The Family Law Act 1975 (Cth) section 21B, however, provides the Chief Justice of the Family Court with considerable discretion as to how to deal with complaints:

> (1B) The Chief Justice may, if a complaint is made about another Judge, deal with the complaint by doing either or both of the following in respect of the complaint:
>
> (a) deciding whether or not to handle the complaint and then doing one of the following:
>
> (i) dismissing the complaint;
>
> (ii) handling the complaint if the Chief Justice has a relevant belief in relation to the complaint about the other Judge;
>
> (iii) arranging for any other complaint handlers to assist the Chief Justice to handle the complaint if the Chief Justice has a relevant belief in relation to the complaint about the other Judge;
>
> (b) arranging for any other complaint handlers to decide whether or not to handle the complaint and then to do one of the following:
>
> (i) dismiss the complaint;
>
> (ii) handle the complaint if each of the complaint handlers has a relevant belief in relation to the complaint about the other Judge.

There are also informal mechanisms available through the Bar. For example:

> A party may express concerns or complaints about delay in the delivery of a judgment. In such a case a party can send a letter to the president of the bar association or the law society in the State or Territory in which the case was heard and request that the president take up the matter with the Chief Justice. The president will then convey the concern or complaint to the Chief Justice without identifying which party complained. The Chief Justice will look into the matter and, if appropriate, take it up with the judge concerned. (Family Court of Australia, 2017)

All these mechanisms have the defect of requiring the initiative of the complainant and immediately identifying the complainant in a situation which is necessarily characterised by a power imbalance. This means they will require a certain level of courage on the part of the complainant if they are a party who is the subject of a reserved decision and/or a practitioner who seeks to appear before that judge in the future. Thus, although in 2019–20 the Family Court received only 21 judicial service complaints, four regarding judicial conduct and 17 regarding delay in delivery of a judgment (Family Court of Australia, 2020a: 29), this does not necessarily indicate that judicial malfunction is rare. Further, as noted earlier, the concept of 'judicial independence' means that there are limits as to what remedies are available. At most, the Chief Justice may, at the end of the official complaints process, refer a complaint directly to the Attorney-General, to be considered by Parliament.

VI. CONCLUSION

Our analysis in this chapter points to serious concerns regarding how Australia's legal system deals with judicial malfunction of federal judges, including judges of the family courts. Further questions beyond the scope of this chapter exist as to whether the 'judicial independence' commonly accepted as a requirement of the separation of powers is in practice a challenge to the separation of powers, due to the absence of any 'checks and balances' in relation to the Executive's processes of judicial appointment (Australian Constitution, section 61). Consistent with this, the ALRC in its current inquiry into judicial impartiality proposed that '[t]he Australian Government should commit to a more transparent process for appointing federal judicial officers that involves a call for expressions of interest, publication of criteria for appointment, and explicitly aims for a suitably-qualified pool of candidates who reflect the diversity of the community' (ALRC, 2021: 26).

While the ALRC has suggested several other options for better addressing issues that we have identified, including transfer of applications for recusal to the duty judge (leaving unaddressed the concern that 'having judges of the same court rule on their fellow judges doesn't sound like a perfect idea, either' (Pelly, 2021)), an orientation program for new judges, ongoing judicial education, and the introduction of 'methodologically sound processes to seek structured [anonymised, aggregated] feedback from court users, including litigants and practitioners, about their satisfaction with the court process, in a way that allows any concerns about experiences of a lack of judicial impartiality to be raised' (ALRC, 2021: 34), all of these amount to tinkering at the edges.

Fixed judicial terms of (say) five years and review of reappointment by an independent body outside the Family Court would make the system more 'systematic' in the sense of replacing judicial officers who had proved unfit for purpose. Complaints being handled by someone independent of the Court (similar to the approach adopted in some other jurisdictions, as noted earlier) would be more systematic than the Court's current internal process, as would automatic triggering of consequences in the event, for example, that a decision was not delivered within three months. These more fundamental changes would, however, require Parliament to act on the recommendation of the independent body, and/or Constitutional amendment to remove section 72(ii) – both of which are highly unlikely to occur. Given this, much would seem to rest on the High Court's decision in *Charisteas* and the work of the ALRC in its review of judicial impartiality and the law on bias (due to report in September 2021) to provide some much-needed boundaries for judges who really should know better.

REFERENCES

ABC News (2021) 'This proposed lawsuit could test whether a judge can be sued for sending someone to jail': www.abc.net.au/news/2020-01-31/proposed-lawsuit-could-test-whether-judge-can-be-sued-for-senten/11910592.

ABS (2016) 'Cultural Diversity in Australia, 2016. 2071.0 – Census of Population and Housing: Reflecting Australia – Stories from the Census, 2016': www.abs.gov.au/ausstats/abs@.nsf/Lookup/by%20Subject/2071.0~2016~Main%20Features~Cultural%20Diversity%20Article~60.

Attorney-General's Department (2021) 'Court appointments': www.ag.gov.au/legal-system/courts/court-appointments.

Australian Constitution.

Australian Institute of Family Studies (2019) 'Parenting arrangements after separation. Research Summary – October 2019': aifs.gov.au/publications/parenting-arrangements-after-separation.

Australian Law Reform Commission (1999) 'Managing Justice: A Review of the Federal Civil Justice System' ALRC Report 89: www.alrc.gov.au/publication/managing-justice-a-review-of-the-federal-civil-justice-system-alrc-report-89.

Australian Law Reform Commission (2019) 'Family Law for the Future: An Inquiry into the Family Law System' ALRC Report 135.

Australian Law Reform Commission (2021) 'Judicial Impartiality: Consultation Paper' CP 1, 2021: www.alrc.gov.au/publication/judicial-impartiality-cp1.

Family Court of Australia (2020) 'Annual Report 2019–2020': www.fcfcoa.gov.au/2019-20-family-court-australia-annual-report.

Family Law Section, Law Council of Australia (2021) 'About us': www.familylawsection.org.au/about-us.

Federal Circuit and Family Court of Australia (2021) 'Judicial Complaints Procedure': www.fcfcoa.gov.au/policies-and-procedures/judicial-complaints.

Gleeson, M (1999) 'The state of the judicature', Address Australian Legal Convention Canberra, 10 October 1999, cited in ALRC 1999, [2.250].

Hanson, P (1996) Member for Oxley. Appropriation Bill (No. 1) 1996–97 Second Reading. 10 September 1996. Parliamentary Debates (Hansard). Commonwealth of Australia: House of Representatives, p 3859: parlinfo.aph.gov.au/parlInfo/search/display/display.w3p;query=Id%3A%22chamber%2Fhansardr%2F1996-09-10%2F0038%22.

Hanson, P (2016) Queensland. First Speech. Commonwealth of Australia, Parliamentary Debates, Senate, Official Hansard, 14 September 2016, pp 937–944: parlinfo.aph.gov.au/parlInfo/download/chamber/hansards/16daad94-5c74-4641-a730-7f6d74312148/toc_pdf/Senate_2016_09_14_4436_Official.pdf;fileType=application%2Fpdf.

Joint Select Committee on Australia's Family Law System (2020) Improvements in family law proceedings, Interim report.

Kaspiew, R, Carson, R, Dunstan, J, Qu, L, Horsfall, B, De Maio, J, Moore, S, Moloney, L, Coulson, M and Tayton, S (2015) *Evaluation of the 2012 Family Violence Amendments*, Synthesis report (Australian Institute of Family Studies, Melbourne, Australia).

Kirby, M (2001) Discipline of federal judicial officers in Australia. The Judicial Group on Strengthening Judicial Integrity, Second Meeting, Bangalore, India 24–26 February 2001: www.hcourt.gov.au/assets/publications/speeches/former-justices/kirbyj/kirbyj_judicialgroup.htm.

Maley, J (2021a) 'Federal Circuit Court judge found to have harassed two young women', *The Sydney Morning Herald* (8 July): www.smh.com.au/national/federal-circuit-court-judge-found-to-have-harassed-two-young-female-staff-20210707-p587sz.html.

Maley, J (2021b) 'Judge who harassed women was barred from court duties after decisions criticised', *The Sydney Morning Herald* (8 July): www.smh.com.au/business/workplace/judge-who-harassed-women-was-barred-from-court-duties-after-decisions-criticised-20210708-p5880s.html.

Pelly, M (2021) 'Should judges be free to decide whether they are biased?' *The Australian Financial Review* (30 April).

PWC (2018) 'Review of efficiency of the operation of the federal courts' Final report (April): www.ag.gov.au/sites/default/files/2020-03/pwc-report.pdf.

Qu, L, Weston, R, Moloney, L, Kaspiew, R and Dunstan, J (2014) 'Postseparation parenting, property and relationship dynamics after five years' (Canberra: Attorney-General's Department): www.ag.gov.au/families-and-marriage/publications/post-separation-parenting-property-and-relationship-dynamics-after-five-years.

The Age (2021) 'Man personally suing judge for compensation over "gross miscarriage of justice"': www.theage.com.au/national/man-personally-suing-judge-for-compensation-over-gross-miscarriage-of-justice-20210108-p56sob.html.

The Victorian Bar (2018) 'Quality of Working Life Survey', Final report and analysis (October 2018): www.vicbar.com.au/sites/default/files/Wellbeing%20of%20the%20Victorian%20Bar%20report%20final%20Oct%202018.pdf.

13

Family Court Proceedings in Parent and Child Matters in Germany: A Binding Setting for Alternative Dispute Resolution

THOMAS MEYSEN

The German approach to family justice in parent and child matters is characterised by a structured interplay between all the professional stakeholders, with the family courts and the child and youth welfare system as main actors. In the case of conflict over contact and custody, separated or divorced parents are expected to make use of so-called counselling centres. These are provided and financed by the child and youth welfare system, and access is free of cost for parents and children. The family court primarily serves in a process-oriented secondary role; it works towards and can order parents' participation in counselling, which does not address the decision itself but looks at the reasons that are hindering parents from coming forth with solutions themselves. The family court guarantees a binding setting in which it must hold a first hearing within a month to sound out the situation and sort out the next steps. Joint counselling (or mediation if desired) is the usual follow up, which could be backed by temporary agreements or orders, further assessment and protection measures in case of violence. The ultimate goal is to enable parents to control the fate of their post-separation parenthood. A majority of judges, lawyers, guardians ad litem, social worker and counsellors (75 per cent) believe the proceedings are practicable, but are less confident about the potential to prevent conflict in first place, with varying views over the question whether the agreements are sustainable, or sceptical about success in high-conflict cases. The incentives for the justice system are significant reductions of direct costs as well as judges' time to work these cases. The burden of family law disputes on the public purse as a whole are not affected, but the policy is seen as the right way to address conflicts in parent and child matters in separated families.

I. THE GERMAN APPROACH: A HISTORICAL INTRODUCTION

A. Family Law Reform in 1998: Family Conflict as Cause in Need of Support

The law of parent and child matters was subject to major reform in 1998 (Deutscher Bundestag, 1996). As a general rule, since then contact with both parents has been declared to be in the best interest of the child.[1] The child and each parent have a right to contact that can be claimed at court.[2] In addition, parents are obliged to refrain from any action that renders more difficult the relationship of the child to the other parent.[3] If parents are or have been married shared custody continues after separation or divorce unless a parent claims sole custody at court and transfer to the applicant is regarded as most conducive to the best interests of the child.[4] Non-married parents can achieve shared custody by declaration.[5]

What seems to be standard nowadays was a paradigmatic change at the time of the reform (Proksch, 2002) that 'did not leave a stone standing' (Schwab, 1998: 457). To find common ground, family conflicts after separation have been framed as a cause for support. The child and youth welfare law defined a parental right to counselling and support in case of separation and divorce[6] as well as in the exercise of contact.[7] Parents shall be supported in the development of a plan for the parental custody and responsibility.[8] Services are accessible independently of a court proceeding. The main providers are the counselling centres (*Erziehungsberatungsstellen*), run by non-governmental organisations or local authorities as a defined unit. The law requires them to be multi-disciplinary and to work with different methods and concepts of counselling, advice and mediation.[9] The services can be used by all parents without cost. They can access the centres themselves and do not need a permit from the child and youth welfare office to do so.[10]

The services of counselling centres are reliably and in a timely way available in all 560 cities and counties with a child and youth welfare office. Larger local authorities are obliged to offer a variety of centres so that parents have a choice, or example between a centre run by a catholic, protestant or non-religious non-governmental organisation. Since national statistics started recording data the number of counselling activities in cases of separation and divorce has risen

[1] Section 1626(3) Civil Code.
[2] Section 1684(1) Civil Code.
[3] Section 1684(2) Civil Code.
[4] Section 1671(1) Civil Code.
[5] Section 1626(1) Civil Code.
[6] Section 17(1) Social Code Book VIII.
[7] Section 18(3) Social Code Book VIII.
[8] Section 17(2) Social Code Book VIII.
[9] Section 28 Social Code Book VIII.
[10] Section 36a(2) Social Code Book VIII.

steadily, increasing by 125 per cent from about 33,000 in 1993 to 74,000 in 2006, with a slight peak after the reform of 1998 (bke 2012: 14–16). Hence, the support services have been provided by the child and youth welfare system. They include professional attendance and counselling for the child and both parents in cases of supervised/protected contact, which is another litigable right of parents laid down in social law.[11]

The link into the family court proceedings remains through the obligatory participation of a social worker from the social services in the child and youth welfare office (*Jugendamt*) in all family court proceedings concerning contact and custody.[12] They represent a specialist authority with their socio-pedagogical expertise and complement the judicial expertise by providing written reports as well as attendance at court hearings. The family justice system did not incorporate any psychosocial idea of conflict resolution. It stayed adversarial and decision-oriented. The ground-breaking shift in German family policy was translated into a complex family law reform that has notions of a 'hair-splitting jurists' oeuvre' in a typical German law tradition attempting to 'judicialise the whole of life' (Schwab, 1998: 472).

B. Family Justice Reform in 2009: Family Court Proceedings as Part of a Process

The reform of 1998 was consistent but still incomplete. It accepted the conflicts after separation and divorce as a need of the children and parents involved, but aligned the family justice system with it. Nevertheless, in a few regions models of interdisciplinary collaboration evolved. The most prominent has been a model and later the practice from Cochem, a small town in Rhineland-Palatine. The family judge went on a nationwide mission propagating the coordinated practice in his court district in which:

- the family court pledged to hold a hearing swiftly;
- lawyers abstained from written pleadings that were conflict exacerbating;
- counselling centres offered the parents a first appointment within two weeks;
- the child and youth welfare office attended every hearing but spared itself the necessity of the usual written opinions; and
- psychological experts promised to work in a solution-oriented manner (Rudolph, 2005).

At the time, consensus had been reached that the fragmented law on family court proceedings needed reform. The legislator constructed a coherent act for

[11] Section 18(3)4 Social Code Book VIII.
[12] Section 50 Social Code Book VIII.

all family matters: the Act on Proceedings in Family Matters and in Matters of Non-contentious Jurisdiction. In the explanatory memorandum one of the legislator's core solutions was the 'acceleration of contact and custody proceedings: introduction of an obligatory first hearing within a short period (one month) to avoid longer contact discontinuities; encouragement of parents' amicable solutions on contact and custody' (Deutscher Bundestag, 2007: 2).

Since the reform came into force in 2009 parents are no longer parties in the family court proceedings but 'participants',[13] as are the child and the guardian ad litem.[14] It is mandatory for first instance family courts to conduct proceedings in matters concerning the child's residence, contact and the surrender and protection of the child as accelerated, as well as prioritised over all other family court matters.[15] First, the case shall be argued with all participants in an 'early hearing' that shall take place not later than a month after the start of the proceedings and may only be postponed due to compelling reasons; the child and youth welfare office is to be heard at this hearing.[16] The 'early hearing' does not pave the path to the fastest possible decision but is intended to decelerate and de-escalate the family conflict dynamics through the acceleration of proceedings (Heinke et al, 2021; Wegener, 2020: 1012). Parents' personal appearance before the court shall be ordered.[17] This allows the judge and the social worker from the child and youth welfare office to sound out the situation and sort out the next steps, which may range from settlement through an agreement to measures to protect the child or a parent (Meysen, 2014a: 532).

In parent and child matters upon separation or divorce, other than in child protection matters,[18] the court shall facilitate agreement of the participants at every phase of the proceedings.[19] It shall inform them about the services of counselling centres as well as of the child and youth welfare office. The court's advice is only semi-voluntary, since it may order the parents to participate in such support services – a decision that can neither be appealed nor enforced.[20] Agreements shall be recorded as court-approved settlements, which carry the same liability as court orders. As a formal participant in the proceedings, any

[13] Section 7 Act on Proceedings in Family Matters and in Matters of Non-contentious Jurisdiction.

[14] Section 158 (3)2 Act on Proceedings in Family Matters and in Matters of Non-contentious Jurisdiction.

[15] Section 155(1) Act on Proceedings in Family Matters and in Matters of Non-contentious Jurisdiction.

[16] Section 155(2) Act on Proceedings in Family Matters and in Matters of Non-contentious Jurisdiction.

[17] Section 155(3) Act on Proceedings in Family Matters and in Matters of Non-contentious Jurisdiction.

[18] Section 157 Act on Proceedings in Family Matters and in Matters of Non-contentious Jurisdiction.

[19] Section 156(1)1 Act on Proceedings in Family Matters and in Matters of Non-contentious Jurisdiction.

[20] Section 156(1)2-5 Act on Proceedings in Family Matters and in Matters of Non-contentious Jurisdiction.

guardian ad litem has to agree as well, and the court will only approve when the agreement is not contrary to the best interests of the child.[21] If no agreement can be reached in the 'early hearing', the court shall discuss an interlocutory order with the participants and the child and youth welfare office. The child shall be heard in person by the judge prior to issuing such an order.[22]

Anne Loschky (2011) framed the professional cooperation as 'fenced voluntariness' which might be termed 'guided autonomy'. Family courts, having such a set of binding measures up their sleeves, can create a setting that puts quite some pressure on parents to face their conflict and the reasons that hinder them to come up with autonomous decisions about their family life. The use of joint counselling has become the expected norm. Lawyers advise parents about counselling and parents may contact the child and youth welfare office or a counselling centre proactively to show their willingness to cooperate. If they do not jointly manage to make use of such services and seek their rights at the family justice system, usually the entry point is the judge motivating or ordering them to do so. If parents reach an agreement in the process of professional counselling they usually return to court to have it approved.

Quantitatively the number of cases in the counselling centres doubled again after the reform. In 2014, in 151,667 of the 309,907 cases advice and support by counselling centres was provided in family conflicts in the parental partnership, after separation and divorce, or disputes about contact and custody (Statistisches Bundesamt, 2016). The number of concluded family court proceedings concerning contact[23] also increased significantly after each of the two reforms. Around 1998 it went up from 21,841 cases in 1997 to 30,547 cases in 2000 and the numbers grew steadily to 36,653 in 2004 and 44,780 in 2008. After the reform of 2009 another peak of 10,000 more cases was reached by 2011 (54,980 in 2011). But from then on numbers have plateaued at a level of around 55,000 proceedings since 2010 (see Table 13.1).

Table 13.1 Concluded family court proceedings regarding contact, from 1997 to 2019

Year	1997	2000	2004	2008	2011	2014	2016	2019
conclusion of proceedings concerning contact	21,841	30,547	36,653	44,780	54,980	56,400	54,349	55,640

Source: Statistisches Bundesamt (1998, 2002, 2005, 2009, 2012, 2014, 2017, 2020).

[21] Section 156(2) Act on Proceedings in Family Matters and in Matters of Non-contentious Jurisdiction.

[22] Section 156(3) Act on Proceedings in Family Matters and in Matters of Non-contentious Jurisdiction.

[23] Proceedings concerning the devolution and withdrawal of custody are counted together with child protection proceedings and, therefore, are not listed here.

Due to a lack of research on the family justice system and its law in action, interpretations need to be made cautiously. Since before 1998 a right to contact was rarely adjudicated if the 'residential parent', usually the mother, did not agree (Hammer, 2021), it is not surprising that mainly fathers took their chance to push through their right to contact. Rising societal expectations towards fathers and their wish not only to take on financial responsibilities but also to be actively involved in the care of their children (Jurczyk and Walper, 2009; Possinger, 2013; Li et al, 2015) could explain the continuous increase of conflicts in families with separated parents reaching the courts. Reasons for the increase in cases after 2009 might be rooted in previous reservations about calling on the court due to the legal situation before reform, with decision-oriented one-shot chances. Additionally, after the reform, initiating family court proceedings includes the incentive that they usually lead to a binding engagement of the other parent in a process working towards a family life after separation that both parents can agree on.

II. LEGALLY SET NORMATIVITY FOR POST-SEPARATION FAMILIES

Societal normativity for post-separation families, cast in a legislative mould, states that contact with both parents is generally in the best interest of the child[24] and leads to a legal actuality that both parents routinely have joint custody (Liebsch, 2017). In that, the law proceeds from the given assumption that a continuation of the parent-child relationship usually has positive effects on the well-being of a child (Sütterly, 2017: 57). The norm cannot appeal to empirical findings in developmental psychology (Kindler, 2009). Nevertheless, the statutory presumption sets the scene for professionals. They do not need to assess whether contact is in the best interests of the child in every single case or what assignment of custody might serve the interests of the child better, but only when there are extraordinary circumstances. Therefore, as Nina Dethloff describes it in one of the leading handbooks for family law, professionals' actions should be oriented towards two interests of the children which are not easy to reconcile with each other:

(i) to regularly maintain a close relationship to both parents; and
(ii) to support the achievement of a conflict-free family setting after separation and divorce (Dethloff, 2018: 433).

The latter leads to another formative norm in the family justice system: reaching parental agreements. Its roots are derived from the constitution and the principle of proportionality. While the state has the role of a 'custodian' when

[24] Section 1626(3) Civil Code.

intruding into family life due to the protection of children from harm,[25] its role is to act as intermediary in cases of parental conflict (Jestaedt and Reimer, 2018; Osthold, 2016: 196 ff). This places autonomy in the hands of the parents, which is to be respected by the state, including the courts, as far as possible. The procedural obligation to work towards the use of counselling/mediation and parental agreements[26] is driven by the goal to be a 'neutral agreement helper' (Hammer, 2020: 1531) for parents to regain independence in their ability to make decisions of substantial significance[27] and about contact (Meysen, 2014b: 550). Consequently, as well as revealingly, the legal procedural framing is called 'agreement proceedings' in the literature (Streicher, 2019: 585).

The incentives for family judges to follow the norm of intermediating consent-oriented proceedings are obvious but rarely openly discussed and has not yet been reflected on in publications. Being in the position of enhancing conflict reduction and enabling the preservation of a 'full family' after parental separation has a positive connotation in society and is in line with an understanding of the state respecting personal liberties, but this is not the only factor. For the family justice system, the proceedings are also resource-efficient and for the judges their workload is reduced. First, in a case where an agreement can be achieved judges can cut down on time-consuming written judgments. Second, if parents do not agree in the early hearing, it is the counselling centres, the child and youth welfare offices or mediators doing the job; these are financed by the local communities and not the states (*Länder*) which are responsible for the justice system. Third, achieving parental agreements spares judges the obligation to hear the child in person. It is mandatory to hear children from the age three or four years and over[28] prior to a preliminary decision[29] or a decision on the merits of the case.[30] Judges usually take note of the duty to hear the child in person (Schmidt, 2020: 271 ff): 95.3 per cent of family judges declared in a national study that they hear children from enrolment onward and the average age for hearing the child was 4.1 years (Karle, 2010). Thus, only 39.6 per cent of children (n=318) answered that the judge heard them in child protection proceedings (Bindel-Kögel und Seidenstücker, 2017, section 168 ff) and in an

[25] Art. 6(2)2 Basic Law for the Federal Republic of Germany.

[26] Section 156(1) Act on Proceedings in Family Matters and in Matters of Non-contentious Jurisdiction.

[27] Section 1687(1)1 Civil Code.

[28] Section 159(1) Act on Proceedings in Family Matters and in Matters of Non-contentious Jurisdiction backed up by the Federal Constitutional Court (eg 26 Sept. 2006 – 1 BvR 1827/06; 23 March 2007 – 1 BvR 156/07; 17 June 2009 – 1 BvR 467/09; 14 Juy 2010 – 1 BvR 3189/09) and the Federal Supreme Court (eg 12 February 1992 – XII ZR 53/91; 15 June 2016 – XII ZB 419/15; 31 October 2018 – XII ZB 411/18).

[29] Section 156(3)3 Act on Proceedings in Family Matters and in Matters of Non-contentious Jurisdiction.

[30] Section 159(2) Act on Proceedings in Family Matters and in Matters of Non-contentious Jurisdiction.

analysis of files (n=343) only in 53 per cent of the files was a hearing of the child documented (Kratky, 2020). The reason for these discrepancies remain unclear but might partly be explained by proceedings that did not end with a judgment.

Overall, judges tend to refrain from openly intruding into family life after divorce and separation but have all the tools to pressure parents to seek counselling/mediation and to more or less freely agree on contact and custody. Surrounded by such normativity, the awareness of a transgression of limits resulting in an encroachment into family life seems to be much more pronounced than for such encroachments resulting from falling short of necessary intervention, as Rüdiger Ernst, presiding judge at the high court of Berlin, points out (Ernst, 2016: 361 f). This particularly shows in cases of child abuse, intimate partner violence and so-called high-conflict cases (see section IV).

III. EMPIRICAL FINDINGS ON PROFESSIONALS' PERCEPTION OF THE PROCEEDINGS

About eight years after the major reform with the introduction of the Act on Proceedings in Family Matters and in Matters of Non-contentious Jurisdiction of 2009, the Federal Ministry of Justice commissioned research to evaluate the proceedings. The quantitative study conducted by Stefan Ekert and Bettina Heiderhoff (2018) appraised the system by asking the views of first instance and high court judges, lawyers, social workers from the child and youth welfare offices and guardians ad litem. Asked about the concept of prioritised proceedings in parent and child matters, the early hearing and the work towards parental agreements,[31] 75.0 per cent rated the system as practicable while 20.1 per cent rated it as not very practicable or, in rare cases (2.6 per cent), rated it as not practicable.[32] Further, 73.7 per cent said the system provided sufficient options with only 10 per cent of judges describing them as insufficient, in comparison to 22 per cent of the guardians of litem and 19 per cent of the lawyers. The differentiation between the various subjects of the proceedings was deemed sufficient by 67.1 per cent of those asked (Ekert and Heiderhoff, 2018: 242 ff, 350).[33]

The system seems to be more characterised by the aim to work towards consensus than the intention to speed proceedings up. Of the professionals, 61.2 per cent believed that more agreements could be achieved while 22.0 per cent thought that this was not the case.[34] Interestingly, judges at the first instance courts were significantly less positive (42.3 per cent) than those who work with

[31] Section 155, 156 Act on Proceedings in Family Matters and in Matters of Non-contentious Jurisdiction.

[32] 4.8 per cent no answer provided; n=656.

[33] 19.3 per cent no answer provided; n=426.

[34] 16.8 per cent no answer provided; n=655.

the families over a longer period of time (64.3 per cent of social workers in child and youth welfare office) or who stand at the side of the child (71.2 per cent of guardians of litem). That proceedings are successfully concluded more rapidly was the perception of 50.2 per cent of those asked,[35] with about 60 per cent of the lawyers and guardians ad litem agreeing (ibid: 244 f, 351). A conflict of objectives between speeding up proceedings and working towards agreements was noted by 36.2 per cent of the professionals,[36] with only 26.1 of the first instance court judges being sceptical but almost 40 per cent of the social workers in the child and youth welfare office, guardians ad litem and high court judges (ibid: 246, 351).

A. Binding Setting to Work Towards Agreements

The right to legal protection is constitutionally secured.[37] Asked whether the proceedings fulfil the right to a decision by the court, 81.2 per cent of the first instances judges agreed[38] but only 46.9 per cent of the social workers in the child and youth welfare offices agreed (17.4 per cent did not answer; n=230); overall, 60.8 per cent agreed.[39] A discussion about this issue is yet to come. Agreements and controvertible judgments were thought to be balanced by 59.4 per cent.[40] The view that the necessity of a court decision could take a back seat was believed by 66.7 per cent[41] and that the proceedings are too much about conflict avoidance by 41.8 per cent[42] (ibid: 247 ff).

Only 13.6 per cent of the high court judges and 27.2 per cent of the first instance court judges thought that escalation of a family conflict could be prevented.[43] Guardians ad litem had a strikingly different view, with 57.3 per cent agreeing this was the case.[44] Of the social workers in the child and youth welfare offices,[45] 61.8 per cent disagreed but many believed that conflicts could be mitigated (57.8 per cent). The overall figure was 59.5 per cent with, again, the guardians ad litem as the most positive (70.1 per cent) and the high court judges the most sceptical (18.2 per cent).[46] Judges took a positive view about the

[35] 17.1 per cent no answer provided; n=655.
[36] 11.4 per cent no answer provided; n=655.
[37] Article 19(4) Basic Law for the Federal Republic of Germany.
[38] 9.1 per cent no answer provided; n=110.
[39] 14.4 per cent no answer provided; n=652.
[40] 12.0 per cent no answer provided; n=652.
[41] 6.6 per cent no answer provided; n=652.
[42] 15.9 per cent no answer provided; n=652.
[43] 22.7 per cent of high court judges / 16.4 per cent of first instance court judges no answer provided.
[44] 2.5 per cent no answer provided; n=239.
[45] 5.7 per cent no answer provided; n=230.
[46] 6.3 per cent no answer provided; n=654.

sustainability of the agreements achieved (76.4 per cent)[47] but this is seemingly an overestimate since the social workers in the child and youth welfare office who are in contact with the families after the court proceedings ended were less optimistic (43.0 per cent;[48] 55.4 per cent overall).[49]

The instruments that are legally set out on how to deal with family conflicts in parent and child matters after separation and divorce were not thought to be suitable for high-conflict cases, ie cases with several court proceedings over a longer period of time (Fichtner et al, 2010), according to about two-thirds of all professionals, with only minor variations between the different professions (67.0 per cent)[50] (ibid: 252 ff). The study did not comment on cases concerning contact or parental custody in which intimate partner violence or child abuse and neglect plays a role.

Cases do not always come to the attention of courts if a parental agreement can be achieved. Judges and lawyers estimated this to happen in just over two thirds of the cases.[51] In just under half of the cases in which parents had made use of non-judicial counselling it was the unanimous view of judges, lawyers and social workers in child and youth welfare offices and by judges and guardians ad litem that an agreement could be reached (ibid: 272 ff).[52] In cases concerning contact it was thought by judges at first instance and guardians that three quarters could be resolved by an agreement that has been approved by the court[53] (ibid: 280 f).

B. Prioritised and Accelerated Proceedings

There seemed to be a broad consensus that proceedings have indeed been accelerated in practice (84.6 per cent).[54] The picture was less clear when it comes to the reduction of the duration of proceedings (58.9 per cent).[55] However, when asked whether the acceleration in parent and child matters had led to a slowing down of proceedings in other matters, only a minority of 38.2 per cent of first instance court judges[56] and 23.6 per cent of lawyers[57] agreed (Ekert and Heiderhoff, 259 ff; 354).

[47] 12.7 per cent no answer provided; n=110.
[48] 8.7 per cent no answer provided; n=230.
[49] 9.5 per cent no answer provided; n=654.
[50] 5.7 per cent no answer provided; n=654.
[51] n=58.
[52] n=217.
[53] n=337.
[54] 7.6 per cent no answer provided; n=649.
[55] 9.4 per cent no answer provided; n=649.
[56] 7.2 per cent no answer provided; n=110.
[57] 21.6 per cent no answer provided; n=51.

The early hearing was approved as reasonable overall by all the professionals (86.8 per cent).[58] When asked if the statutory provisions could be realised in practice almost a third of the first instance court judges answered 'almost always' (30.0 per cent), a little less than a half 'in a majority of cases' (46.4 per cent) and only a smaller number 'in about half of the cases' (10.9 per cent) or a 'minority of cases' (1.8 per cent) and none said 'almost never'.[59] The information from the other professionals was quite similar, with a shift between 'almost always' towards 'in a majority of cases' (13.7 per cent) in the answers of lawyers[60] and a slightly higher number of social workers in child and youth welfare offices managing to get in line with the provisions in 'about half the cases' (14.5 per cent).[61] Requests for an adjournment were said to be rejected 'almost always' by 11.8 per cent, 'in a majority of cases' (29.1 per cent), 'in about half the cases' (8.2 per cent), 'a minority of cases' (37.3 per cent), or 'almost never' (8.2 per cent) by the first instance court judges,[62] and the guardians ad litem as well as the lawyers gave similar answers (ibid: 264 ff.).

The early hearing was said to have 'deescalating effects' by 63.9 per cent of professionals;[63] 60.4 per cent thought that it has 'conflict resolving effects'[64] with first instance court family judges being even more confident (66.4 per cent);[65] and 48.9 per cent of all professionals reported 'conflict preventing effects'.[66] When asked about the effect on the duration of the proceedings, it was seen as shortening the duration by 38.6 per cent of the professionals, 50.9 per cent saw no change, and 10.4 per cent believed it prolonged proceedings. A minority of professionals thought that there are cases in which an early hearing is counterproductive (35.9 per cent)[67] with judges being most sceptical (46.4 per cent)[68] and lawyers least sceptical (19.6 per cent)[69] (ibid: 267 ff).

C. Interdisciplinary and Multi-agency Setting in Family Court Proceedings

The interplay between professionals in this binding setting was found overall to achieve better outcomes, with 30.8 per cent strongly agreeing and another 30.3 per cent agreeing to some extent.[70] Lawyers were the least optimistic

[58] 7.0 per cent no answer provided; n=622.
[59] 4.5 per cent no answer provided; n=110.
[60] 5.9 per cent no answer provided; n=51.
[61] 4.9 per cent no answer provided; n=227.
[62] 5.5 per cent no answer provided; n=110.
[63] 10.3 per cent no answer provided; n=644.
[64] 10.6 per cent no answer provided; n=644.
[65] 15.5 per cent no answer provided; n=110.
[66] 11.8 per cent no answer provided; n=644.
[67] 18.9 per cent no answer provided; n=644.
[68] 18.2 per cent no answer provided; n=110.
[69] 21.6 per cent no answer provided; n=51.
[70] 15.5 per cent no answer provided; n=650.

(42.3 per cent)[71] and social workers in the child and youth welfare offices the most convinced (69.0 per cent).[72] The cooperation between the professional partners received a very high positive rating, with 84.5 per cent of professionals perceiving each other as living up to their task.[73] They saw themselves as fit for their role in the cooperation model to an extent of 80.1 per cent.[74] But a vast majority still called for more training to be offered (76.9 per cent)[75] while only a minority thought that their workload allowed for enough time to spare for training (40.3 per cent) particularly the judges and social workers (Ekert and Heiderhoff, 253 ff; 352 f).[76]

D. Reflections on the Evaluation Study

The study with its rather small number of participants, ie 110 first instance court family judges at the maximum in a country as large and regionally diverse as Germany, and with its solely quantitative approach, can only give indications of what could or should be explored and discussed further. But the results point to quite a broad accordance and compliance with the legal requirements in family court proceedings. In particular the professional coordination and cooperation gets high approval rates across the field. There are profound indications that the prioritisation and acceleration of proceedings in parent and child matters as well as the primary orientation to work towards parental agreements has positive effects on progress and duration of the proceedings. Also, a majority of professionals believe deescalating effects are achieved. This seems to be a base on which further differentiation could be built. The latter obviously is seen as necessary, in particular in high-conflict cases as well as in case of child abuse and intimate partner violence (see section IV).

IV. CONCLUSIONS: POTENTIAL FOR FURTHER ADVANCEMENT

All the tools necessary for a highly functional interplay between legal and psycho-social professionals and institutions in proceedings about contact and custody after separation and divorce are in place. The binding setting is legally structured and organisationally secured. Although the lack of knowledge about the views of the children and parents is a problem, the system seems to work for 'regular' cases. Differentiation seems necessary in cases of high conflict and

[71] 19.3 per cent no answer provided; n=52.
[72] 12.7 per cent no answer provided; n=229.
[73] 4.6 per cent no answer provided; n=284.
[74] 7.6 per cent no answer provided; n=186.
[75] 7.6 per cent no answer provided; n=186.
[76] 4.8 per cent no answer provided; n=169.

violence. Recent studies and policy discourses point out significant potential for improvement of practice as well as the legal framework for family relationships after separation and divorce in cases where children and parents are affected by intimate partner violence (Frauenhauskoordinierung and bff, 2019; Kotlenga and Nägele, 2016: 11 ff; Bündnis Istanbul-Konvention, 2021: 106 ff, 159). In such proceedings the judges' intermediary role does not provide for protection and the child's best interests (Liebsch, 2017).

Nevertheless, continuity in the relationship with the main attachment person(s) is currently still loaded with such high normativity (Sütterly, 2017: 72) that the character of the attachment and the quality of the relationship tend to slip out of sight in professional dealings with family conflicts about contact and custody. Currently contact and joint custody is held to be in the best interests of the child until the opposite is proven (see section II). This rebuttable presumption is not yet complemented with a presumption after thorough assessment that in cases of child abuse, intimate partner violence or high conflict joint custody or (unprotected) contact could only be ordered if responsibility for protection against violence and disproportionate burden could be taken on by the court. In line with Arts 31 and 51 of the Istanbul Convention the prioritised and accelerated proceedings could and should be primarily oriented towards establishing facts in an interdisciplinary risk assessment and risk management to prevent the rights and safety of the child being jeopardised. Working towards agreements is contraindicated prior to determination of the relevant facts (Schirrmacher and Meysen, 2021). The current procedural law allows for exceptions but does not shift the focus explicitly. But if integrated into family law and the Act on family court proceedings the binding interdisciplinary setting could, in the future, serve all cases well.

REFERENCES

Bindel-Kögel, G and Seidenstücker, B (2017) 'Ergebnisse der Fallerhebung in den beteiligten Jugendämtern' in Münder, J (ed), *Kindeswohl zwischen Jugendhilfe und Justiz. Zur Entwicklung von Entscheidungsgrundlagen und Verfahren zur Sicherung des Kindeswohls zwischen Jugendämtern und Familiengerichten* (Weinheim, Basel, Beltz Juventa) 123–88.

Bundeskonferenz für Erziehungsberatung eV (bke) (2012) *Familie und Beratung. Memorandum zur Zukunft der Erziehungsberatung* (Fürth: bke).

Bündnis Istanbul-Konvention (2021) *Alternativbericht zur Umsetzung des Übereinkommens des Europarats zur Verhütung und Bekämpfung von Gewalt gegen Frauen und häuslicher Gewalt* (Berlin).

Dethloff, N (2018) *Familienrecht* (32nd edn) (München, CH Beck).

Deutscher Bundestag (1996) 'Gesetzentwurf der Bundesregierung. Entwurf eines Gesetzes zur Reform des Kindschaftsrechts (Kindschaftsrechtsreformgesetz – KindRG) vom 13.6.1996', *Bundestags-Drucksache 13/4899* (Bonn).

Deutscher Bundestag (2007) 'Gesetzentwurf der Bundesregierung. Entwurf eines Gesetzes zur Reform des Verfahrens in Familiensachen und in den Angelegenheiten der freiwilligen Gerichtsbarkeit (FGG-Reformgesetz – FGG-RG) vom 7.9.2007', *Bundestags-Drucksache 16/6308* (Berlin).

Ekert, S and Heiderhoff, B (2018) *Die Evaluierung der FGG-Reform. Abschlussbericht zum Forschungsvorhaben*, published by the Federal Ministry of Justice and for Consumer Protection (Mönchengladbach, Forum Verlag Godesberg).

Ernst, R (2016) 'Psychologische Sachverständigengutachten in Kindschaftssachen. Formulierung und Beantwortung der Beweisfrage(n)' in *Familien-Rechtsberater (FamRB)* 361–64.

Fichtner, J, Dietrich, P, Halatcheva, M, Hermann, U and Sandner, E (2010) *Kinderschutz bei hochstrittiger Elternschaft. Wissenschaftlicher Abschlussbericht* (Munich, German Youth Institute).

Frauenhauskoordinierung eV and Bundesverband Frauenberatungsstellen und Frauennotrufe Frauen gegen Gewalt eV (bff) (2018) 'Umgang und Gewaltschutz im Konflikt – professionelle Perspektiven: Dokumentation der Fachveranstaltung am 9 November 2017 in der Berliner Stadtmission' (Berlin: Frauenhauskoordinierung & bff).

Hammer, S (2020) '§ 156 Hinwirken auf Einvernehmen' in H Prütting and T Helms (eds) *FamFG. Gesetz über das Verfahren in Familiensachen und in den Angelegenheiten der freiwilligen Gerichtsbarkeit. Kommentar* (5th edn, Cologne, Otto Schmit) 1527–60.

Hammer, S (2021) 'Entwicklungslinien im Sorge- und Umgangsrecht bei Getrenntleben der Eltern' in *Zeitschrift für das gesamte Familienrecht (FamRZ)* 905–17.

Heinke, S, Wildvang, W and Meysen, T (2021) 'Kindschaftssachen nach häuslicher Gewalt: Praxishinweise für die Verfahrensführung und Mitwirkung' in T Meysen (ed), *Kindschaftssachen und häusliche Gewalt. Umgang, elterliche Sorge, Kindeswohlgefährdung, Familienverfahrensrecht* (Heidelberg, SOCLES) 96–139.

Jestaedt, M and Reimer, P (2018) 'Artikel 6 Abs. 2 und 3 GG' in W Kahl, C Waldhoff and C Walter (eds), *Bonner Kommentar zum Grundgesetz* (loose-leaf) (Munich, CH Beck).

Jurczyk, K and Walper, S (eds) (2009) *Gemeinsames Sorgerecht nicht miteinander verheirateter Eltern: Empirische Studien und juristische Expertisen* (Wiesbaden, Springer VS).

Karle, M, Gathmann, S and Klosinski, G (2010) *Rechtstatsächliche Untersuchung zur Praxis der Kindesanhörung nach § 50b FGG: Abschlussbericht* (Cologne: Bundesanzeiger).

Kindler, H (2009) 'Umgangsregelung im Einzelfall – Psychologische Aspekte' in *Familie, Partnerschaft, Recht (FPR)* 150–52.

Kotlenga, S and Nägele, B (2016) 'Gewaltschutz in Fällen von Nahraumgewalt – die Situation von Frauen mit spezifischen Bedarfen verbessern. SNaP – Specific Needs and Protection Orders' Policy Paper (Göttingen).

Kratky, N (2020) *Familienrechtliche Verfahren zum Kinderschutz: Eine Gerichtsaktenanalyse zur Rolle von elterlicher psychischer Gesundheit, Alleinerziehung und des Kindeswillens im Verfahrensverlauf* (Darmstadt, Technische Universität Darmstadt).

Li, X, Zerle-Elsäßer, C, Entleitner-Phleps, C and Schier, M (2015) *Väter 2015: Wie aktiv sind sie, wie geht es ihnen und was brauchen sie? Eine aktuelle Studie des Deutschen Jugendinstituts* (München, DJI).

Liebsch, K (2017) 'Gemeinsame elterliche Sorge bei hochstrittigen Sorgerechtsfällen – ein Technologie des Kindeswohls' in F Sütterly and S Flick (eds), *Der Streit ums Kindeswohl* (Weinheim, Basel, Beltz Juventa) 189–206.

Loschky, A (2011) 'Die Beratung mit angeordneter Teilnahme' in K Menne and M Weber (eds), *Professionelle Kooperation zum whole des Kindes. Hinwirken auf elterliches Einvernehmen im familiengerichtlichen Verfahren (FamFG)* (Weinheim, Basel, Beltz Juventa), s 137–150.

Meysen, T (2014a) '§ 155 Vorrang- und Beschleunigungsgebot' in T Meysen (ed), *Praxiskommentar Familienverfahrensrecht. Einführung, Erläuterungen, Arbeitshilfen* (2nd edn, Köln, Bundesanzeiger Verlag) 528–37.

Meysen, T (2014b) '§ 156 Hinwirken auf Einvernehmen' in T Meysen (ed), *Praxiskommentar Familienverfahrensrecht. Einführung, Erläuterungen, Arbeitshilfen* (2nd edn, Köln, Bundesanzeiger Verlag) 545–55.

Osthold, FR (2016) *Die rechtliche Behandlung von Elternkonflikten* (Baden-Baden, Nomos).

Possinger, J (2013) *Vaterschaft im Spannungsfeld von Erwerbs- und Familienleben: 'Neuen Vätern' auf der Spur* (Wiesbaden, Springer VS).

Proksch, R (2002) *Rechtstatsächliche Untersuchung zur Reform des Kindschaftsrechts* (Köln, Bundesanzeiger Verlag.

Rudolph, J (2005) '"Cochemer Praxis" – ein Handlungsmodell zur interdisziplinären Zusammenarbeit im Familienkonflikt' in *Forum Familienrecht (FF)*, 167–71.

Schirrmacher, G and Meysen, T (2021, in print) 'Impulse zur Weiterentwicklung von Kindschafts- und Familienverfahrensrecht für einen kindeswohlorientierten, effektiven Schutz vor Gewalt' in *Zeitschrift für das gesamte Familienrecht (FamRZ)*, pp 1929–34.

Schmidt, J-R (2020) *Will das Kind sein Wohl? Beiträge zur Rechtsgeschichte des 20*, Jahrhunderts 113 (Tübingen, Mohr Siebeck).

Schwab, D (1998) 'Elterliche Sorge bei Trennung und Scheidung der Eltern. Die Neuregelung des Kindschaftsrechtsreformgesetzes' in *Zeitschrift für das gesamte Familienrecht (FamRZ)*, 44–8, 457–72.

Statistisches Bundesamt (1998) *Familiengerichte 1997. Arbeitsunterlage* (Wiesbaden, Statistisches Bundesamt).

Statistisches Bundesamt (2002) *Rechtspflege. Familiengerichte 2000. Fachserie 10 / Reihe 2.2* (Wiesbaden, Statistisches Bundesamt).

Statistisches Bundesamt (2005) *Rechtspflege. Familiengerichte 2004. Fachserie 10 / Reihe 2.2* (Wiesbaden: Statistisches Bundesamt).

Statistisches Bundesamt (2009) *Rechtspflege. Familiengerichte 2008. Fachserie 10 Reihe 2.2* (Wiesbaden, Statistisches Bundesamt).

Statistisches Bundesamt (2012) *Rechtspflege. Familiengerichte 2011. Fachserie 10 Reihe 2.2* (Wiesbaden, Statistisches Bundesamt).

Statistisches Bundesamt (2014) *Rechtspflege. Familiengerichte 2012. Fachserie 10 Reihe 2.2* (Wiesbaden: Statistisches Bundesamt).

Statistisches Bundesamt (2016) *Statistiken der Kinder- und Jugendhilfe. Erzieherische Hilfe, Eingliederungshilfe für seelisch behinderte junge Menschen, Hilfe für junge Volljährige. Erziehungsberatung 2014* (Wiesbaden: Statistisches Bundesamt).

Statistisches Bundesamt (2017) *Rechtspflege. Familiengerichte 2016. Fachserie 10 Reihe 2.2* (Wiesbaden: Statistisches Bundesamt).

Statistisches Bundesamt (2020) *Rechtspflege. Familiengerichte 2019. Fachserie 10 Reihe 2.2* (Wiesbaden: Statistisches Bundesamt).

Streicher, M (2019) 'Teil III: Elterliche Sorge und Umgang. § 6 Verfahrensrecht' in D Schwab and R Ernst (eds), *Handbuch Scheidungsrecht* (8th edn, Munich, CH Beck) 551–98.

Sütterly, F (2017) 'Normative Paradoxien der rechtsstaatlichen Sorge um das Kindeswohl' in F Sütterly and S Flick (eds), *Der Streit ums Kindeswohl* (Weinheim, Basel, Beltz Juventa) 52–87.

Wegener, S (2020) '§ 156 FamFG Hinwirken auf Einvernehmen' in S Heilmann (ed), *Praxiskommentar Kindschaftsrecht. BGB – FamFG – SGB VIII – RPflG – HKÜ – IntFamRVG* (2nd edn, Cologne, Reguvis) 1007–36.

14

What is a Family Justice System for? Concluding Observations and Next Steps

MAVIS MACLEAN

WE HAVE THOUGHT hard and long about this question, which we think lies behind current widespread anxiety about the working of family justice systems, as it is so difficult to evaluate or make progress without a clearer view of the aims and objectives involved: What *is* a family justice system for? After hearing from thoughtful and experienced analysts and practitioners from Canada, Europe and Australia, not surprisingly we have no clear single answer. But, as we had hoped, we do now have a number of new and exciting questions to consider and to help us in the search for new ways forward. In these closing observations we will try to draw these together and add further examples from recent experience, including issues arising from the Covid-19 pandemic experience. Rather than simply continuing the current debate about the relative merits and disadvantages of decision-making in family matters in or outside the courts through forms of alternative dispute resolution, we are beginning to identify deeper underlying issues in different jurisdictions associated not only with issues of the cost of access to justice, but also with the conflict between promoting individualisation and concern to protect the vulnerable. There also seems to be a growing awareness of the role of a justice system in not only adjudicating individual disputes where there are disagreements about some aspect of family life, especially when parents separate, but also in law-based decision-making where issues of public concern are becoming more prevalent, including domestic abuse and the protection of children. The individual conflicts may arise from individual problems which may be amenable to help with individual parenting skills, or addiction issues. But the resort to court may also be influenced by more broadly based social needs for help with housing or sufficient income, requiring not just individual attention but acceptance of how family law not only supports individuals but can contribute to social policy on a larger scale.

In England and Wales, for example, we have recently seen, largely through the energy and commitment of Judge Nick Creighton, the development of a helping court known as FDAC (the Family Drug and Alcohol Court). These courts have been piloted and successfully evaluated for the Ministry of Justice and now work in several areas. Where a question of risk to a child arises as a result of drug or alcohol dependency, the court can provide a high level of support over time to a parent at risk of losing a child to public care. The court provides ongoing counselling and support, and sees the parent frequently, congratulating them on progress whenever possible. It is a costly process for the court service, but is expected to produce considerable savings to the public purse in other ways through relieving pressure on Children's Services and the National Health Service.

But when we go beyond the controlling function of law where there is a public safety interest into the realm of helping families with private disputes, we go beyond the traditional role of the courts and enter a new area, where the court process comes closer to the kinds of decision-making required of the medical professions when seeking the best possible future outcome 'in the best interests' of a child. The Children Act 1989 in England and Wales is widely respected as having taken an important step in bringing together public and private matters, and requiring any court making a decision in any matter where a child is concerned to give 'paramount consideration' not to any idea of parental rights, which are replaced in this Act by the concept of parental responsibility, but to the welfare of that child. This is known as the 'welfare paramountcy principle'. But of course this is not a simple process. Individual values come into play: religious considerations, for example, where one parent may argue for a particular form of religious upbringing, or a particular form of education as a primary concern. In disputes over custody and visitation, where there are new demands from fathers' groups seeking shared parenting and growing concerns from mothers about safety issues, the Act had to be amended in 2014 to say that a continuing relationship with both parents after separation will be assumed to be in the best interests of the child 'unless there is evidence that it would not'. So … the wider the area of responsibility the court is given, the more difficult it becomes to provide the firm decision-making associated with judicial adjudication. The English judges have no special expertise in child development. Nor do they have a staff of such experts at their disposal. They are however, advised by the Children and Family Court Advisory and Support Service (CAFCASS), which is supported by, but independent from, the Ministry of Justice, and from local Children's Services. So while the struggle to contain the increasing cost of decision-making in family justice continues partly by encouraging decision-making by family members outside the courts – autonomy and economy in tandem – we now have a clearly visible second axis, where we need to find a balance between justice and future welfare.

Our original question arose in the context of widespread international dissatisfaction with the institutions of the family justice systems, clustered around the increasing level of demand on the family courts, and the associated impact on the public purse. Although access to justice is widely valued and incorporated in human rights documents such as the European Convention on Human Rights, there is also widespread frustration at the way in which individual family problems so often develop into disputes which cannot be resolved without help from outside the family, and for which families turn to the courts. This concluding chapter will try to learn from the different strategies employed in different jurisdictions, and draw together the common issues including those highlighted during the Covid-19 crisis. The best research does not always provide answers to old problems by looking back, but can try to identify the next set of issues emerging, and begin to enable us to look ahead to new solutions (see Rein, 1970: 461–64).

I. CUTTING COSTS BY DISCOURAGING ACCESS TO COURT

… but does this mean access to the court as decision maker? Or as guarantor of compliance? Or as a pathway to help and support? Does it rely on using triage? Or does it require reducing or changing the role of lawyers?

The first chapters of this volume looked at the boundaries of court responsibility, beginning with Rachel Treloar's account (chapter one) of recent Canadian developments, where judicial policy has long been admired for developing practical solutions to the problem of increasing demand, in family and other civil courts. The Canadian use of websites reporting existing child support decisions which enable parties to see what most families find acceptable and perhaps follow suit has been widely praised but requires careful preparation. In British Columbia recent attempts to deal with increasing demand in family matters have not taken the approach of trying to change the central position of the courts, but instead have aimed to reduce their workload and make them more accessible and friendly by adding a range of services designed to help those in conflict by offering information and early resolution services. But Treloar describes how these additional services are present in the private sector, and can charge fees, and although offering help do so at a cost to the parties. This enables the court to limit its own contribution, but may leave the parties without the resources to go to the court.

Encouragement to use services associated with the court for dispute resolution is also the strategy of the new Federal Circuit and Family Court of Australia, established in September 2021. The former specialist family court and the federal magistrates service have been replaced by a unified court service aiming to offer a faster, more efficient service, but again doing so by increasing the involvement of peripheral private sector services. The official announcement set out the way to 'Separate Smarter', listing the decisions which will need to be made, and how to reach at least a temporary agreement, starting with a link to the subsidised Family Relationship Advice Line. The introduction states: 'Most people don't need to come to court … there is no need unless it is not safe to make your own agreement, or after making a genuine attempt to resolve your dispute through Family Dispute Resolution agreement still has not been reached.' However, as in British Columbia, the Australian Family Dispute Resolution Practitioners are also in the private sector and charge a fee. The practice directions for the new court[1] set out a requirement for the applicant to give evidence of having taken 'genuine steps' to reach agreement before approaching the court. There is concern among legal practitioners about what this will mean, especially in the context of reaching financial agreements where advice is likely to be needed and the lack of good advice could have a major impact on the more vulnerable parties, and particularly women. As in British Columbia, parties may now be spending a considerable sum on this kind of advice, rather than proceeding directly to court and having matters considered in a single appropriate forum, partly because in Australia the waiting time to reach court had become disproportionately long. But there is concern among academics about cases where there is a power imbalance or coercive control, and about what is meant by 'consent' in these situations. In British Columbia the family education and assessment services may be used outside the court in the private sector and fees are charged. But Australia has taken a step further in preparing to require attendance at two peripheral conflict resolution services before allowing an application to be made to the family courts. The desired outcome in both jurisdictions is a reduction in public expenditure on court services. The concern being expressed by practitioners and academics, especially in Australia, is that after paying for the required alternative dispute resolution (ADR) that parties will simply not be able to afford to make an application to the court. They will be in effect priced out the justice system, however well intentioned the additional services may be.

In London, also, at the time of writing (October 2021) a similar pathway is under discussion. Following a recent decision by the Civil Justice Council that ADR could be required before an application to court can be made in certain defined civil matters, the government quickly became interested in this procedure as a way of increasing the low take up of family mediation in private family law matters, and to discourage the continuing level of resort to court (even without legal aid since the Legal Aid, Sentencing and Punishment of Offenders Act 2012). The government's increasingly energetic measures to encourage higher take up of mediation now include the gift of vouchers for £500 per case to get a family mediation process started.[2] The total cost to a couple is, however, likely to be at least £2k for all-issues mediation (although note that these figures are estimates only as there appear to be no national statistics, even from the Family

[1] See Federal Circuit and Family Court of Australia, FAMILY CASE MANAGEMENT, Central Practice Direction September 2021.

[2] See www.gov.uk/guidance/family-mediation-voucher-scheme.

Mediation Council), including documents prepared by the mediator such as an open financial statement or a memorandum of understanding, to which must be added the legal costs of drafting a consent order which a court would accept, which would probably be at least £1,500 … and also court fees of £550. The cost-saving implications of going to mediation remain rather unclear. And if a slightly different change in practice was to be was encouraged whereby a family solicitor could be consulted by both parties to negotiate an agreement, at perhaps £300–400 an hour, and thereby avoid a contested court hearing, the total cost might be little different. It is important to be clear that while mediation is clearly a dispute resolution process, seeing a solicitor may not be. It may instead be an information and advice seeking process, which may begin at the earlier stage in a separation where there may be matters to arrange or problems to solve but these have not yet become disputes, particularly with one practitioner seeing both clients. For one solicitor to act for both parties in a family law matter is not forbidden by the profession as a reserved activity, and is clearly acceptable if the parties both understand and wish it and have an overriding common interest, which for those with children is likely to be the case. A skilled solicitor negotiating with two clients may be able to achieve a fair and informed settlement quickly and cheaply, which can be used without further advice to seek a consent order from the court to ensure compliance.

There does appear to be a need to be rather more careful about defining concepts and issues … in particular to note the differences between problems where people want help to find solutions, and disputes where people want help to reach settlement or failing that seek adjudication that will provide an answer with certainty about compliance. Parties are looking for information, advice and support, rather than simply a mediated agreement in these matters of private law which are of no public interest to the state.

So the out-of-court route for family matters in private law – particularly for adult issues – can include both solicitors and mediators, and there may well be ways of reducing access to court although not necessarily access to the lawyers who can help parties to avoid dispute. But if we add in the public law matters such as domestic violence and child protection which, as discussed in earlier chapters, are thought to be increasing in France, Australia, England and Wales, and Spain, then there is often a need to get to court fast and without cost or procedural barriers.

II. ACCESS THROUGH TRIAGE TO AN ADMINISTRATIVE ROUTE SUPPORTED BY EXPERTS?

The chapter from Denmark (chapter two) describes a very different approach to enabling a family justice system to cope with a high incidence of family matters by using triage to direct a case to the expert administrative route, and to ensure rapid access to justice in public law cases by dividing cases needing justice from those needing welfare-based conflict management. The newly established Administrative Agency of Family Law can direct complex cases rapidly to the newly established Family Court which delivers justice. Other matters requiring conflict management are to be dealt with by the Administrative Agency, which offers family mediation and counselling, and whose Child Unit is responsible for the protection of children through social work intervention including out-of-home placement if necessary. This is a complex structure, and requires close cooperation between the two departments, which may take time to develop fully. But the family justice system retains responsibility for helping with all family matters while diverting appropriate cases away from court to the administrative arm of the justice system, … and has not privatised access to help with private matters.

III. CUTTING COSTS THROUGH NEW WAYS OF USING THE COURTS

In the Netherlands (chapter three), yet another route to reducing pressure on family courts has been developed by reducing the level of legal intervention in the private arrangements to be made by couples who separate. The duration of the legal requirement for spousal maintenance, which may ameliorate the financial disparity between mothers and fathers who separate, has been reduced. This withdrawal reflects social attitudes to the normalisation of divorce, and to the inappropriateness of state interference in post-separation agreements, and a move away from legal support which had been increasingly reflecting state support for gender equality. But, sadly, gender inequality in earning capacity persists, and has led to a third of single mothers becoming dependent on state benefits after separation. A similar situation can be seen Switzerland (chapter four) where private agreements are encouraged and ratified by courts, but do not reflect constitutional norms of gender equality, thus giving rise to problems for single parents, mainly mothers. Again, this raises the question of whether the work of a family justice system should be considered as a separate item in the public accounts subject to private decision-making, or considered in the context of the impact of these private decisions on other costs including public expenditure on welfare, housing and health care.

The two chapters which follow indicate recent changes to the range of those expected to participate in a family justice system, and in particular the absence of two groups: one whose role has traditionally been considered essential, and one the very group of applicants whose presence is being discouraged elsewhere. Chapter five describes how in France the courts continued to deal with family matters as the move towards using mediation failed, despite the high level of qualifications achieved by the mediation profession in France. The work of managing conflict is still carried out in the courtroom, but is now largely done by lawyers without the judges. And in chapter six we heard for the first and only time of concern that family courts as an organ of the state are not used often enough in Poland, where family life is regarded as private, and those with problems choose to accept the guidance of their family or their church. This may have serious but so far unmeasured impacts on child welfare and levels of domestic violence.

In Spain (chapter seven) the role of mediators has varied across the different autonomias, but nationally is held to be absolutely unacceptable for any matters where there is risk of gender violence or harm to children. In the Netherlands (chapter eight) the courtroom also remains central, but a court-based non-adversarial procedure for dealing with parenting conflicts has been piloted. This has introduced the role of an active judge who intervenes in the process in court. And a new concern has been acknowledged with the way problems continue to re-emerge even after a divorce or separation agreement has been reached. It is becoming clear that parents who achieve dispute resolution, whether in court or outside, may not be protected from becoming involved in high-conflict court procedures long after the court-based process has finished, as post-divorce parental conflicts and re-litigation can result from non-compliance with the parenting arrangements made. This adds a further dimension to our justice versus welfare balance, if family conflicts may last a lifetime, or even include cross-generational matters of inheritance.

IV. NEW DEVELOPMENTS

New players are still appearing on the family justice scene. In chapter nine we heard of community involvement in achieving access to the courts in England. In chapter ten we heard from Buenos Aires about the range of support used by the courts in domestic violence cases, and in Istanbul (chapter eleven) about the arrival of high status religious advisers to the courts. And there are also new roles emerging for key traditional participants. In Germany (chapter thirteen) the family courts do not appear to try to limit access, but instead encourage quick access to prevent a problem from getting worse due to delay. Judges are trained to stand back from judicial decision-making and instead, wherever possible, provide a safe space for couples in difficulty while they access free counselling (*not* mediation unless requested). The judge waits for their own decision to emerge, which will then be given the authority of the court to ensure compliance. An attractive solution, although we did also hear of the gaps in local welfare provision, and the difficulty of securing cooperation between the different agencies.[3] And in the chapter from Australia (chapter twelve) we heard of the problems which can arise when the most highly qualified and respected members of the family justice system, the judges, do not always abide by the behavioural rules expected of them … in a recent case, for example, having

[3] We are grateful to Barbara Willenbacher who alerted us to these issues.

a close relationship with the representative of one of the parties appearing. Perhaps this is an occupational hazard in a jurisdiction where the senior judiciary are drawn from a small close-knit group of lawyers who have known each other and worked together since their student days.

To conclude:

In one sense our picture of the family justice system has no boundaries: we have seen that a court can refuse to accept applications without evidence of attempts to settle; it can call in other sources of authority such as religious advisers or child development experts to advise on the decision to be made; it can provide access to counselling or mediation if requested and wait for the parties to agree; it can take into account the long term future of a child or family; and it can decide what is best for a child, or simply send the case back to an administrative agency. The context is decisive. In Poland, where the secular courts were the public province of the unwelcome communist regime for many years, courts were underused while church and family were seen as safe but private places; in France the career judges were akin to government servants and could be redirected away from court work leaving it to the advocates; in England lawyers were thought to be avaricious and adversarial and not to be trusted to seek agreement; and in Turkey the secular courts were not trusted by the government without religious supervision. While in the famously moderate societies of Switzerland and the Netherlands social norms favoured individual choice and the state looked for gender equality, sadly economic gender disparity makes for private decision-making which fails to support the economically vulnerable. And in Australia, Belinda Fehlberg and Richard Ingleby have shown us how vulnerable the judiciary are to charges of incompetence or lack of vigilance … and how difficult it is to deal with such lapses.

But there are common threads … justice *is* different from social normativity even if not too different; there *is* a need for information, advice, and support if parties are to be left to reach their own decisions, and also the need for a source of strength to secure compliance with an agreement reached whether privately or publicly. And there *is* a distinction between private quarrels with equality of arms and those where there may be potential oppression of weaker parties and risk to the vulnerable, particularly children. It is not surprising that it is so difficult – and often costly – to devise a system which can deal with all of these needs. Perhaps we should look across the range of needs, not seeking to prioritise court or out-of-court work, but instead trying to bring together the helpful features of the different elements, for example both mediation and legal support, as in legally assisted mediation … and trying to understand the impact on other aspects of life and for society as a whole of the outcomes of the family justice system reached by whatever route.

After the onset of the Covid-19 pandemic and the need to close many courts to the public, stop social workers from visiting children and their families, and rely on remote hearings with digital assistance, we saw an extraordinary degree of resilience in our ability to continue to manage family matters, particularly the urgent ones where there is risk of harm to the vulnerable. In England and Wales, for example, child protection cases continued to be decided, though some high-asset divorce settlements were required to wait.

There were some interesting differences in the response to the situation from practitioners. For example, in England where the legal profession is divided into barristers who are court advocates and solicitors who prepare cases and work closely with the parties, the division of work changed. Because solicitors no longer needed to travel to courts for live hearings, and wait for long periods for a judge to be available, they were able to do more of the work on a case from home, and were less likely to call in a barrister. In a small study in 2020, Robert George and I interviewed a group of barristers, solicitors and family judges. We found solicitors continuing to work closely with clients, inviting them into their offices for support during online hearings, and being available for phone calls at all hours of the day every day of the week (Maclean and George, 2021). The younger barristers were completely without work for some weeks at the beginning of the pandemic, but then began to develop remote working skills. Some firms of solicitors are so satisfied with online working that they are thinking of giving up their very expensive office city centre office buildings, and reducing costs to clients by working from home. The judges have not been troubled, as some thought might happen, by trying to measure the reliability of a witness without being face to face and observing their expressions and demeanour. The consensus view seems to have been accepted that facial expression and honesty are perhaps not always closely related. But several judges reported the stress of not having sufficient social distance between themselves and the parties. One judge said: 'I find it very hard to take a woman's children away from her in a child protection case while I can hear my own children playing in the garden outside.'

There was also concern about the variation in access to resources in the courts. The higher courts were well supplied with good internet connections, equipment and technical support. The local magistrates' courts, however, sometimes had to rely on mobile phones. And though there was some evidence from the special education tribunals that some parents were finding it easier to give evidence from home than in a formal courtroom, it was widely agreed that there was something unacceptable about a parent hearing that their child was to be taken into local welfare authority care while they were sitting alone on a park bench with a mobile phone. The concept of making justice available began to be replaced by debate about what would constitute good enough justice … were there some unacceptable elements in remote working? On the other hand, the advantages to everyone of not needing to travel makes it likely that online working will continue for some kinds of work such as administrative hearings for making directions, or uncontested matters on paper. But not care proceedings. There were differences of opinion about domestic violence cases, where a survivor might be protected from coming face to face with a perpetrator in a courtroom. We heard more than once accounts of online cases where a woman was asked by phone if she was alone at home (ie not under duress) to give her evidence, when a deep male voice replied 'Yes!' But if we return to the cost perspective, it is possible that the continuation of some online working may help reduce pressure on the courts.

As lawyers, even though we are sociologists of law, we should close with the thoughts of Encarna Roca Trias, Deputy President of the Constitutional Court in Madrid, who took part in our workshop. Although pressure of work during the pandemic has made it difficult to contribute a chapter for publication, she has asked us to include the thoughts she expressed in the paper she gave in September 2021. She asked us to remember always the enduring and permanent role of the judiciary in family conflict, and at the same time the need to guarantee the human rights of those involved in family disputes. Perhaps we may also keep in mind what has been called by Martha Cover, a senior family barrister in London, 'the magic of the court'. She asks us to remember that a court is a place where people from different backgrounds, with difference skills and experience, aims and objectives meet … not for a common experience like making music together … and not for a trial of strength … but to find a way through a set of complex and conflicting points of view to find a just and acceptable outcome for adults in dispute … and to promote at all times the welfare of any children involved. The lack of face to face hearings takes away the opportunity for brief encounters between the different parties and their representatives, the exchange of new items of information, and the possibility of seeing what line of argument might be acceptable to the other side. This extra layer of increased communication and understanding of each other acts as a form of social lubrication and is present in all social interaction … but it has a clearer measurable impact at the apex of disagreement, the court hearing. We still know so little about the longer term impact of adjudication, mediation or negotiation. It is time to try harder to look at law in context over time. We seem to have lost ground in the study of law and economics of law, where we badly need better information, and analysis rather than simply accounts of how much the family justice system costs. But there are now not only sociologists of law, but also, for example, epidemiologists of law in London, at the UCL Legal Epidemiology Unit, which has measured the progress of children involved in court hearings over time, noting their returns to court after both involvement in both public and private law cases, and the outcomes for the children. For example, they found that children whose first legal involvement was in a public law case were less likely on returning to court to be found in public law and more likely to be involved in a private law case (Jay et al, 2020). The explanation could be that the public law case had led to some form of welfare intervention which had protected the child from further public law matters. So we are seeing a broader range of social science intervention in thinking hard about family justice … and even exercises like the 'Law Reform Now' project in the University of Birmingham in collaboration with the Law Commission to identify the priority areas for a law reform programme for each coming year.[4]

We seem to be moving towards asking for more from a family justice system than individual case resolution, or even certainty of compliance with an individual decision. Perhaps we are becoming more inclined to see family justice as part of social policy, not just the rule of law; not only looking for ways to avoid problems from becoming disputes, but also seeking to resolve disputes in a way which will avoid recurrence, and can be brought to the attention of policy makers. Clearer normativity might clarify decision-making, and changes to ways of accessing employment, income, housing, education and health could aid prevention, but forensic quasi-criminal process in matters which have a criminal element such as domestic abuse or child protections remain essential. The cost of family justice will of course remain important, but we would be the poorer if it were to become the only important variable in our analysis.

REFERENCES

Jay M, Pearson R, Wijlaars L, Olhede, S and Gilbert, R (2020) *Using Administrative Data to quantify overlaps between public and private children law in England* (UCL Legal Epidemiology Unit, London).

Maclean, M and George, R (2021) 'Family practice during Covid and access to justice', *Family Law*, 51.

Rein, M (1970) *Social Policy: Issues of Choice and Change* (NY, Random House).

[4] Law Reform Now, University of Birmingham and the Law Commission, September 2021.

Index

Lightning Source UK Ltd.
Milton Keynes UK
UKHW020020250822
407730UK00003B/154

9 781509 950973